EXPLORERS & DISCOVERERS

EXPLORERS & DISCOVERERS

From Alexander the Great to Sally Ride

Volume
Ch-He

Peggy Saari
•
Daniel B. Baker

U·X·L

AN IMPRINT OF GALE RESEARCH INC.,
AN INTERNATIONAL THOMPSON PUBLISHING COMPANY

I(T)P

NEW YORK • LONDON • BONN • BOSTON • DETROIT • MADRID
MELBOURNE • MEXICO CITY • PARIS • SINGAPORE • TOKYO
TORONTO • WASHINGTON • ALBANY NY • BELMONT CA • CINCINNATI OH

Explorers and Discoverers

From Alexander the Great to Sally Ride

Peggy Saari and Daniel B. Baker

Staff

Carol DeKane Nagel, *U·X·L Developmental Editor*
Thomas L. Romig, *U·X·L Publisher*

Shanna Heilveil, *Production Associate*
Evi Seoud, *Assistant Production Manager*
Mary Beth Trimper, *Production Director*

Pamela A. E. Galbreath, *Page and Cover Designer*
Cynthia Baldwin, *Art Director*

Margaret A. Chamberlain, *Permissions Supervisor (Pictures)*

The Graphix Group, *Typesetter*

∞™ This book is printed on acid-free paper that meets the minimum requirements of American National Standard for Information Sciences—Permanence Paper for Printed Library Materials, ANSI Z39.48-1984.

ISBN 0-8103-9787-8 (Set)
ISBN 0-8103-9798-6 (Volume 1)
ISBN 0-8103-9799-4 (Volume 2)
ISBN 0-8103-9800-1 (Volume 3)
ISBN 0-8103-9801-X (Volume 4)
Printed in the United States of America

Published simultaneously in the United Kingdom
by Gale Research International Limited
(An affiliated company of Gale Research Inc.)

I(T)P™   U•X•L is an imprint of Gale Research Inc.,
          an International Thomson Publishing Company.
          ITP logo is a trademark under license.

Contents

Chronology of Exploration

Explorers by Place of Birth

Index

Volume 2: Ch-He

Volume 3: Hi-Pi

Chronology of Exploration

Explorers by Place of Birth

Index

Volume 4: Po-Z

Preface

Explorers and Discoverers: From Alexander the Great to Sally Ride features biographies of 171 men, women, and machines who have expanded the horizons of our world and universe. Beginning with ancient Greek scholars and travelers and extending to twentieth-century oceanographers and astronauts, *Explorers and Discoverers* tells of the lives and times of both well-known and lesser-known explorers and includes many women and non-European explorers whose contributions have often been overlooked in the past. Who these travelers were, when and how they lived and traveled, why their journeys were significant, and what the consequences of their discoveries were are all answered within these biographies.

The 160 biographical entries of *Explorers and Discoverers* are arranged in alphabetical order over four volumes. Because the paths of these explorers often crossed, an entry about one explorer may refer to other explorers whose biographies also appear in *Explorers and Discoverers*. When this occurs, the other explorers' names appear in bold letters and are followed by a parenthetical note to see the appropriate entry for further information. The 176 illustrations and maps bring the subjects to life as well as provide geographic details of specific journeys. Additionally, 16 maps of major regions of the world lead off each volume, and each volume concludes with a chronology of exploration by region, a list of explorers by place of birth, and an extensive cumulative index.

Comments and Suggestions

We welcome your comments on this work as well as your suggestions for individuals to be featured in future editions of *Explorers and Discoverers*. Please write: Editors, *Explorers and Discoverers,* U·X·L, 835 Penobscot Bldg., Detroit, Michigan 48226-4094; call toll-free: 1-800-877-4253; or fax: 313-961-6348.

Introduction

Explorers and Discoverers: From Alexander the Great to Sally Ride takes the reader on an adventure with 171 men and women who have made significant contributions to human knowledge of the earth and the universe. Journeying through the centuries from ancient times to the present, we will conquer frontiers and sail uncharted waters. We will trek across treacherous mountains, scorching deserts, steamy jungles, and icy glaciers. We will plumb the depths of the oceans, land on the moon, and test the limits of outer space. Encountering isolation, disease, and even death, we will experience the exhilaration of triumph and the desolation of defeat.

Before joining the explorers and discoverers, however, it is worthwhile to consider why they venture into the unknown. Certainly a primary motivation is curiosity: they want to find out what is on the other side of a mountain, or they are intrigued by rumors about a strange new land, or they simply enjoy wandering the world. Yet adventurers often—indeed, usually—embark on a journey of discovery under less spontaneous circumstances; many of the great explorers were commissioned to lead an expedition with a specific mission. For instance, Spanish and Portuguese states sent **Christopher Columbus, Vasco da Gama,** and the sixteenth-century *conquistadors* on voyages to the New World in search of wealth.

Explorers also receive support from private investors. Prince **Henry the Navigator** financed expeditions along the coast of Africa. The popes of Rome sent emissaries to the Mongol khans. The Hudson's Bay Company, through the development of fur trade, was largely responsible for the exploration of Canada. **Joseph Banks** and the Royal Geographical Society backed the great nineteenth-century expeditions to the African continent. In each of these cases the explorer's discoveries resulted in lucrative trade routes and increased political power for the investor's home country.

Religion has been another strong motivating force for exploration. Famous Chinese travelers such as **Hsüang-tsang,** who was a Buddhist monk, went to India to obtain sacred Buddhist texts. **Abu Abdallah Ibn Battutah,** a Muslim, explored the Islamic world during a pilgrimage to Mecca. The medieval travel writer and rabbi **Benjamin of Tudela** investigated the state of Jewish communities throughout the Holy Land. Later, Christian missionaries **Johann Ludwig Krapf, Annie Royle Taylor,** and **Susie Carson Rijnhart** took their faith to the indigenous peoples of Asia and Africa.

Explorers have been inspired, too, by the quest for knowledge about the world. **Alexander von Humboldt** made an expedition to South America that collected a wealth of scientific information, while **James Cook** is credited with having done more than any other explorer to increase human knowledge of world geography. **Charles Darwin**'s famous voyage to South America aboard the Beagle resulted in his revolutionary theory of evolution.

Perhaps the foremost motivation to explore, however, is the desire to be the first to accomplish a particular feat. For instance, for nearly three centuries European nations engaged in a competition to be the first to find the Northwest Passage, a water route between the Atlantic and Pacific oceans, which the Norwegian explorer **Roald Amundsen** successfully navigated in 1903. Similarly, in the 1950s the United States and the Soviet Union became involved in a "space race," which culminated in 1969 when **Neil Armstrong** became the first human to walk on the moon.

Sometimes the spirit of cooperation can also be an incentive. During an 18-month period of maximum sunspot activity, from July 1957 through December 1958, 67 nations joined together to study the solar-terrestrial environment. Known as the International Geophysical Year, the project resulted in several major scientific discoveries along with the setting aside of Antarctica as a region for purposes of nonmilitary, international scientific research.

Although daring individuals throughout history have been driven by the desire to be first, the achievement began to take on special meaning with the increasing participation of women in travel and exploration during the nineteenth century. Pioneering women such as **Hester Stanhope, Mary Kingsley,** and **Alexandra David-Neel** broke away from rigid social roles to make remarkable journeys, but their accomplishments have only recently received the recognition they deserve. Since the advent of the aviation age in the early twentieth century, however, women have truly been at the forefront of exploration. **Amelia Earhart, Amy Johnson,** and **Beryl Markham** achieved as many flying "firsts" as their male colleagues; Soviet cosmonaut **Valentina Tereshkova** and U.S. astronaut **Sally Ride,** the first women in space, have made important contributions to space exploration.

By concentrating on biographies of individual explorers in this book we seem to suggest that these adventurers were loners who set out on their own to singlehandedly confront the unknown. Yet possibly the only "one-man show" was **René Caillié,** the first Westerner to travel to the forbidden city of Timbuktu and return alive. As a rule, explorers rarely traveled alone and they had help in achieving their goals. Therefore, use of an individual name is often only shorthand for the achievements of the expedition as a whole.

Famous explorers of Africa like **Richard Burton, John Hanning Speke, David Livingstone,** and **Henry Morton Stanley,** for instance, were all accompanied by large groups of servants and porters. In fact, the freed African slave **James Chuma,** who was the caravan leader for Livingstone and several other explorers, has been credited with the success of more than one expedition. Similar stories occur in other areas of exploration. For example, **Robert Edwin Peary** is considered to be the first person to reach the North Pole, yet he was accompanied by **Matthew A. Henson,** his African American assistant, and four Inuit—Egingwah, Seeglo, Ootah, and Ooqueah.

Explorers and Discoverers tells the stories of these men and women as well as others motivated by a daring spirit and an intense curiosity. They ventured forth to rediscover remote lands, to conquer the last frontiers, and to increase our knowledge of the world and the universe.

A final note of clarification: When we say that an explorer "discovered" a place, we do not mean she or he was the first human ever to have been there. Although the discoverer may have been the first from his or her country to set foot in a new land, most areas of the world during the great periods of exploration were already occupied or their existence had been verified by other people.

Picture Credits

The photographs and illustrations appearing in *Explorers and Discoverers: From Alexander the Great to Sally Ride* were received from the following sources:

On the cover: John Smith; **The Granger Collection, New York:** Beryl Markham and Matthew A. Henson.

UPI/Bettmann: pages 1, 129, 306, 375, 406, 489, 555, 611, 657, 699, 733, 742, 817, 856; **Norwegian Information Service:** page 14; **NASA:** pages 26, 30, 31, 34, 351, 400, 588, 723, 779, 844, 847; **The Granger Collection, New York:** pages 43, 44, 52, 61, 81, 86, 107, 122, 133, 141, 144, 145, 150, 164, 179, 187, 193, 209, 225, 282, 285, 311, 321, 325, 330, 334, 336, 345, 355, 359, 393, 424, 428, 433, 449, 460, 474, 499, 508, 512, 524, 560, 578, 589, 632, 638, 704, 744, 757, 772, 783, 806, 811, 830, 836, 852, 864; **The Bettmann Archive:** pages 169, 176, 268, 303, 341, 464, 494, 528, 623, 653, 695, 735, 767, 809, 828, 867; **Novosti Press Agency, Moscow:** page 378; **Hulton Deutsch Collection Limited:** page 418; **AP/Wide World Photos:** pages 538, 800;

NASA/Jet Propulsion Laboratory: page 585; UNHCR: page 604; Archive Photos/American Stock: page 610; UPI/Bettman Newsphotos: pages 739, 871.

Maps

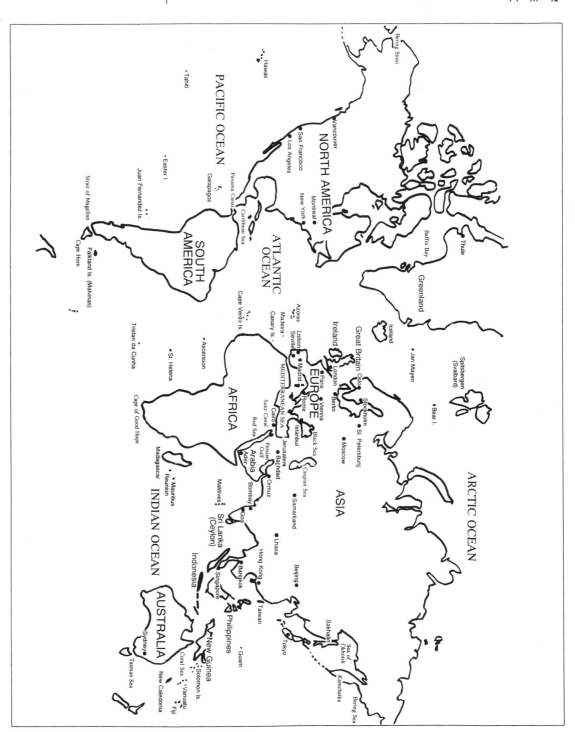

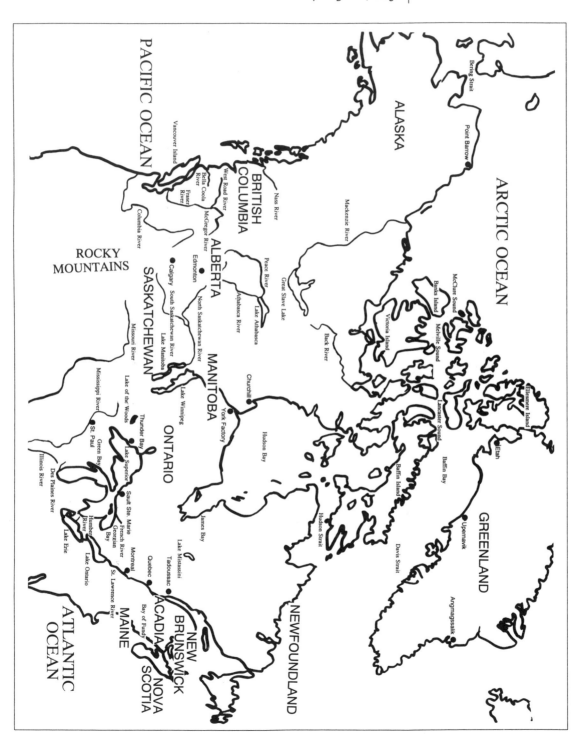

Americas—United States of America.

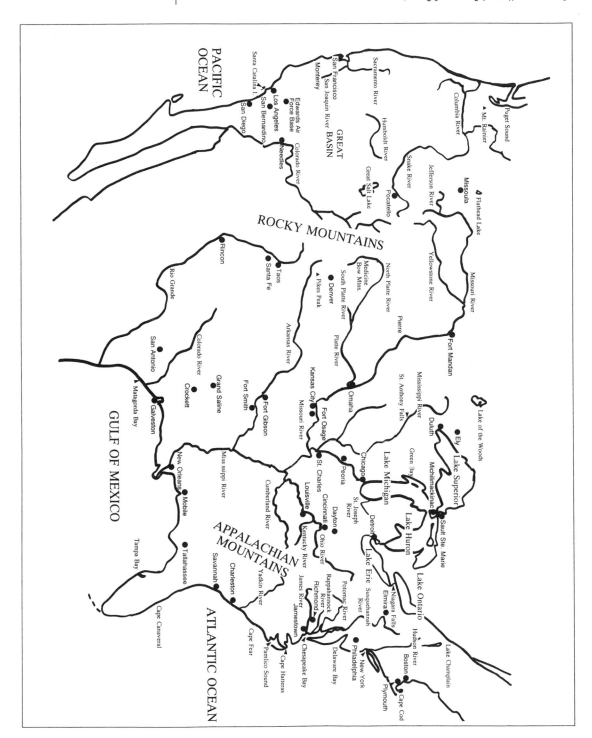

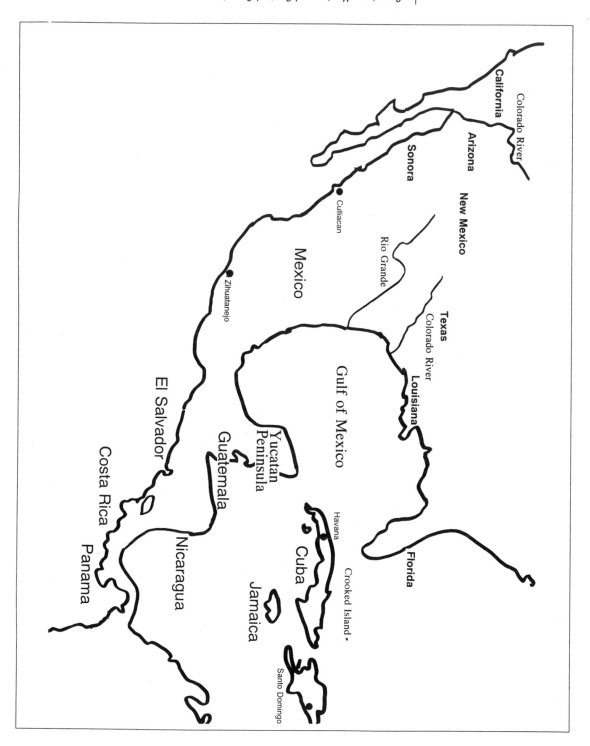

Cartagena
Margarita Island
Gulf of Paria
Lake Maracaibo
Caracas
Venezuela
Magdalena River
Guyana
Berbice River
CUNDINAMARCA
Orinoco River
Demerara River
Colombia
Devil's Island
Meta River
Mount Roraima ▲
Cayenne
Buenaventura
Paramaribo
French Guiana
Bogota
Uraricoera River
Maroni River
ESMERALDAS
Guaviare River
RORAIMA
Itany River
Aguarico River
Casiquiare Canal
Courantyne River
Quito
Rio Branco
Jari River
Ecuador
Andoas
Amazon River
Rio Negro
Guayaquil
Napo River
Amazon River
Manaus
Belem
Iquitos
Tefe (Ega)
Parintins
Sao Luis
Leticia
MARANHAO
Maranon River
Madeira River
Tapajos River
Cabo Sao Roque
Huallaga River
Acre River
Juruena River
Xingu River
Mt. Husacaran ▲
Abuna River
Roosevelt River
Tocantins River
Recife
RONDONIA
Paranatinga
Brazil
Callao
Urubamba River
Araguaia River
Bahia
Lima
Guapore River
Machu Picchu
Cuzco
Cuiaba
Brasilia
Arequipa
La Paz
Goias
Bolivia
MATO GROSSO
Andes Mountains
Mt. Illampu
MINAS GERAIS
Sucre
Paraguay River
Tarma
Potosi
Ouro Preto
GRAN CHACO
Sao Paulo
Pacific Ocean
Atacama Desert
Pilcomayo River
Asuncion
Rio de Janeiro
Paraguay
Copiapo
Encarnacion
Coquimbo
RIO GRANDE DO SUL
Parana River
Argentina
Uruguay
Valparaiso
▲ Mt. Aconcagua
Santiago
Buenos Aires
Atlantic Ocean
Chile
Rio de la Plata
Concepcion
Rio Colorado
Arauco
Rio Negro
Lake Musters
Lake Colhue Huapi
PATAGONIA
Punta Arenas
Falkland Islands (Malvinas)

Americas–South America.

ATLANTIC
OCEAN

Tangier
Fez
Rabat

Tunis

Tunisia

Tripoli

Morocco

Ghadames

Canary Islands

Sahara Desert

In-Salah

Marzuq

Tassili-n-Ajjer

FEZZAN

Cape Bojador

Ahaggar Mountains

Ghat

Cabo Blanco

Mauritania

Air Mountains

Tibesti Massif

Agadez

Timbuktu

Senegal River

Sinbing

Mali

Gao

WADU

Lake Chad

Senegal

Silla

Djenne

Niger River

Kano

N'djamena

Goree
Island

Pisania

Bamako

Segu

Sokoto

Kukawa

Gambia River

Volta River

BORNU

Bijagos Islands

Nigeria

Chari River

Sierra
Leone

Freetown

Ghana

Badagri

Bussa

Lokoja

Benue River

Central
African
Republic

Liberia

Lagos

Togo

Brass Town

Cape Palmas

Africa and the Middle East—Northwest Africa.

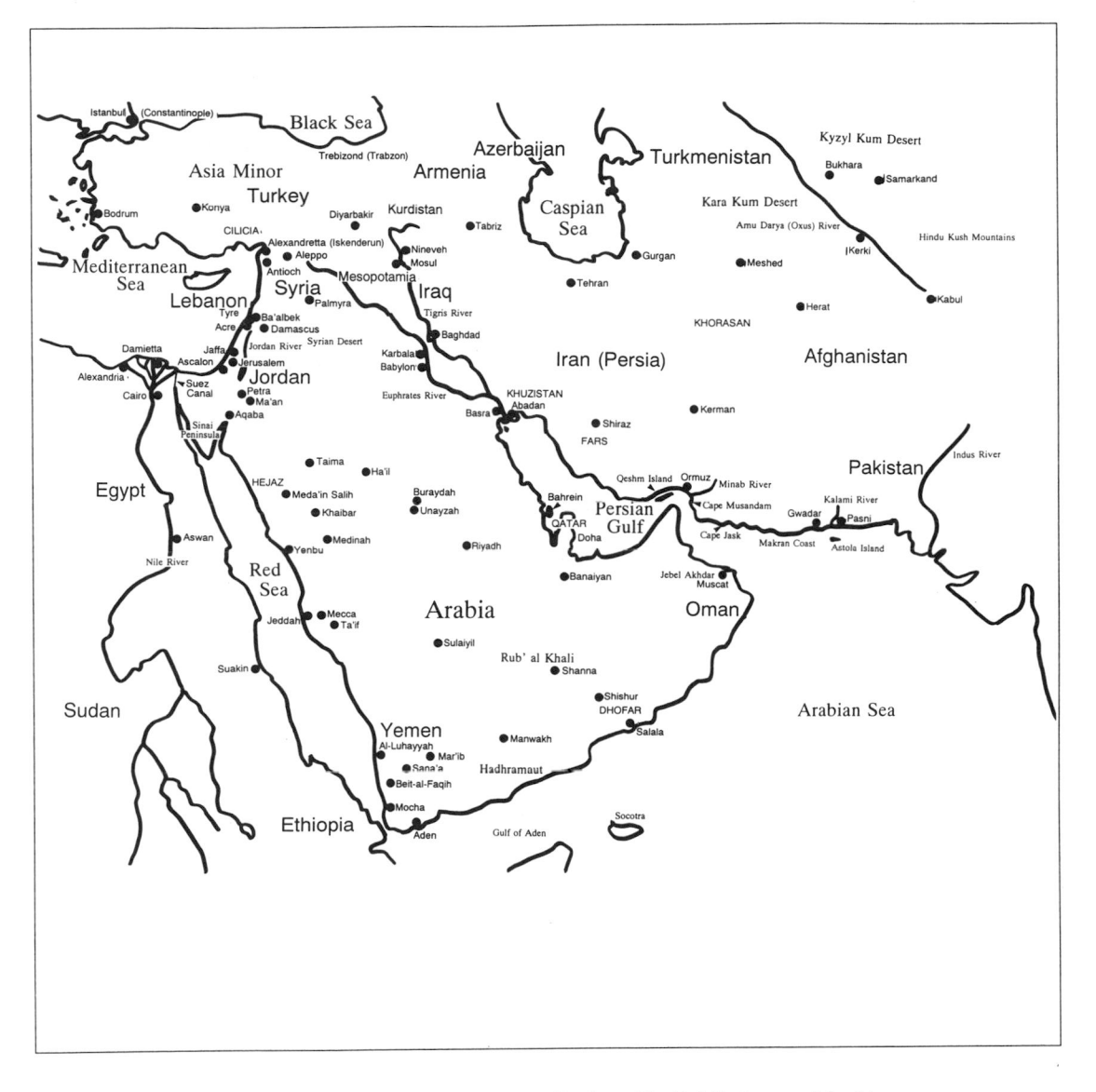

Africa and the Middle East—The Middle East and Arabia.

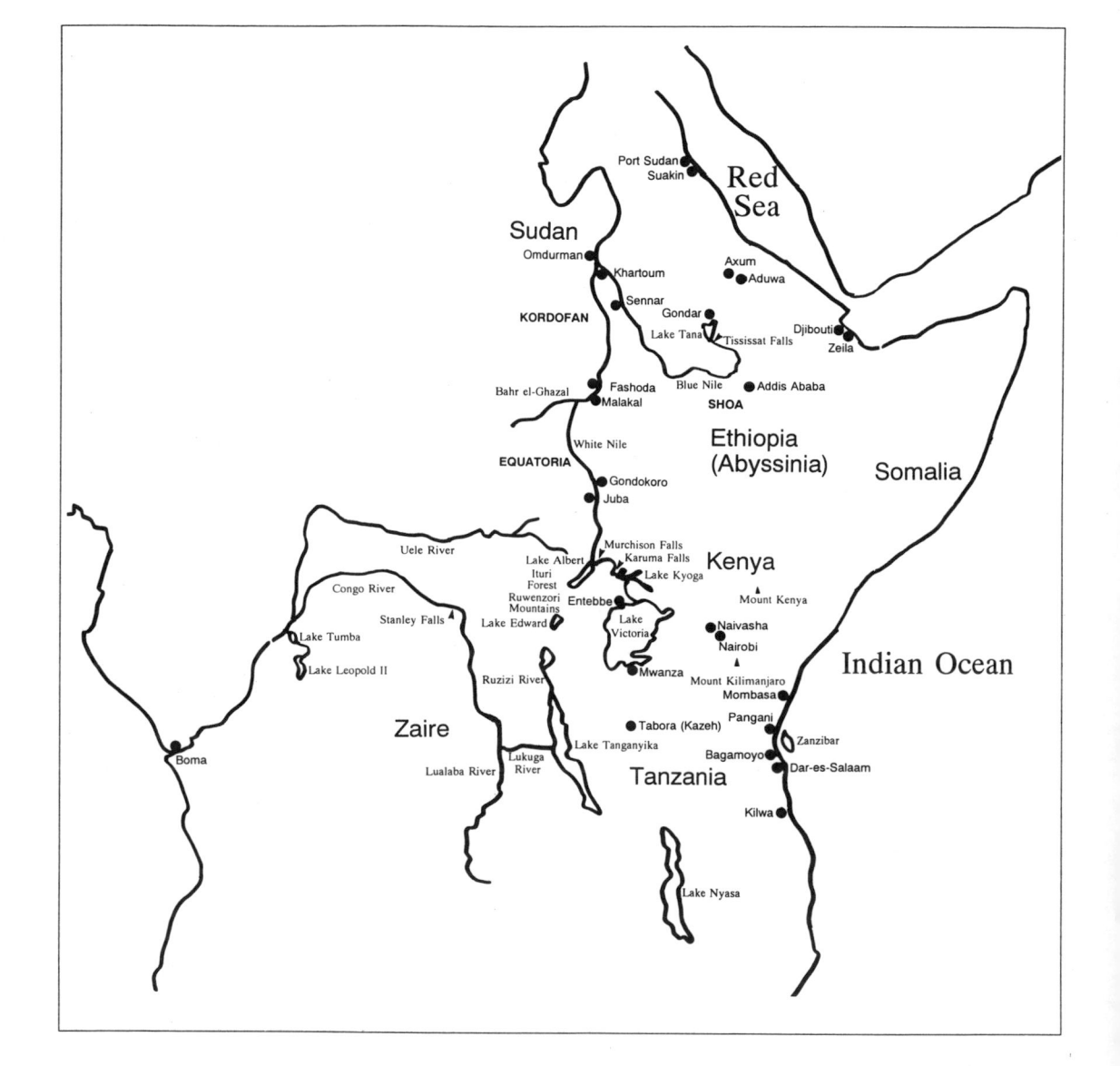

Africa and the Middle East—Eastern Africa.

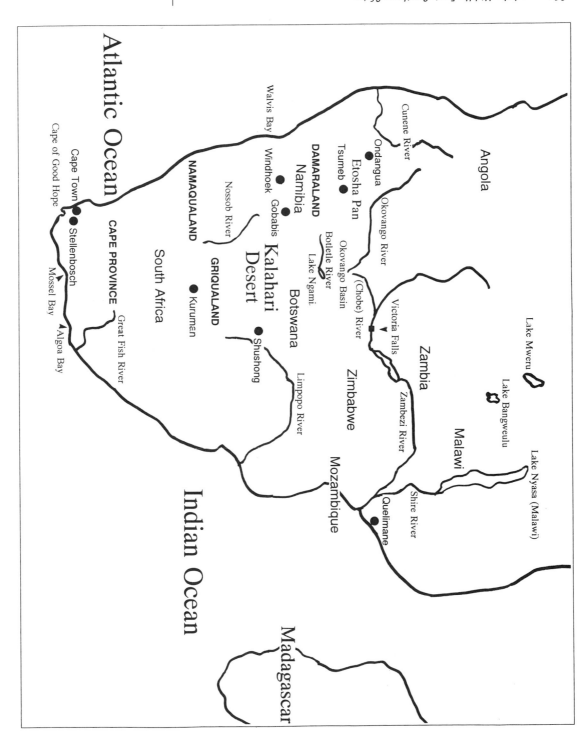

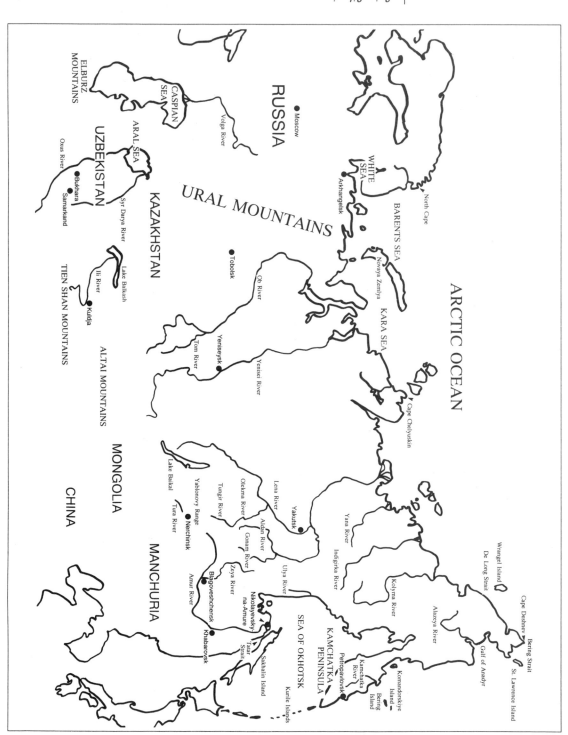

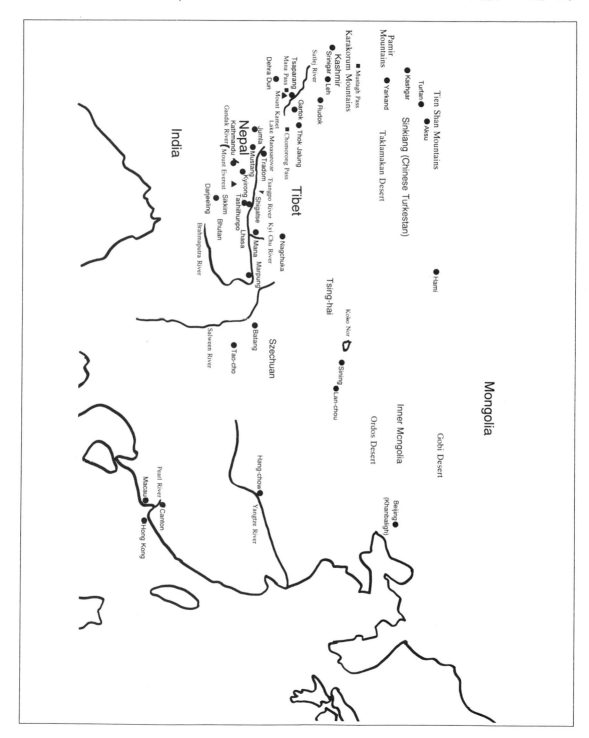

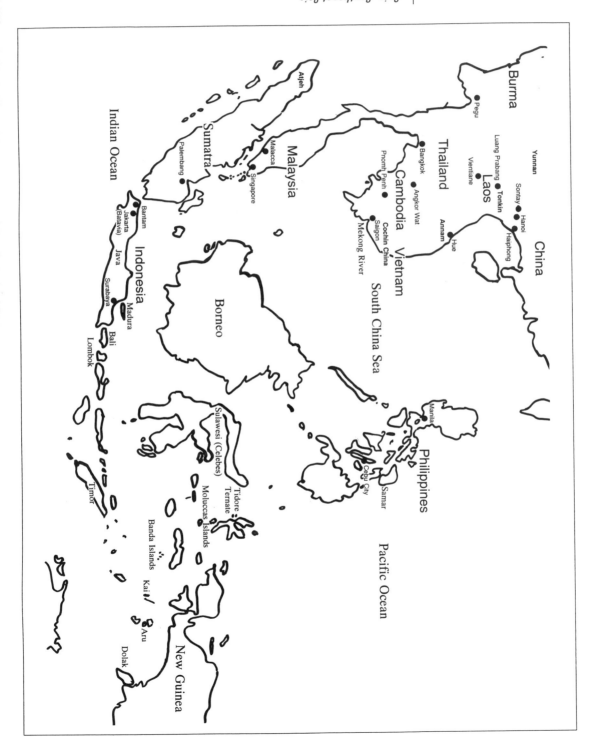

Burma
Pegu
Thailand
Bangkok
Yunnan
Luang Prabang • Tonkin
Vientiane
Laos
Sontay
Hanoi
Haiphong
China
Annam
Hue
Phnom Penh
Angkor Wat
Cambodia
Cochin China
Saigon
Mekong River
Vietnam
South China Sea
Malacca
Singapore
Malaysia
Sumatra
Palembang
Indian Ocean
Atjeh
Bantam
Jakarta
(Batavia)
Java
Surabaya
Madura
Bali
Lombok
Indonesia
Borneo
Sulawesi (Celebes)
Timor
Tidore
Ternate
Moluccas Islands
Banda Islands
Kai
Aru
Dolak
New Guinea
Manila
Cebu City
Samar
Philippines
Pacific Ocean

Pacific Ocean–Oceanea.

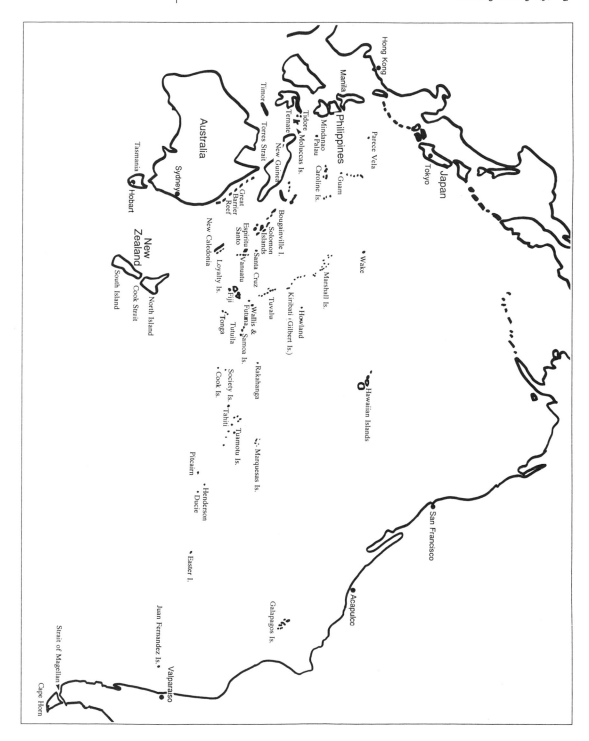

Pacific Ocean–Australia.

SIBERIA

Lena River

Kara Sea

Novaya Zemlya

Arkhangelsk

White Sea

Kolyma River

Cape Chelyuskin

Severnaya Zemlya

Barents Sea

Vardohus

Laptev Sea

North Cape

Ostrova De-Longa

Franz Josef Land

Tromso

Svalbard (Spitsbergen)

Lofoten Islands

ARCTIC OCEAN

King's Bay

North Pole +

De Long Strait

Jan Mayen Island

Gulf of
Anadyr

Wrangel Island

Cape Dezhnev

Cape Columbia

Bering Strait

GREENLAND

Point Barrow

Cape Thomas Hubbard

Iceland

Kane Basin

Etah
Thule
Thule Air Base

Ringnes I.

Ellesmere
Island

Upernavik

Melville I.

ALASKA

Angmagssalik

Banks I.

Viscount
Melville
Sound

Devon I.

Lancaster Sound

Baffin Bay

North
Magnetic
Pole

Mackenzie River

Amundsen Gulf

Victoria I.

Prince
Regent
Inlet

Brattahlid

Godthab

Cape
Farewell

King William Island

Foxe
Basin

Davis Strait

Julianehab

Cumberland Sound

Arctic Region.

Antarctic Region.

EXPLORERS & DISCOVERERS

H.M.S. *Challenger*

Set sail December 21, 1872,
Portsmouth, England
Docked May 24, 1876,
England

The idea for the H.M.S. *Challenger* expedition, which investigated the physical and biological properties of the world's oceans, began with two British naturalists, William B. Carpenter and Charles Wyville Thomson. Having already dredged in the North Atlantic Ocean off the coast of Britain, they realized a wealth of information could be obtained from the oceans if they were examined in a systematic way.

Prompted by Carpenter, the Royal Society, the major scientific society in Great Britain, asked the British Admiralty to supply a ship and crew to make such a voyage. The request was granted. Naval command was given to Sir George Nares, while Thomson was put in charge of scientific research. The instructions given to these men were to:

> investigate the physical condition of the deep sea throughout the three great ocean basins, that is, to ascertain their depth, temperature, circulation, etc. to determine the distribution of organic life throughout

The H.M.S. Challenger *expedition, which conducted the first scientific exploration of the world's oceans, pioneered the science of descriptive oceanography.*

the areas traversed, at the surface, at intermediate depths, and especially at the deep ocean bottom.

Investigation of the oceans

Nares and Thomson were provided a 226-foot-long combination steam and sailing vessel, which they named the *Challenger*. The party set sail from the British naval harbor at Portsmouth on December 21, 1872. During the course of the expedition, the ship stopped every 200 miles and stayed in place to record ocean depths, to dredge for animal life, and to take the temperature of the ocean at different depths. It performed these operations at 362 stations, dredging as deep as 5,486 meters (18,000 feet).

The *Challenger* expedition was the first to systematically record the differences between the Atlantic and Pacific oceans. The Pacific, for example, is considerably deeper and has a clay bottom. *Challenger* scientists found the first deposits of manganese, a potentially valuable mineral, in the mid-Atlantic on March 7, 1873, at a depth of 1,500 fathoms (9,000 feet); they later found manganese on the floor of the Pacific as well.

Traveling every ocean except the Arctic and crossing the equator six times, the voyage covered 69,000 nautical miles (79,000 statute miles). The expedition took a two-month break in Australia in March and April 1874 so the scientists could spend their time ashore studying freshwater biology. While cruising in the Pacific in 1875, the ship encountered ocean depths so much greater than had been thought possible that their thermometers, used to measure the ocean temperature at various depths, broke under the unexpected pressure. The varying measurements of the ocean floor convinced the geologists of a revolutionary idea—there were mountain ranges under the sea.

Major discoveries

The *Challenger* returned to England on May 24, 1876, carrying "a great freight of facts." Besides adding 715 new genera and 4,717 new species to man's knowledge of marine zoology, *Challenger* scientists found life at depths much greater than ever before suspected. They also revealed the physical and chemical nature of the ocean floor, obtained seawater for chemical analysis, and gained new information about the circulation of the ocean currents. They mapped the contours of ocean basins, including the Atlantic Ridge and the Challenger Deep, located in the western Pacific Ocean in the Mariana Trench. The report of the *Challenger* expedition took 23 years to compile and filled 50 volumes.

Samuel de Champlain

Born c. 1567,
Brouage, France

Died December 25, 1635,
Quebec, New France (now Canada)

Samuel de Champlain, a Frenchman who explored eastern North America, was involved in the founding of French colonies in Acadia and Quebec.

After visiting New France, a French colony that became the country of Canada, Samuel de Champlain convinced the French government that the land in North America had potential for settlement and commercial development. Now considered the father of New France and the founder of Quebec, Champlain made 12 journeys to New France to explore and consolidate French holdings in the New World. Champlain wrote six books about his expeditions and the importance of New France. Serving for a time as the king's lieutenant in New France, he lived to see Quebec established on both shores of the St. Lawrence River.

Champlain was born in the small seaport town of Brouage on the west coast of France in about the year 1567. It is thought that he was born a Protestant and at some point converted to Catholicism during a period of bitter rivalry between Protestants and Catholics over which religion would control the government.

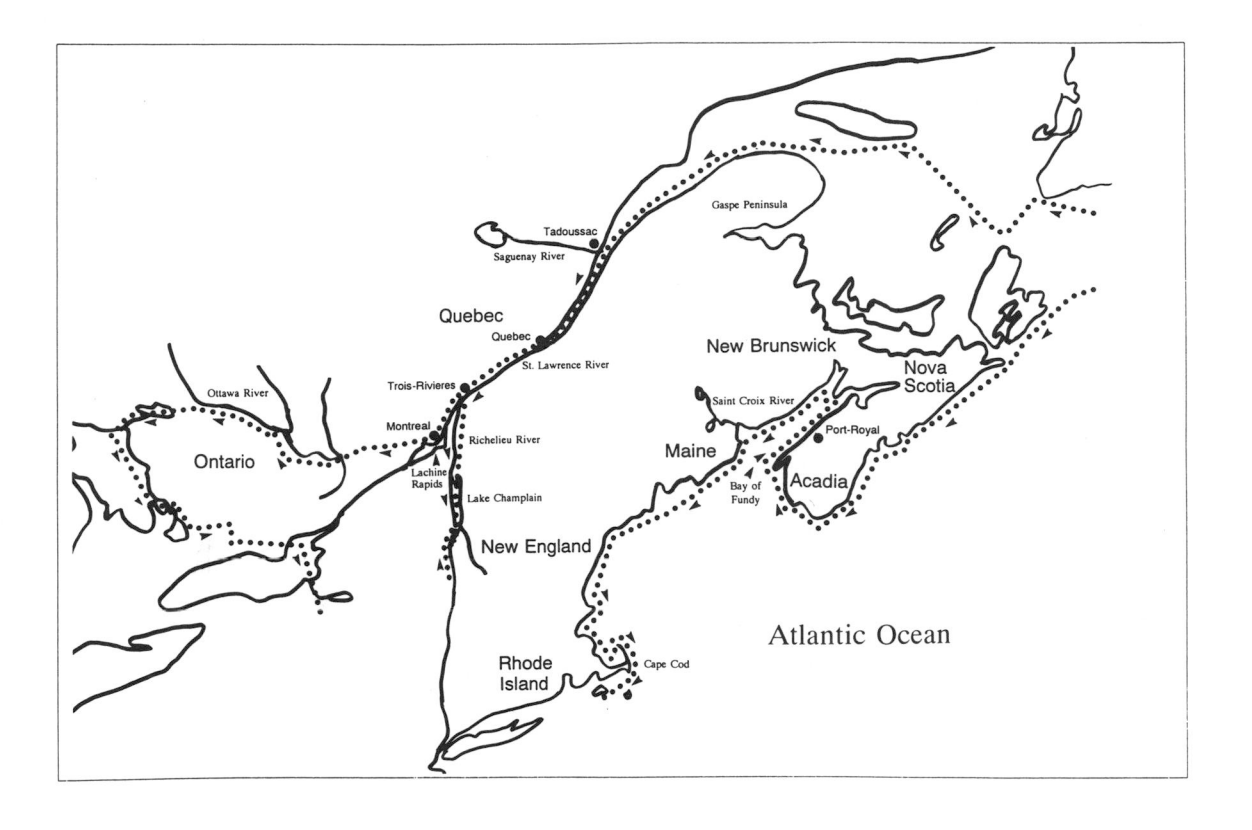

Champlain went to sea at an early age and learned navigation and cartography, or the drafting of maps and charts. Until 1598 he fought as a sergeant on the side of Protestant King Henry IV in the religious wars; he then made a voyage of two and a half years to the West Indies. Although Champlain was born a commoner, his reputation as a navigator earned him an honorary title in Henry's court.

Champlain explored eastern Canada and New England; he was the first person to chart the Atlantic coast from the Bay of Fundy to Cape Cod.

Joins expedition to New France

In 1603 Champlain was invited to join the expedition of François Gravé Du Pont to visit the River of Canada, now called the St. Lawrence River. The expedition landed at Tadoussac, a summer trading post where the Saguenay River runs into the St. Lawrence. Champlain sailed with the expedition up the St. Lawrence past the sites of Quebec, Trois-Rivières, and Montreal. He immediately realized that these lands could be colonized and made a source of wealth for the French king; he also learned of the existence of the Great Lakes. The French found the land sparsely inhabited by Native Americans, some of whom were friendly toward the Europeans while others were not. He wrote about the customs of the Native Americans in a report which was published in France.

Returning to Tadoussac in July, the expedition sailed around the Gaspé Peninsula into a region Champlain called Acadia, probably named for Arcadia, the mythical paradise of the ancient Greeks. Champlain urged the French government to explore Acadia, now known as Nova Scotia. The region reportedly had rich mines and some speculated it might even be the key to finding the elusive Northwest Passage, the water route between the Atlantic and Pacific oceans that the major world powers had long been seeking.

As a result of his efforts in New France, Champlain was chosen in 1604 to be the geographer on an expedition to Acadia. Led by Lieutenant-General Pierre de Monts, who had a monopoly on the fur trade in the region, the party of explorers and settlers sailed to Acadia. Traveling down the coast of New Brunswick, they stopped at the Saint Croix River and built a small fort on a site that is now almost exactly on the border between the United States and Canada. The first winter was disastrous: scurvy, a disease caused by lack of vitamin C in the diet, killed nearly half of the party. The following winter they moved across the Bay of Fundy to Port Royal, now called Annapolis Royal in Nova Scotia. This was to become the center of settlement for the French Acadians.

Explores present-day New England

During the next three years Champlain went off on his own trying to find an ideal site for colonization. He sailed along the coast of Maine and traveled as far as 150 miles inland. On another trip, he sailed down the coast of New England as far as Martha's Vineyard off Cape Cod. Although the English were exploring in the same area and eventually established the Plymouth Colony in 1620, Champlain was the first European to give a detailed account of the region. He is credited with discovering Mount Desert Island as well as most of the major rivers in Maine.

Since the French did not find a spot they particularly liked, they returned to Acadia to build a more permanent fort at Port Royal. De Monts returned to France but Champlain stayed with the settlers in Acadia. In September 1606, he made another exploration to the south as far as Rhode Island. During the following winter the French made the best of their isolated situation by forming the Order of Good Cheer, which sponsored banquets and games and amateur shows. In 1607, when Henry IV canceled de Monts's trading privileges, the entire colony was forced to return to France. Before he left Champlain had accurately charted the Atlantic coast from the Bay of Fundy to Cape Cod.

Founds Quebec City

In 1608 Champlain had secured backing for his most ambitious project in the New World, the beginning of a permanent settlement at Quebec City. Arriving in July, the party, which included 32 colonists, built a fort and faced their first hard winter. Only nine people survived to welcome the reinforcements that arrived in June of the following year. Champlain continued his exploration of Canada by traveling up the St. Lawrence and Richelieu rivers to the lake that now bears his name, Lake Champlain. In 1609 he joined the Hurons and their allies in a great battle against a marauding band of Iroquois on Lake Champlain near present-day Crown Point, New York. The French and Hurons defeated the Iroquois, thus leading to 150 years of hostilities between the French and the Iroquois, one of the most powerful tribal nations in North America.

Iroquois Confederacy

The Iroquois Confederacy was founded around 1570 by the prophet Deganawidah and his disciple Hiawatha, who was the subject of a famous poem by Henry Wadsworth Longfellow. The purpose of the confederacy, which consisted of five tribes known as the Five Nations—the Mohawk, Oneida, Onondaga, Cayuga, and Seneca—was to stop intertribal warfare and end the practice of cannibalism (eating human flesh). The Five Nations, numbering about 5,500 people, lived in upper New York State.

In the early seventeenth century the Iroquois had the most advanced culture in the Eastern region; descent was matrilineal, meaning that family members took the mother's name, and women held a high status in their society. The men trapped and hunted and women tended gardens; they lived in bark-covered huts known as longhouses. The main Onondaga village was the capital of the council of the Five Nations, who were noted for their political organization and military power. Today the Iroquois in the United States and Canada number around 29,000.

Jean Nicollet

Jean Nicollet had been living among the Huron, Algonquin, and Nipissing tribes since 1618 as an interpreter and negotiator of their fur trade with French companies. In 1634 Champlain sent Nicollet on a diplomatic mission to the Winnebago tribe who lived along the shores of Green Bay in the present-day state of Wisconsin. The Winnebago were not friendly with the Algonquin and it was feared that they would direct their trade to the English. Since the theory was that the route to the Great Lakes might also lead to China, Nicollet set out wearing a Chinese robe embroidered with flowers and birds.

Nicollet left Quebec in mid-July 1634 and traveled via the Ottawa River, Lake Nipissing, and the French River to Lake Huron, where he passed through the straits of Michilimackinac to Lake Michigan, then proceeded down to Green Bay. He was the first European to follow this route, which was to become the main passage for French fur traders to the West. One of the great scenes of North American exploration is Nicollet coming ashore in Green Bay dressed in his flowery Chinese robe. Impressing the tribesmen with his elaborate costume, Nicollet successfully completed his mission by signing a treaty of peace between the Winnebago and the French.

Named Lieutenant in New France

In 1612 Champlain returned to France. On the basis of his report, the king decided to make Quebec the center for French fur trading in North America. Around this time Champlain married Hélène Broullé, the daughter of the secretary to the king's chamber. During the next few years, Champlain frequently traveled back and forth from Canada to France. While in Canada he pursued his explorations and tried to nurture the colony in Quebec, but political intrigues in France demanded all his diplomatic skills. When the fur trade faltered, he had to muster support for the colony. He came out of this skirmish the victor, having been made a lieutenant in New France by the new king, Louis XIII.

When Champlain returned to Canada in 1613, he explored the Ottawa River to Allumette Island, opening the route that was to be the main river road to the Great Lakes for the next two centuries. By this time the French had made favorable treaties with many of the Native American tribes, and the fur trade prospered. Champlain was able to spend time on other aspects of governing the colony. In 1615 he returned from France with the first Catholic missionaries who came to convert the Native Americans to Christianity. During that summer he saw the Great Lakes for the first time.

Position threatened by politics

The Iroquois presence remained troublesome. When the French, allied with the Hurons and Algonquins, unsuccessfully attacked an Iroquois stronghold at a site in modern-day New York State, Champlain was seriously wounded. He spent the winter recuperating among his old friends, the Hurons. When he returned to France in 1616 he found that politics at court had once again weakened his position, and he lost the position of lieutenant in New France. In order to regain his position he proposed an ambitious plan to colonize Quebec, establish agriculture, and search for the Northwest Passage. He gained the king's support and spent part of 1618 in Quebec.

Champlain's problems in France were not yet over. Plagued by lawsuits and political manipulations, he again appealed to the king. This time he was appointed commander and spent the following years trying to strengthen the colony. His authority gained momentum when the most powerful man in the French government, the Cardinal de Richelieu, formed the Company of One Hundred Associates to rule New France with Champlain in charge.

Exiled to England

In 1629 Quebec was attacked and forced to surrender to a party of English privateers. Champlain was exiled to England, where he spent the next four years defending the importance of New France and writing accounts of his life. When a peace treaty was signed between England and France in 1632, Champlain was restored to his former position. In 1634 he sent Jean Nicollet, a French trapper and trader, to the West to extend French claims in the region that is now Wisconsin. Having suffered from various health problems since 1633, Champlain died in Quebec on December 25, 1635.

Chang Ch'ien

Born c. 160 B.C.

Died 114 B.C.

Chang Ch'ien was a Chinese diplomat who made the first recorded trip of a Chinese into central Asia and opened up the "Silk Road" trade route with Rome.

When Wu-Ti, a member of the Han dynasty, became the emperor of China in 140 B.C., the country was threatened on its northern border by the Hsiung-nu "barbarians," known in the West as the Huns. The new emperor tried to deal with this threat by organizing military alliances against the Hsiung-nu. He asked for volunteers to carry out a diplomatic mission to the Yüeh-chih nomads in central Asia. His challenge was accepted by Chang Ch'ien, a young court official from the city of Hanzhong. The Yüeh-chih were Indo-Scythian tribesmen, ancestors of modern Afghans and Tajiks, who had taken over control of central Asia after the disintegration of the empire of **Alexander the Great** (see entry).

Held captive by the Hsiung-nu

In 138 B.C. Chang Ch'ien and his entourage, which included a Tatar slave named Kan Fu, traveled west through the Chinese province of Gansu. They were captured by members of the Hsiung-nu tribe and taken to their headquarters in the Altai Mountains. Chang Ch'ien was kept in captivity for ten years; during that time he married and had a son. After he was able to escape he made his way southward, traveling through Fergana in the area that is now Uzbekistan to Bactria in present-day Afghanistan. Chang Ch'ien also visited northern Pakistan around the city of Peshawar, which was then ruled by the Yüeh-chih. He finally reached the Yüeh-chih capital of Heyuchi, where he stayed for a year. However, he could not persuade the Yüeh-chih to join with the Chinese in fighting the Hsiung-nu.

Returns to China

In 126 Chang Ch'ien returned home by a more southerly route. Hoping to avoid the Hsiung-nu, he went south of the Kunlun Shan range to the lake at Lop Nor and then to the Tsaidam, a swampy region in the Tsinghai province. Once again he was captured, but this time he escaped after only one year. In 126 B.C. he returned to the Wu-Ti's court, bringing with him his wife and Kan Fu. Chang Ch'ien reported to the emperor not only about the countries he had visited but also about places he had heard of, including India, the Caucasus Mountains, Persia, Mesopotamia, and the Roman provinces in Asia. He proposed setting up trading relations with India via the Chinese province of Szechwan. Wu-Ti sent out four missions to achieve this goal, but they all failed.

Chang Ch'ien was given a title of nobility and took part in a campaign against the Hsiung-nu in 122 B.C. During an attack, however, he failed to come to the aid of his commander. For this dereliction he was fined and reduced to the rank of private. After the Chinese inflicted a major defeat on the Hsiung-nu the following year, Chang Ch'ien was restored to the emperor's favor.

Heads diplomatic mission

Chang Ch'ien proposed another diplomatic mission, so Wu-Ti sent him to Wusun in the valley of the Ili River in what is now Chinese Turkestan and Kazakhstan. Although the mission was a diplomatic failure, it did have one significant result: while in Wusun Chang Ch'ien sent out to neighboring countries envoys who carried gifts of silk produced in China. These silks gradually found their way to the West and opened the so-called Silk Road—the overland trade route through Central Asia between China and the Roman Empire. The route extended from Merv, which is present-day Mary, in Turkmenistan, through northern Iran to Ecbatana; from there it went to the city of Seleucia-Ctesiphon near Baghdad, through northern Mesopotamia and Syria to the port of Antioch, 6,000 miles from China.

Following his mission to Wusun, Chang Ch'ien returned to China, where he was appointed head of the Office of Foreign Affairs. He died the following year, in 114 B.C.

Cheng Ho

Born c. 1371,
Kunyang, K'un-ming, China

Died c. 1433,
Calicut, India

When Cheng Ho (or Zheng He) was a young boy, he was made a servant of the Chinese emperor. He then rose to become an important military leader and admiral. Although his expeditions to Southeast Asia, India, Arabia, and the east coast of Africa contributed significantly to Chinese knowledge of these areas, the government failed to recognize the advantages to be gained from this information. The history of the centuries that followed might have been different had the Chinese taken better advantage of the voyages of Cheng Ho.

Taken from home as a child

Cheng Ho was born into a Muslim family in the city of Kunyang in the K'un-ming province of southwestern China. When he was ten years old, the Muslims of K'un-ming rebelled against their Chinese rulers. The Chinese put down the rebellion, however, and Cheng Ho was one of a few local children who were selected to be castrated and serve as eunuchs in the

Cheng Ho was a Chinese admiral who led seven large naval expeditions from China to Asia, India, Arabia, and Africa.

Eunuchs

The practice of employing eunuchs, or young boys who have been castrated, as servants in wealthy households and royal courts dates back to ancient times, although it was not so common in the Muslim world as it was in the Byzantine and Ottoman empires. Eunuchs frequently became powerful leaders, like Cheng Ho; another example was the Byzantine general Narses. Because eunuchs were castrated they had high voices, and they were often used in choirs; this custom began in Constantinople and was adopted by European opera companies in the eighteenth century. *Castrati* sang in the papal choir at the Vatican in Rome until the nineteenth century.

court of the Chinese emperor. Cheng Ho became a servant to a prince named Chu Ti. As Cheng Ho grew older, he accompanied Chu Ti on various military campaigns against the Mongols on the northern border. He eventually became one of the prince's most valued military leaders and advisers.

Heads naval operations

In 1402, after leading a successful insurrection, Chu Ti was crowned emperor. Now known as Yung-lo, the emperor put Cheng Ho in charge of several naval expeditions to foreign lands. Yung-lo suspected that the previous emperor might have fled across the sea, so he directed Cheng Ho and others to pursue evidence of his whereabouts. In 1405 Cheng Ho set out on his first voyage from the mouth of the Yang-tse River with an enormous fleet that was said to contain 65 large and 255 small vessels and a total crew of 27,800. The party sailed south across the South China Sea, anchoring at Qui Nhon in what is now Vietnam.

Makes several more voyages

In one of his first important acts as a leader Cheng Ho defeated the famous Chinese pirate Chen Tsu-i in battle. He took Chen Tsu-i prisoner, sending him to Nanking to be executed. Cheng Ho continued on to Sri Lanka and the port of Calicut, in south India. He returned to China in 1407. During that same year Cheng Ho set out on his second voyage to Calicut, then the center of the spice trade in southern India. After leaving Calicut, Cheng Ho's expedition stopped in Thailand and Java before returning to China in 1409.

Goes to Southeast Asia and Africa

During his third voyage, from 1409 to 1411, Cheng Ho

made excursions to Thailand, Malacca on the coast of Malaya, Sumatra, and Sri Lanka. After having some trouble with the king of Sri Lanka, Cheng Ho was taken prisoner and sent back to China. For his fourth voyage, from 1413 to 1415, Cheng Ho took his fleet even farther: dividing the ships into several squadrons, he sent some to Sri Lanka and Bengal and others to the Maldive Islands off the southwest coast of India, to Hormuz (the main port of Iran), and to the south coast of Arabia. On the fifth voyage (1417-19) the fleet went to the Ryukyu Islands between Japan and Taiwan, to Brunei on the north coast of Borneo, and to the island of Java. Squadrons continued on to the shores of East Africa, visiting Mogadishu, Brava, and Juba in Somalia; Malindi and Mombasa in Kenya; the island of Zanzibar and ports in Tanzania and Mozambique. The sixth expedition (1421-22) expanded upon the previous one, visiting states between Brunei and Zanzibar, and stopping at the ports of Brava and Mogadishu.

Loses royal backing for voyages

Before Cheng Ho returned from his sixth expedition, Yung-lo died. Cheng Ho had lost his major supporter. Officials at the court began to lobby to stop Cheng Ho's voyages, arguing that the expeditions were unnecessary and wasteful. They claimed that the "Middle Kingdom"—as China was then called because the Chinese believed they occupied the middle of the earth and were surrounded by barbarians—had nothing to gain by dealing with other countries. However, the new emperor, Chu Chan-chi, approved one last voyage.

From 1433 to 1435 Cheng Ho revisited many places on the coast of Africa, traveling as far north as the Strait of Hormuz, which lies between the Persian Gulf and the Gulf of Oman. The party was given gifts and tributes for the Chinese emperor from rulers of many lands they had visited. Cheng Ho died during this trip, in the port of Calicut; his body was taken back to China to be buried in Nanking.

Left legacy for European explorers

In 1431 Cheng Ho had erected a monument in a Taoist

temple, upon which he inscribed a description of his accomplishments. Discovered in 1937, the monument provides a poetic account of his explorations. It states in part:

> [We have] gone to more than thirty countries large and small. We have traversed more than one hundred thousand li [a li is about one-third of a mile] of immense water spaces and have beheld in the ocean huge waves like mountains rising sky-high, and we have set eyes on barbarian regions far away hidden in a blue transparency of light vapors.

It remains a mystery why the Chinese did not follow up on the explorations of Cheng Ho. About 70 years after the admiral's death, **Vasco da Gama** (see entry) and other Portuguese and European navigators began to explore the areas Cheng Ho had previously visited. The Chinese could have profited from Cheng Ho's voyages, perhaps especially from their knowledge of Africa. Instead, it was the Europeans who became the important maritime powers of the next several centuries.

Médard Chouart des Groseilliers

Born 1625,
Northern France

Died 1698,
Sorel, Quebec

Pierre Esprit Radisson

Born c. 1636,
Avignon, France

Died c. 1710,
London, England

Radisson and Groseilliers

Médard Chouart des Groseilliers was born in northern France on his parents' farm, which was called Les Groseilliers, or the Gooseberry Bushes. He went to New France, which is now Canada, at an early age, probably as a soldier. Groseilliers married in Quebec City and stayed there to raise a family. After his first wife died, he remarried in 1653 and moved to the town of Trois Rivières. His second wife's half-brother, Pierre Esprit Radisson, was to become Groseilliers's companion on many of his trips. The two have been known as "Gooseberries and Radishes" to generations of Canadian schoolchildren.

Pierre Esprit Radisson was born in Avignon in the south of France sometime around 1636. His half-sister immigrated to Canada, and Radisson either went with her or joined her there later. The first mention of him comes in 1651 when he was captured by the Iroquois, a confederation of Native American tribes. Taken by members of the Mohawk tribe to a village near present-day Schenectady, New York, he was adopted

Médard Chouart des Groseilliers and Pierre Esprit Radisson were Frenchmen who explored the area north of Lake Superior; they realized the potential of the fur trade in Hudson Bay and were responsible for the founding of the

by an Iroquois family. Radisson stayed there until he escaped to the Dutch trading post at Fort Orange, which is now Albany, New York, in 1653. He returned to his home in Trois-Rivières, Canada, in 1654.

By the time of Radisson's return the French and Iroquois had reached a peace agreement. In 1657 he went on a French missionary trip to Onondaga near Syracuse, New York, as an interpreter. Growing tired of the missionaries, the Iroquois plotted to kill them. Somehow Radisson learned of their plot and, according to accounts at the time as well as legends that formed afterward, Radisson is supposed to have convinced the Iroquois to attend a big feast where they were drugged long enough for the Frenchmen to make their escape.

Groseilliers finds trade route

Ever since the founding of New France, the French had been at war with the Iroquois. In the early 1650s the Iroquois annihilated the Huron tribe, who had become Christianized allies of the French. This victory cut off New France from much of the fur trade in the interior, which was the main source of economic support for the colony. Following a truce between the French and the Iroquois in 1654, Groseilliers was commissioned to lead a two-year expedition to the interior.

The exact route of this trip is unknown, but the most interesting result is that when he returned to New France with an impressive quantity of furs, he claimed to have found an overland route to Hudson Bay. Groseilliers's companions on the trip are also unknown; although historians have assumed that Radisson was in the party his presence has not been verified. Groseilliers undertook another expedition to the interior in 1658, and this time Radisson went with him.

Punished for initiative

In August 1658 Groseilliers and Radisson left Montreal on a voyage that took them to Lake Superior and then to Lake Courte Oreille, which is near the present-day village of Radisson, Wisconsin. They spent the winter with Huron and Ottawa refugees who had been driven off their lands by the Iroquois. During their stay the two Frenchmen were the first Europeans to meet members of the Sioux tribe. Traveling to the north shore of Lake Superior in the spring, they learned from Cree tribesmen about the wealth of furs that could be found in the country around Hudson Bay.

Groseilliers and Radisson returned to Trois-Rivières nearly five years later with a large supply of furs and knowledge about a trading route beyond the lands of the Iroquois. Instead of being welcomed, however, Groseilliers was put in jail, both he and Radisson were fined, and their furs were confiscated. The French authorities charged that they had left the colony without a government license. As a result of this incident Groseilliers and Radisson went to work for the British; this shift in loyalties would have a major influence on the history of North America.

Hudson's Bay Company formed

In the spring of 1663 Groseilliers and Radisson left New France with the intention of traveling down the St. Lawrence River and taking the sea route to Hudson Bay. For some reason they ended up in Boston, Massachusetts; from there they made two unsuccessful efforts to reach Hudson Bay. Then, with the blessing of the governor of Massachusetts, they went to England to convince King Charles II of the advantages of opening fur trade in the north.

During the voyage to England the Frenchmen's ship was captured by a Dutch pirate and they were rerouted to Spain. From Spain they journeyed overland to England. After some effort, Groseilliers and Radisson were able to convince the king to sponsor an expedition to Hudson Bay. They left England in 1668 aboard separate ships; when Radisson's ship, the *Eaglet,* was damaged in a storm, Radisson returned to England. While waiting for Groseilliers to come back from America, he wrote his book *Voyages.* Groseilliers's trip to Hudson Bay was successful: he returned with a valuable cargo of furs and reports of the vast potential for profitable trade in the area. As a result the Hudson's Bay Company was chartered on May 2, 1670.

Médard Chouart des Groseilliers
Pierre Esprit Radisson

Shift allegiance back to France

Within a month Groseilliers and Radisson embarked again for Hudson Bay, and again they traveled on separate ships. Radisson went to the mouth of the Nelson River on the west coast of Hudson Bay in what is now Manitoba. After building a trading post, he took possession of the land in the name of the king of England. Although he had to abandon the post, this claim became the basis for the British possession of the bay and its tributaries.

During the next few years Radisson and Groseilliers made several trading voyages to Hudson Bay. By this time the French were becoming alarmed at the encroachments of the British into Canada. In 1675 a Jesuit priest named Albanel, who had been captured by the English, convinced the two men to return to French allegiance. Taking his advice, Groseilliers and Radisson sneaked across the English Channel to France and presented themselves to the French court. When they were sent back to Canada, the governor of New France, the Count de Frontenac, refused to help them because he mistrusted them. Groseilliers returned to his farm and Radisson went back to France.

Radisson drifts for awhile

Once he was in France Radisson found that no one was interested in his schemes for trade in Canada. The best job he could find was as a midshipman on a French naval expedition to capture Dutch colonies on the west coast of Africa and in the Caribbean. The expedition left France in 1677, but most of the ships were wrecked on a hidden reef in the Caribbean. Having barely survived, Radisson returned to France in 1678, again without any source of income.

Disappointed by his bad luck, Radisson went back to England, where he tried to convince his wife—before leaving for Africa he had married the daughter of a prominent English businessman—to go with him to either France or Canada. When her family refused to let her go, Radisson returned to Paris alone. This time his fortunes improved.

The trappers work for France

The French backers of a new company, the Compagnie du Nord, hired Radisson to lead a French expedition to the Nelson River. Since the Hudson's Bay Company was planning to do the same thing, it is possible that Radisson brought this information back with him from England, spurring the French to action. In any case, when Radisson arrived in Hudson Bay there were ships from England as well as one from Massachusetts. Radisson was joined by Groseilliers and the two men outwitted their opponents by capturing the trading post and furs for France.

When they arrived in Quebec, however, they were told they would have to pay taxes on their furs. Disputing this assessment, they took their case to Paris. The French government, which was unwilling to risk an incident with Britain, refused to support the two adventurers. Groseilliers went back to Canada, and there is no further account of him until his death in 1698. But Radisson, apparently weary of French mistreatment, decided to go to England. He was helped to escape from France by a French Protestant who was being persecuted for his religion and wanted to get to England; he thought that if he arrived with Radisson it would help his prospects.

Radisson rejoins Hudson's Bay

In 1684 Radisson went back to work for the Hudson's Bay Company. On his first trip he was sent to the Nelson River where his nephew, Groseilliers's son, was in charge of the French post Radisson had founded. He convinced the young man to change sides and take his great stock of furs to England. As they were leaving the bay, they just missed being caught by French ships that had come to foil the plot.

Back in London, Radisson attended the coronation of King James II. Radisson's nephew, regretting his change of allegiance, made several efforts to escape to France but he was caught every time. In the meantime, the French had put a price on Radisson's head. Radisson made his last trip to Hudson Bay from 1685 to 1687. Just before leaving England, he mar-

Médard Chouart des Groseilliers
Pierre Esprit Radisson

ried the daughter of the French Protestant who had helped him out of France; presumably his first wife had died.

In 1687 Radisson returned to England for the last time. He settled down in the suburbs of London. He was given stock in the Hudson's Bay Company and an annuity. These payments led to a quarrel with the company that turned into a lawsuit, which Radisson won in 1697. His second wife died during delivery of their fifth child; he married a third time and had three more children. Radisson made his will on June 17, 1710, and died shortly thereafter.

James Chuma

Born c. 1850,
Lake Nyasa, Africa

Died 1882,
Zanzibar, Tanzania

James Chuma and David Susi ▶

hrough his assistance to European explorers, James Chuma contributed to knowledge of southeastern Africa, especially the area that today is known as Tanzania. Like **Sidi Mubarak Bombay** (see entry), he was a member of the Yao tribe that lived on the shores of Lake Nyasa in southeastern Africa. Chuma was the son of a fisherman named Chimilengo and his wife, Chinjeriapi. During a war among local tribes, Chuma was captured and eventually sold to a Portuguese slave trader. He was rescued from slavery by a fellow Yao named Wekotani. Together they attended the mission school founded by Anglican Bishop Charles Frederick Mackenzie at Magomero. While at the school Chuma became the servant of a Reverend Henry Rowley, to whom he introduced a Yao delicacy, whole-fried rat.

Hired by Livingstone

In 1864 Chuma and Wekotani moved to another mission school at Shanapur, India, about 100 miles northeast of Bom-

James Chuma, a freed African slave who worked as a servant for Scottish explorer David Livingstone and as a caravan leader for others, was honored by the Royal Geographical Society for helping to carry Livingstone's body out of Africa.

bay. Chuma flourished there, becoming healthier and learning to read and write in English. He and Wekotani met the Scottish physician and explorer **David Livingstone** (see entry), who had recently returned from an expedition to the Zambezi River in southeastern Africa. Livingstone hired them as his personal servants; on December 10, 1865, Chuma was baptized and given the name James Chuma.

At first Livingstone was pleased with Chuma and Wekotani, but by August 1866 they had begun to exasperate him with their youthful antics. An entry from Livingstone's journal reads:

> Chuma and Wekotani are very good boys but still boys utterly. ... I had them about me personally till I was reduced to the last fork and spoon. ... They showed an inveterate tendency to lose my things and preserve their own. If I did not shout for breakfast I got it sometime between eleven and two o'clock. I had to relieve them of all charge of my domestic affairs.

Returns to Lake Nyasa

Livingstone took Chuma and Wekotani on an expedition from the Mozambique port of Quelimane back to their home on Lake Nyasa, a journey that lasted five months. Once again among his own people, Wekotani announced his desire to stay behind and marry. He was the first of many African members of the party to abandon the expedition, leaving only nine of the original 36 at the end of a month. Chuma was among those who stayed with Livingstone.

Livingstone and his remaining followers met a party of Arabs in January 1867 and traveled with them for more than a year. During this time, they went to Lake Mweru, on the border between Zambia and Zaire, and then headed toward Lake Bangweulu.

Stages mutiny

On April 13, 1868, Chuma and the other Africans staged a mutiny, refusing to continue any farther with the expedition.

All of the men feared going into Kazembe (now in eastern Zambia), which was a notorious haunt of slave traders. Chuma had reasons of his own: he bore a grudge against Livingstone, who had docked his pay in 1865; he also did not want to leave David Susi, a fellow servant who had joined Livingstone in 1861. Susi was one of the ringleaders of the Africans' revolt against going into the dangerous territory to the south. Livingstone proceeded on to Kazembe without the Africans.

Chuma and Susi did not work for Livingstone from April to November of 1868. But when Chuma returned to Lake Bangweulu after a trip, he and Susi joined the other men in asking to be reinstated. At first Livingstone denied their request but he finally relented; he wrote in his journal:

> I have taken all the runaways back again—after trying the independent life they will behave better. Much of their ill conduct may be ascribed to seeing that ... I was entirely dependent on them—more enlightened people often take advantage of men in similar circumstances, though I have seen pure Africans come out generously to aid one abandoned to their care. Have faults myself.

Rejoins Livingstone

Livingstone took his party from Lake Bangweulu to Ujiji on the eastern shore of Lake Tanganyika. They stayed there until the following October. Livingstone wanted to explore the Lualaba River, which flows out of Lake Tanganyika, but only Chuma, Susi, and one other of his supporters were willing to go along.

Livingstone went back to Ujiji in October 1871. It was there that he had his famous meeting with Welsh explorer and journalist **Henry Morton Stanley** (see entry) on November 10. The two Europeans explored Lake Tanganyika with Chuma, Susi, and Bombay serving as rowers. They then traveled to the town of Tabora, which is now in central Tanzania, where Chuma was on hand to see Stanley off on March 14, 1872. The following June Chuma was married to one of Livingstone's cooks, Ntaoeka. The expedition set out for the interior in August, armed with supplies provided by Stanley.

Carries Livingstone's body to Zanzibar

In January 1873 Livingstone's expedition began the return trip to Lake Bangweulu, with Chuma in charge of the advance party. Livingstone became ill on the trip. By April, he was too weak to walk and had to be carried by Chuma, Susi, and some of the other servants. The Scots explorer was found dead in his hut by Susi on the morning of May 1, 1873.

Chuma and Susi decided to take Livingstone's body, along with his papers, maps, and instruments, to Zanzibar on the coast of the Indian Ocean. They cut out his heart and other internal organs, burying them on the site where he died, then embalmed the body. The party of about 60 Africans departed, carrying Livingstone's remains. In the long walk that followed, both Susi and Chuma became ill and the party was stalked by wild animals. Near Lake Tanganyika they encountered a hostile tribe, which engaged them in a fierce battle. In spite of these obstacles, Chuma and Susi persisted, finally reaching the town of Kumba Kumba in familiar territory.

Meets relief party

At Kumba Kumba they met a friendly Arab caravan and learned that a relief expedition sent to find Livingstone was at Tabora. Chuma was sent ahead with a letter to Verney Lovett Cameron, the leader of the expedition, informing him of Livingstone's death. Warning of trouble ahead in Ugogo, Cameron advised Chuma to bury Livingstone's body; determined to reach their destination, however, Chuma and Susi continued on toward the coast. After walking over 1400 miles for nine months, the party reached Zanzibar on February 3, 1874. The British consul resupplied the Africans and paid the bearers their back wages.

Honored in England

From Zanzibar, Jacob Wainwright, another of Livingstone's associates, accompanied Livingstone's body to England, where it was buried with great ceremony at Westminster Abbey. The inscription on the tombstone acknowledges the role of Chuma and the other Africans in returning Livingstone to his home country: "Brought by faithful hands over land and sea here rests David Livingstone." Following the funeral, Chuma and Susi and their wives were brought to England at the expense of one of Livingstone's friends. They met Livingstone's son and were introduced to the well-known Africanist Horace Waller. After talking with Chuma and Susi, Waller wrote, "I found them actual geographers of no mean attainments." The Africans attended a meeting of the Royal Geographical Society in June 1874; a few weeks later they were given special medals by the society.

Chuma and Susi stayed with Waller for four months, telling him the history of the expedition and helping him edit Livingstone's journals, which would eventually make Livingstone a hero in England. Chuma built a model of Livingstone's grass hut and presented it to the explorer's family. In a ceremony on August 17, 1874, the Royal Geographical Society presented silver medals inscribed "Faithful to the End" to the 60 Africans in commemoration of their remarkable feat.

Leads trips to interior of Africa

Chuma and Susi returned to Zanzibar in late 1874 and worked as guides to missionaries who were establishing missions in East Africa. Chuma was recruited in August 1875 by the Universities Mission to lead several caravans to the interior. The first set out in November 1875, followed by another in June 1876. In October 1876, with 70 porters under his command, Chuma helped to start a mission station at Masasi in southern Tanzania. He returned to Zanzibar twice for supplies and led a new party to Masasi in June 1877. On his return to Zanzibar in December of that year Chuma met with the British consul to give an assessment of the situation in the interior.

Joins Thomson

In January 1879 Keith Johnston and **Joseph Thomson** (see entry) organized an expedition to explore the lakes of central Africa. They hired Chuma as the caravan leader but rejected Susi for employment because Thomson, who had discovered that Susi had drinking problems, felt he would be a bad influence on Chuma. Susi was later hired by Stanley and took part in founding stations in the Belgian Congo.

The party left Zanzibar in May 1879 with 150 porters and guides. In June Johnston died of malaria, leaving Thomson in charge of the expedition. Although he was only 21 years old and had no experience as a head explorer—he was a geologist—Thomson decided to continue. Chuma served as caravan commander and chief negotiator with the tribes they encountered along the route to the interior. They reached Lake Nyasa in September, exploring the northern end of the lake before continuing to Lake Tanganyika, where they arrived in November.

Praised by Thomson

The relationship between Thomson and Chuma had become a source of amusement on the journey. Because Thomson was so young he depended on Chuma when making decisions; he was so dependent, in fact, that he was nicknamed "Chuma's white man."

Thomson wrote about Chuma in his journal:

Among the Zanzibar porters there is certainly none equal to Chuma as a caravan leader, especially for white men. His long experience under Livingstone as an interpreter of the geographical questions so necessary to be asked, gave him a very fair notion regarding these things, so that he is able at once to pick up a European's meaning when an ordinary native would only look at him in blank perplexity. He is well acquainted with English, and about a dozen native dialects ... Full of anecdote, and fun, and jollity, he was an immense favorite with the men, and yet he preserved such authority over them that no one presumed to disobey his orders.

Dies after successful mission

The party arrived safely back in Zanzibar in July 1880.

Chuma was awarded another silver medal by the Royal Geographical Society for his contribution to the expedition. But by the time the medal was presented to him, Chuma was ill with tuberculosis. He made out his will on September 25, 1882, leaving his few possessions to his wife and friends. Shortly thereafter he died in the mission hospital in Zanzibar.

Christopher Columbus

Born 1451,
Genoa, Italy

Died May 20, 1506,
Valladolid, Spain

Christopher Columbus was an Italian mariner who sailed in the service of the king and queen of Spain; he made four voyages to the Caribbean and South America between 1492 and 1504.

The life of Christopher Columbus is one of contrasts—great triumphs marked by even greater defeats. Despite Columbus's downfall in his own time and the divided reaction to the five hundredth anniversary of his voyage in the United States, Columbus was an accomplished seaman who crossed the Atlantic Ocean using his own genius in a daring feat.

Columbus was born Cristoforo Colombo, the son of Domencio Colombo and Suzanna Fontanarossa in Genoa, Italy, some time in the fall of 1451. For at least three generations his family had lived in Genoa, where they manufactured and traded woolen fabrics. Little is known about Columbus's early life. He, his three brothers, and their sister possibly received some education through their father's guild. More than likely, Columbus was ashamed of his humble origins. In 1479, to improve his social status, he married Felipa Perestrello de Moniz, a Portuguese noblewoman with modest wealth. She died soon after giving birth to a son, Diego. Years later

Columbus and Beatriz Enriquez de Harana, a much younger woman, were parents of Ferdinand, Columbus's biographer, though the couple never married.

Goes to sea as a teenager

By his own account, Columbus became a seaman at a young age, probably in his early teens. By his twenties, he was a skilled sailor with enough knowledge to pilot his own boat. In May 1476 Columbus was a crew member in a convoy attacked by French pirates near the southern Portuguese port of Lagos. Columbus's ship was wrecked and many of the crew killed; fortunately Columbus was able to swim six miles to shore. After recuperating, Columbus traveled to Lisbon, Portugal, where his younger brother Bartholomew operated a book and map store. Columbus educated himself in the store, studying navigation and the art of cartography, or mapmaking.

A devout Catholic, Columbus also studied religion, absorbing ideas that would determine his later view of himself as an explorer. He saw God's hand at work on Earth, and when he made his voyage across the Atlantic Ocean he felt God's hand guiding him; in fact he saw himself as God's messenger in the New World. Columbus interpreted events in his life—being saved from shipwreck and landing near the Rock of Sagres, the home of the academy for sailors founded by Prince **Henry the Navigator** (see entry)—as signs of God's plan.

Formulates "great idea"

Columbus participated in a voyage to Iceland and beyond in February of 1477. In 1478 he served as captain of a merchant ship that sailed to the island of Madeira on an unsuccessful trading mission. Sometime in the early 1480s he made a voyage to the Portuguese trading fortress of Sâo Jorge da Mina in what is now Benin on the west coast of Africa. On his return Columbus began to formulate his "great idea": that it would be faster and easier to travel to Asia by sailing westward across the Atlantic than by sailing around Africa and across the Indian Ocean, as the Portuguese were then trying to do.

Contrary to legend, all educated fifteenth-century Europeans knew that the earth was a sphere, but no one had any idea about the size of the earth, and most theories underestimated the earth by one-third its actual size. In making his arguments, Columbus guessed at the distances between landmasses, making them much closer than they actually are. Columbus also assumed the Asian continent was much wider than it is, but this was an understandable error. In the fifteenth century geographers believed the earth was one huge landmass, consisting of Europe, Africa, and Asia, surrounded by water. For example, he claimed that the distance from Lisbon to Japan would be about 2,400 nautical miles. It is actually more than 10,000.

Columbus named his plan "The Enterprise of the Indies," because sailing west would lead to the eastern shore of Asia. This idea did not originate with Columbus, and the thought of sailing across the Atlantic Ocean, known as the "green sea of gloom," was full of danger and risk, although success would guarantee fame and glory. Besides the obvious physical risk of such a voyage, the mental and emotional strain was apparent too. Yet the belief in a distant land full of unlimited supplies of gold outweighed the dangers.

Seeks Spanish support

Starting in 1484, Columbus tried to persuade the Portuguese king, João II, of the workability of his idea; the king consulted his court advisers, who concluded Columbus's estimates of distance were far too inaccurate. By this time, Columbus's wife had died, and he left Portugal with his son Diego. They traveled by ship to the Spanish port of Palos de la Frontera near the Portuguese border. Columbus placed Diego in a boarding school run by Franciscan monks at the monastery of La Rábida while he traveled around Spain trying to arrange an audience with the Spanish court. The Franciscans, who were interested in establishing foreign missions, gave Columbus a letter of introduction to an influential Spanish nobleman, the count of Medina Celi.

Columbus traveled to the city of Córdoba in January 1486 but missed the Spanish king and queen. He found support among the Genoese colony in the city. He also met a young peasant woman named Beatriz Enriquez de Harana, who became his mistress; two years later they had a son named Ferdinand. When the Spanish monarchs returned to Córdoba in May 1486, Queen Isabella agreed to receive Columbus. Known as the "Catholic Sovereigns," King Ferdinand and Queen Isabella through marriage brought together Castile and Aragon as they worked to make Spain a Catholic nation. In 1492 they would conquer the Moors in Granada and by royal decree would expel all Jews who refused to convert to Catholicism. They would also support the Spanish Inquisition, aimed at converting, punishing, or even killing all those who disagreed with the Roman Catholic church, including nonbelievers and Jews. Columbus's plans fit into their scheme to make Spain an imperial power, and Isabella shared Columbus's enthusiasm for spreading Christianity.

Plan reviewed by royal commission

Queen Isabella appointed the Talavera Commission to study the practicality of Columbus's idea. Although the commission could not come to any decision, it thought enough of Columbus's idea to give him a modest annual salary while it deliberated. Columbus continued to seek support from other monarchs. Early in 1488 he wrote to the Portuguese king, who invited him back to Lisbon.

Columbus traveled to Portugal, only to be present in December 1488 for the return of **Bartolomeu Dias** (see entry), who had rounded the Cape of Good Hope at the southern end of Africa. The Portuguese had finally found the passageway to India and no longer had any interest in Columbus's plan. Columbus's brother Bartholomew sold his business and traveled to England and France to try to get support there, without success.

Plan rejected

In late 1490 the Talavera Commission issued a report calling Columbus's idea unsound and judging his understand-

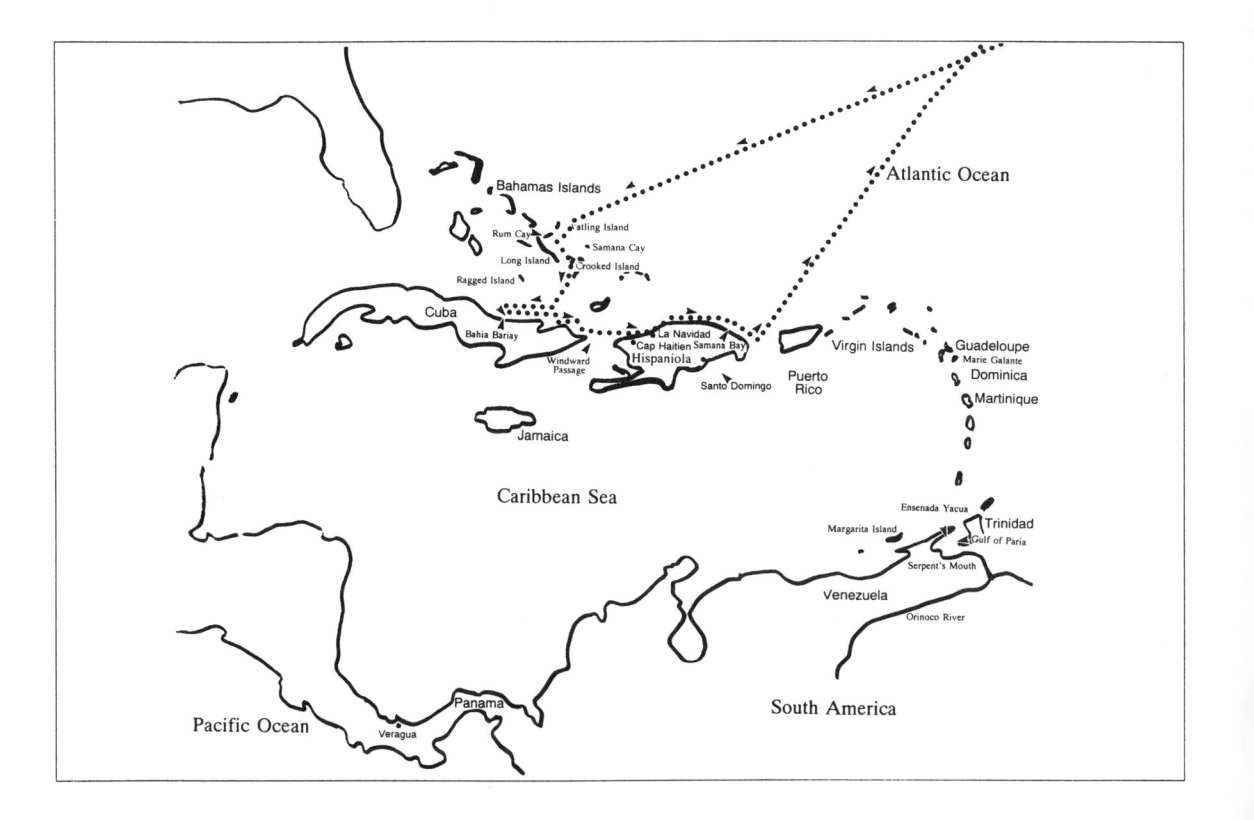

The map shows the Caribbean region with the following labels: Atlantic Ocean, Bahamas Islands, Rum Cay, Watling Island, Samana Cay, Long Island, Crooked Island, Ragged Island, Cuba, Bahia Bariay, Windward Passage, La Navidad, Cap Haitien, Samana Bay, Hispaniola, Santo Domingo, Puerto Rico, Virgin Islands, Guadeloupe, Marie Galante, Dominica, Martinique, Jamaica, Caribbean Sea, Ensenada Yacua, Margarita Island, Trinidad, Gulf of Paria, Serpent's Mouth, Venezuela, Orinoco River, South America, Panama, Veragua, Pacific Ocean

ing of the earth's size and the practicality of a ship sailing such a vast distance unlikely. Columbus returned to the monastery of La Rábida, where the monks urged him to approach Queen Isabella once more. After she consented to see him, in December 1491 Columbus traveled to the royal court outside the city of Granada, where the Spanish were engaged in the last battle to defeat the Muslim Moors, who then ruled southern Spain.

The Royal Council that reviewed Columbus's proposal finally recommended refusal because Columbus had increased his demands: he now wanted to be admiral and viceroy of any lands he discovered. Queen Isabella reluctantly agreed with the recommendation; in January 1492 Columbus made plans to leave Spain and try his luck in France. When Columbus was four miles outside the Spanish camp a messenger caught up with him and told him that through the intervention of Luis de Santangel, a court official, Queen Isabella had changed her mind: she would sponsor the voyage. Six years of persistence had paid off.

Prepares for voyage

In April 1492 Queen Isabella and King Ferdinand signed an agreement with Columbus, called the Capitulations, to sponsor him on a voyage of exploration. Columbus would be named admiral, would become the governor of any lands he discovered, and would have the right to 10 percent of any merchandise obtained in the new lands, free of taxes; these rights would be hereditary in his family.

Columbus returned to the port of Palos and secured three ships—the *Niña,* the *Pinta,* and the *Santa Maria*—with a crew of about 90 men and boys. The *Santa Maria,* at 100 feet in length, was the largest of the three ships; the *Niña* and the *Pinta* were 70-foot caravels. The fleet sailed on Friday morning, August 3, 1492, passing the entrance to the Tinto River at 8:00 A.M.

Embarks on voyage—conditions not good

By undertaking a voyage into unknown waters, Columbus had to overcome profound obstacles and disadvantages. Although the ships carried an ample supply of food, there was no way to keep it safe from contamination because of unsanitary conditions and rodents and cockroaches. Food was rationed and limited to one hot meal a day; crew members slept in whatever available dry spot could be found. Boredom and fear of the unknown were obvious psychological problems. For this reason Columbus kept two sets of logs—an actual record of distance traveled and a false log that reduced the distance.

The voyage was off to a good start, though, because Columbus had discovered the best possible Atlantic route on his first try. Ideal weather, with clear skies and steady winds, combined with Columbus's genius for traveling in unchartered waters with little more than a compass, had made this turn of events possible. Also, Columbus had a knowledge of dead reckoning, a method of plotting a course and measuring distance traveled, which contributed to his success.

Visits Canary Islands

Columbus took his fleet first to the Canary Islands off the African coast. He knew from previous sailing experience that the winds blew from the east at that latitude, where he expected Japan to be. The *Pinta* had to undergo some repairs at Las Palmas, the main port of the Canaries, delaying departure until September 6; still winds kept the Canaries in sight until September 9.

From that point onward the ships had remarkably good winds, traveling as much as 150 miles a day and advancing 182 miles on one day. On September 16 the fleet came to the edge of the giant seaweed fields later named the Sargasso Sea. On September 17 the crew noticed that for the first time the North Star was east of where their compasses said that north should be. Columbus explained this, correctly, saying, "it appears that the Star moves like other stars, and the compasses always point true." Starting on September 19, light winds restricted travel to 234 miles over the next five days.

Land finally sighted

By now, if Columbus's original theories had been correct, land should have been in sight; in fact, at one point the crew members thought they spotted land, but it turned out to be a low-lying cloud bank. The wind picked up on September 26 and the ships traveled 382 more miles by October 1. The wind increased again, and the ships traveled 710 miles between October 2 and October 6. On October 10 the crew became mutinous and wanted to turn back. The following day, however, signs of land became apparent—branches with green leaves and flowers floating in the water—and the crewmen calmed down.

At about 10 P.M. on the night of October 11 Columbus thought he saw firelight on the horizon. At about 2 A.M. on the morning of October 12, the lookout on the *Pinta,* Rodrigo de Triana, saw white cliffs in the moonlight and called out "Tierra! tierra!" Later Columbus awarded himself the honor of first sighting land because he had seen the firelight in the distance.

Reaches islands near North America

The fleet had landed on a small island in the Bahamas. The natives called it Guanahani, but Columbus renamed it San Salvador (Holy Savior); the consensus has been that it was the island later known as Watling. However, recent evidence has shown that a small island farther south, Samana Cay, may be a likelier location. Columbus stayed on the island for two days, meeting with members of the Taino tribe, who were the inhabitants. Not knowing where he was, and always assuming that he had reached Asia, or the "Indies," he called them Indians.

From San Salvador Columbus spent several days exploring the Bahamas, visiting Rum Cay, Long Island, Crooked Island, Hog Cay, and other islands. None fulfilled the visions of wealth and material civilization Columbus had imagined. When the Native Americans told him about another much larger island named Colba (Cuba), he decided it must be part of China or Japan. He left his anchorage at Ragged Island on October 17 and on the morning of October 28 he sighted Bahía Bariay on the north coast of Cuba.

Explores Cuba and Haiti

For the next month, Columbus sailed along the north coast of Cuba. Always looking for gold, he sent two of his men into the interior to visit the reputed capital of the land, which he thought would be the city of the Great Khan (Beijing). They actually found a small village and brought back the first specimens of the tobacco plant Europeans had ever seen. While Columbus's ships were sailing along the northern coast of Cuba, Martín Alonso Pinzón suddenly departed in the *Pinta,* without telling Columbus, sailing eastward to Great Inagua Island to follow up a rumor of gold.

Columbus, with the *Santa Maria* and the *Niña,* left the coast of Cuba on December 5, 1492, and sailed across the Windward Passage to another large island, which he named Hispaniola because it reminded him of Spain. The first landfall was at the Haitian town now called Môle St. Nicolas, named by Columbus because he landed there on December 6, the feast day of St. Nicholas.

Meets Native Americans

Sailing eastward along the north coast of Hispaniola on December 17, Columbus was rewarded for all his troubles. He was met by a young chief, or *kaseke,* who was wearing gold ornaments, which he was willing to trade for European goods. Farther east Columbus met a more important chief who had even larger pieces of gold. Columbus entertained him and his people on board the *Santa Maria* on Christmas eve not far from the modern Haitian city of Cap Haitien. After the festivities, everyone went to sleep—then the *Santa Maria* hit a coral reef.

In spite of efforts to save her, the ship began to founder. Helped by the chief and his followers, the Spanish were able to unload most of the Spanish goods and carry them to shore. Making the best of a bad situation, Columbus founded the first European settlement in the Americas. He named it La Navidad after the birthday of Christ; it was on a small bay where the Haitian village of Limonade-Bord-de-Mer now stands.

Turns back toward Spain

Columbus sailed from La Navidad on January 4, 1493, on the *Niña,* leaving 21 men behind under the command of Diego de Harana, the cousin of his mistress. Two days later he found the *Pinta,* and the two ships sailed along the north coast of the Dominican Republic until they reached Samaná Bay on the eastern end of the island. They left from there for Spain on January 18.

Columbus sailed north and then east, a direction that, unknown to him, took the ships into the best prevailing winds. Good weather aided their progress until they reached the Azores, where the two ships ran into a bad storm, separating them. Columbus anchored off the Portuguese island of Santa Maria; unfortunately, most of his crew were temporarily put in jail by the local governor, who thought they were returning from an illicit voyage to West Africa.

Honored for achievement

Once Columbus left the Azores on February 24, he again

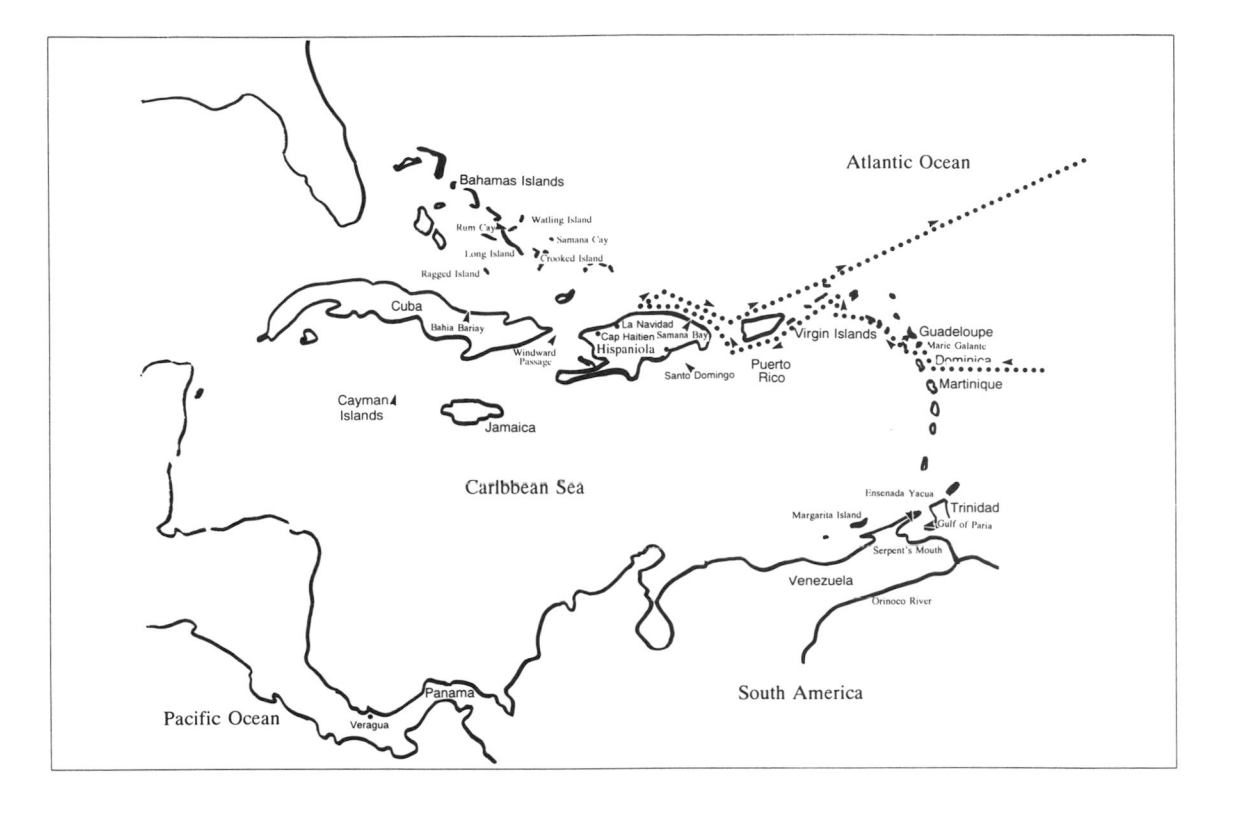

During his second expedition, 1493-96, Columbus explored the islands of the Caribbean Sea.

encountered storms, which drove the ships northward toward the mainland at Cabo da Roca at the mouth of the Tagus River in Portugal. He was summoned by King João II, who received the first report of the discovery of America. After repairing the *Niña,* Columbus reached Palos on March 15. He had already sent a report of his voyage to Queen Isabella and King Ferdinand while he was in Portugal and sent another copy from Palos. On April 7 he received a letter from the king and queen, who expressed their pleasure at his accomplishments. They invited him to meet them in Barcelona to start immediate preparations for a new voyage.

Columbus reached the court at Barcelona on April 20, and stayed there for three months as news of his discoveries began to travel through Europe. He was given various titles and honors by the king and queen. Detailed plans were made for a second voyage, and negotiations were begun to divide the world into Spanish and Portuguese spheres. A less positive event, however, was that the Native Americans who came back with

Columbus began to spread syphilis in Europe, much as the Europeans spread smallpox and measles to the Americas.

Makes second voyage to America

Columbus's second voyage to America was on a much larger scale than the first. There were 17 ships, the flagship was once again named the *Santa Maria*—but it was considerably larger than its namesake—and there were about 1,200 to 1,500 men aboard. They left the Spanish port of Cadiz on September 25, 1493, stopped for ten days in the Canary Islands during the first part of October, and then sighted land on the morning of November 3. Because the day was Sunday, Columbus named the island Dominica.

Columbus did not land on Dominica but headed north to the small flat island of Marie Galante. He anchored the next day off the large island of Guadeloupe, where he encountered the first Caribs, a Native American people who were different from the Arawaks he had met in the Bahamas and Hispaniola and who were warriors. On the island of St. Croix in the Virgin Islands, Spaniards in a boat were attacked by Caribs in a canoe. One of the Spaniards and one of the Caribs were killed; the other Caribs were captured and taken to Spain as slaves. Columbus's fleet reached Puerto Rico on November 19 and anchored off the west coast at Añasco Bay for three days.

Builds fort at present-day Dominican Republic

Sailing from Puerto Rico the Spanish reached the settlement at La Navidad on the night of November 27. When they went ashore the next morning, they found it in ruins and the unburied bodies of Spaniards everywhere. No one knows what had happened, although it was supposed either the demands the Spanish had made on the Arawaks had turned them against the Europeans or the Spanish had fought among themselves, or it had been a combination of the two. Abandoning the site, Columbus took his new colonists 75 miles to the east to a small, shallow bay where he built a trading fort called Isabela, in what is now the Dominican Republic. It turned out not to be a good location, but Columbus laid out a main square with a church and "royal palace" and constructed 200 huts for the settlers.

Makes false claim of discovering Asia

Four days after landing at Isabela, Columbus sent **Alonso de Ojeda** (see entry) into the interior mountains, where he found gold. Columbus then sent a load of gold and what he thought were spices with 12 ships back to Spain. Columbus took three ships and sailed to the south coast of Cuba, then south to the island of Jamaica, and finally back north to Cuba, where he coasted along the entire south shore to the western end of the island. On June 12 a curious incident occurred. Columbus gathered all his men together and made them swear to an oath that the land they had been traveling along was not an island but part of the mainland of Asia. He was still convinced, or was trying to convince himself, he had found the "Indies."

Fights with Native Americans

On his way back, Columbus revisited Jamaica and sailed along the south coast of Hispaniola. He intended to visit Puerto Rico, but illness forced him to return to Isabela on September 29, 1494, where he found that his brother Bartholomew had arrived from Spain. The Arawak natives of Hispaniola had realized that the arrival of the Spanish meant their destruction, and they had collected a large force to try to drive the intruders off the island. At the end of March 1495 Columbus, Bartholomew, and Ojeda led a force into the interior that defeated the Native Americans. They enslaved the surviving tribesmen, who fell to European diseases and quickly died out.

In the meantime, news had reached Spain that the colonists at Isabela were not doing well; Columbus returned to Spain on March 10, 1496, to explain developments in the New World to Ferdinand and Isabella. He left his brother in charge of the colony, but Bartholomew quickly abandoned Isabela and moved the Spanish headquarters to the south side of the island at Santo Domingo.

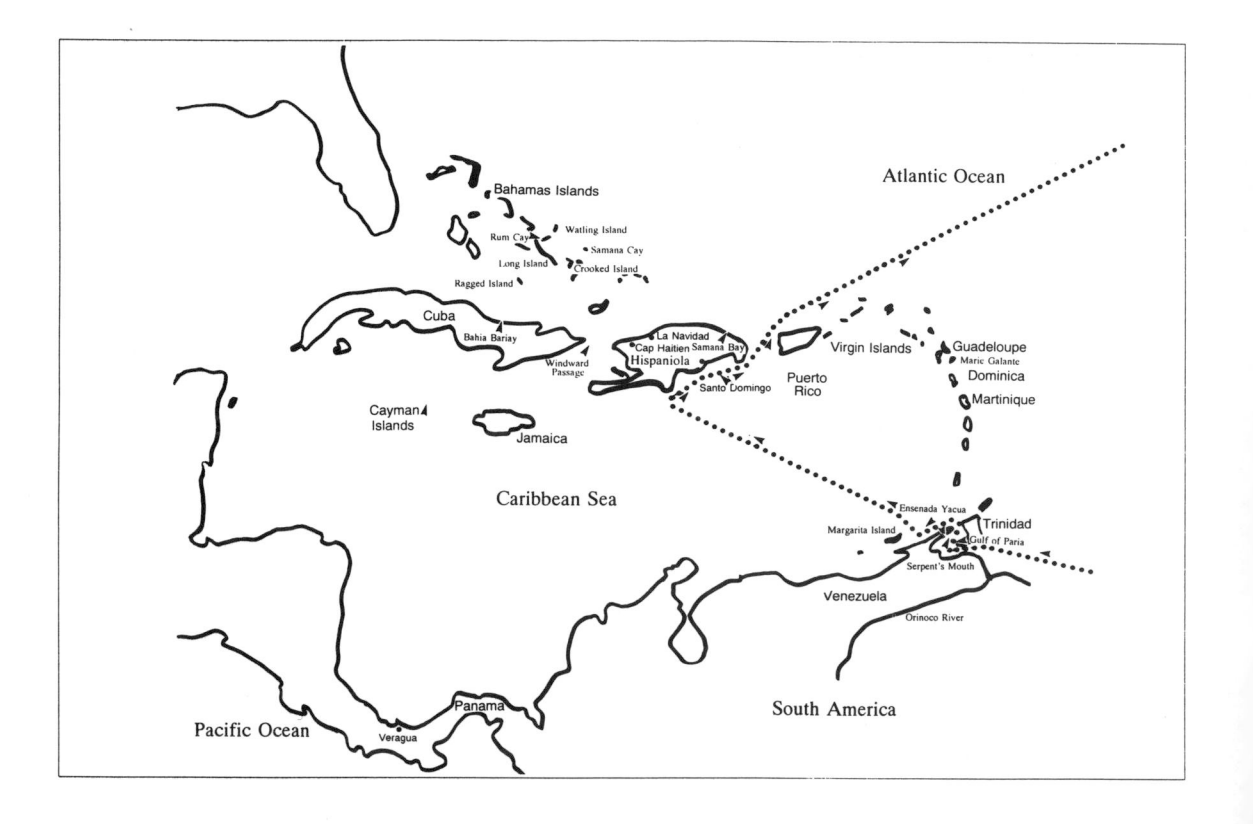

On his 1498 voyage Columbus reached South America.

Lives as monk

Columbus traveled to Spain on the *Niña* once again, accompanied by one other small ship. When he landed in Cadiz, he did something puzzling: he adopted the coarse dress of a Franciscan friar and stayed at stark and strictly ordered monasteries. Columbus lived a monk's existence for two years while in Spain, trying to convince Ferdinand and Isabella to send him out on a third voyage of discovery. He finally got an audience during the summer or early fall of 1496, and the royals agreed to put him in charge of a small provisioning fleet to Hispaniola in mid-1497. The fleet did not actually leave until May 30, 1498, because Columbus had trouble finding ships and supplies.

Makes important discoveries on third expedition

Deciding to take a more southerly course, Columbus

landed on the island of Trinidad on August 1. The next day he sailed into the Gulf of Paria, which separates Trinidad from Venezuela. He passed the mouth of the great Orinoco River, realizing almost at once he had reached a continental landmass—this was his first view of the mainland of the Americas. On August 4, after the Spanish ships were almost sunk by a tidal wave or tidal bore, Columbus decided to leave the entrance to the Gulf of Paria as quickly as possible. He named the spot the Boca del Sierpe, the Serpent's Mouth.

From there Columbus sailed north to a little bay on the mainland called the Ensenada Yacua. When he and his officers went ashore they became the first Europeans since **Leif Eriksson** (see entry) to set foot on the mainland of America. Columbus then sailed along the coast of Venezuela, which he declared to be the Terrestrial Paradise. He also concluded from his observations of the North Star that the world was not a perfect hemisphere; he was the first to reach this realization. The Spanish also discovered the pearl fisheries off Margarita Island. Columbus then turned north and reached the south coast of Hispaniola near Santo Domingo on August 21, where he was met by Bartholomew. He stayed on the island and administered the gold mines found in the interior.

Arrested and sent back to Spain

Ferdinand and Isabella had been hearing unfavorable reports about the administration of Hispaniola by the Columbus brothers. In July 1500 they sent Francisco de Bobadilla to replace Columbus as the new governor. When Bobadilla arrived in Santo Domingo, he found the Spanish inhabitants in a state of rebellion; he immediately arrested Christopher, Diego, and Bartholomew Columbus. He put them in chains and sent them back to Spain, where they arrived at the end of October 1500. Columbus stayed in chains for five weeks after his return until he was released by Ferdinand and Isabella on December 12. He was ordered to report to the court at Granada, where he was received on December 17.

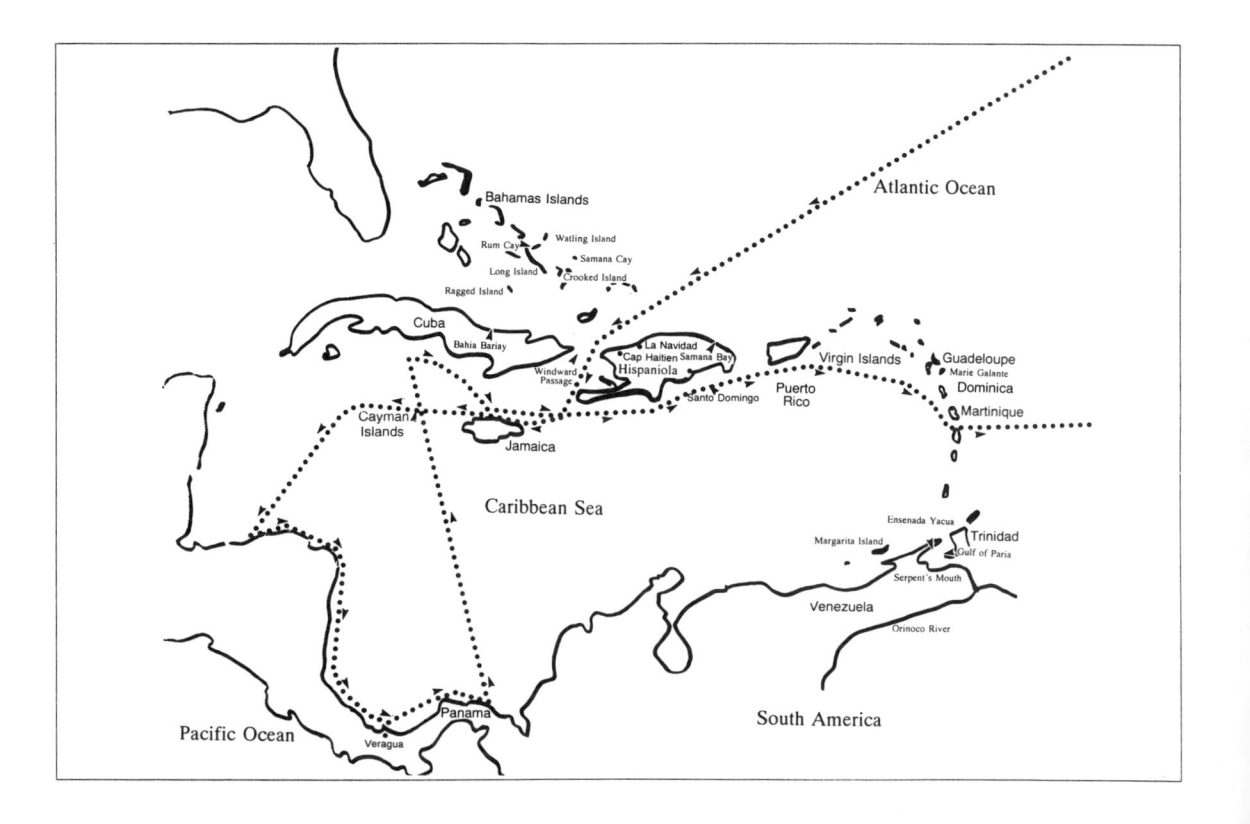

Map labels: Atlantic Ocean, Bahamas Islands, Watling Island, Rum Cay, Samana Cay, Long Island, Crooked Island, Ragged Island, Cuba, Bahia Bariay, La Navidad, Cap Haitien, Samana Bay, Windward Passage, Hispaniola, Santo Domingo, Virgin Islands, Guadeloupe, Marie Galante, Dominica, Puerto Rico, Martinique, Cayman Islands, Jamaica, Caribbean Sea, Ensenada Yacua, Trinidad, Margarita Island, Gulf of Paria, Serpent's Mouth, Venezuela, Orinoco River, South America, Pacific Ocean, Panama, Veragua

Makes his "high voyage"

Columbus took his final and most ambitious voyage from 1502 to 1504, sailing around Cuba and along the coast of South America.

Columbus explained his side of the story and requested restoration of all his titles, including that of governor. The king and queen said they would make a judgment, which was not announced until September 1501. Columbus was allowed to keep his title of Admiral of the Ocean Sea, but a new governor, Nicolás de Ovando, was appointed and sent out to Santo Domingo with a great fleet.

Columbus asked to be allowed to lead another voyage of exploration; his request was granted on February 26, 1502. Columbus sailed from Cadiz on May 9, 1502, with four small ships and a crew of 143 men and boys, including his younger son Fernando and his brother Bartholomew. Columbus called this his "high voyage" because he traveled so far and encountered so many places unknown to the Europeans. He arrived in Santo Domingo on June 29 in the middle of a hurricane, but Governor Ovando would not let him enter the harbor.

Realizes continent is not Asia

Columbus sailed across the Caribbean to the coast of Honduras, running into another storm. He then journeyed southward along the coast of Central America looking for a passageway west. When he reached Panama, he was close to the Pacific, but it would be a few years until **Vasco Núñez de Balboa** (see entry) would actually cross the isthmus. Columbus now realized he had found a continent different from Asia, and that the as-yet-unnamed Americas stood between Europe and the "Indies."

Columbus tried to found a new colony at a place called Veragua in western Panama. As one of the rainiest places in the world and inhabited by Native Americans hostile to the Europeans, it proved unsuitable for settlement. Columbus left on Easter Sunday, April 16, 1503, and sailed eastward to what he thought was the longitude of Santo Domingo. He then turned north but ended up first in the Cayman Islands and next on the western end of Cuba on May 12.

Forced to run leaky ships aground

By now Columbus's two remaining ships were in bad condition, with leaks and missing sails. It took them until June 10, 1503, to fight their way eastward across the south coast of Cuba. Then Columbus decided that if he was to make any progress before his ships sank, he would have to risk sailing into the open sea. When the ships started leaking heavily Columbus was forced to turn to Jamaica and run both ships aground on June 23, 1503.

Columbus and crew were forced to spend a year at St. Ann's Bay in Jamaica. They were rescued by sending Diego Mendez by canoe across the Jamaica Channel to Hispaniola. He reached Santo Domingo in August 1503, but Governor Ovando would not let him charter a rescue ship. Columbus was faced with a mutiny on New Year's Day 1504, when a group of men tried to leave on their own but were forced to return. On February 28, 1504, Columbus tricked the Native Americans by correctly predicting a lunar eclipse, thereby getting food from them.

Makes difficult voyage back to Spain

At the end of March 1504 Columbus learned from a passing Spanish ship that Governor Ovando knew of Columbus's predicament but refused to let him be rescued. This led to a pitched battle between Columbus's followers and the mutineers on May 29. Luckily, Diego Mendez was finally able to charter a vessel and reached Jamaica at the end of June 1504. The boat, a small caravel, leaked so badly that it took six and a half weeks to get back to Santo Domingo, where Columbus chartered another boat and left for Spain on September 12, 1504. He did not arrive until November 7.

Keeps ties with court until his death

Columbus, now ill, retired to a house in Seville. He received word of Queen Isabella's death on November 26. He was financially secure, since he had received a share of Spain's newfound gold in Hispaniola. He stayed in Seville until he recovered, then was received by King Ferdinand at Segovia in May 1505. Columbus failed to convince the king to sponsor another voyage. Following the court as it traveled around Spain, he moved into a house in the city of Valladolid in April 1506. There he wrote his last will on May 19, making his son Diego his principal heir. He died the following day.

James Cook

Born 1728,
Whitby, England
Died February 14, 1779,
Hawaiian Islands

James Cook was born in 1728 near Whitby in northern England, the son of a Scottish farm laborer. After working as a farmer's helper and a grocer's assistant, Cook went to sea at the age of 18, which was then considered late. He was apprenticed to a Whitby shipowner who lodged the boy in his own home when he was ashore and encouraged him to study. When Cook was only 25, he was offered the command of a collier, a coal transport vessel, choosing instead to join the Royal Navy as an ordinary seaman. His ability was quickly recognized, and he was soon promoted to the rank of master, or warrant officer.

Charts St. Lawrence River

During the Seven Years' War with France, Cook saw active service in Canada and was present at the siege of Quebec. His meticulous charting of the St. Lawrence River, a major contribution to the British victory, testified to his

Captain Cook was an English explorer who led three expeditions to the Pacific Ocean, Antarctica, and the Arctic, and discovered the Hawaiian Islands. His explorations greatly increased the knowledge of world geography.

patience and skill as a marine surveyor. The data he gathered were so accurate that his charts were used for over a century. After the war he surveyed the coast of Newfoundland where his skill and industry gave him a deserved reputation as the best pilot in the navy. During this time he also observed an eclipse of the sun and wrote a paper about it for the Royal Society, something unheard of for a noncommissioned officer. The governor of Newfoundland recommended Cook for his first command, on the schooner *Greenville,* and in the winter of 1767-68 he sailed the ship from Newfoundland to England.

Readies for search for Terra Australis

In 1768 the British Royal Society requested that a ship be sent to the Pacific to study the transit of Venus across the sun. The observation of this phenomenon, due on June 3, 1769, was needed to determine the distance of the sun from the earth, and the Royal Society had calculated that the best vantage point for doing so was the newly discovered island of Tahiti. The British admiralty at once seized the opportunity as a convenient cover for a thorough search for the territory that was shown on maps as Terra Australis, or the great southern continent. The French were then active in the Southern Hemisphere, having already settled the Falkland Islands, and if there really were a rich southern continent, the British wanted to be there first.

The admiralty suggested that Cook be given command of the ship and the Royal Society agreed, having already known of his work in Newfoundland. After being promoted to the rank of lieutenant at the age of 40, Cook was able to select his own ship and chose an unusual vessel, a flat-bottomed collier from Whitby. From his experience as an apprentice on the run between Yorkshire and London, Cook knew that a collier could maneuver well along tidal coasts. Its shallow draft was ideally suited for sailing channels of uncertain depth and if the ship happened to go aground, the flat-bottomed hull would allow it to rest there without much risk of turning over.

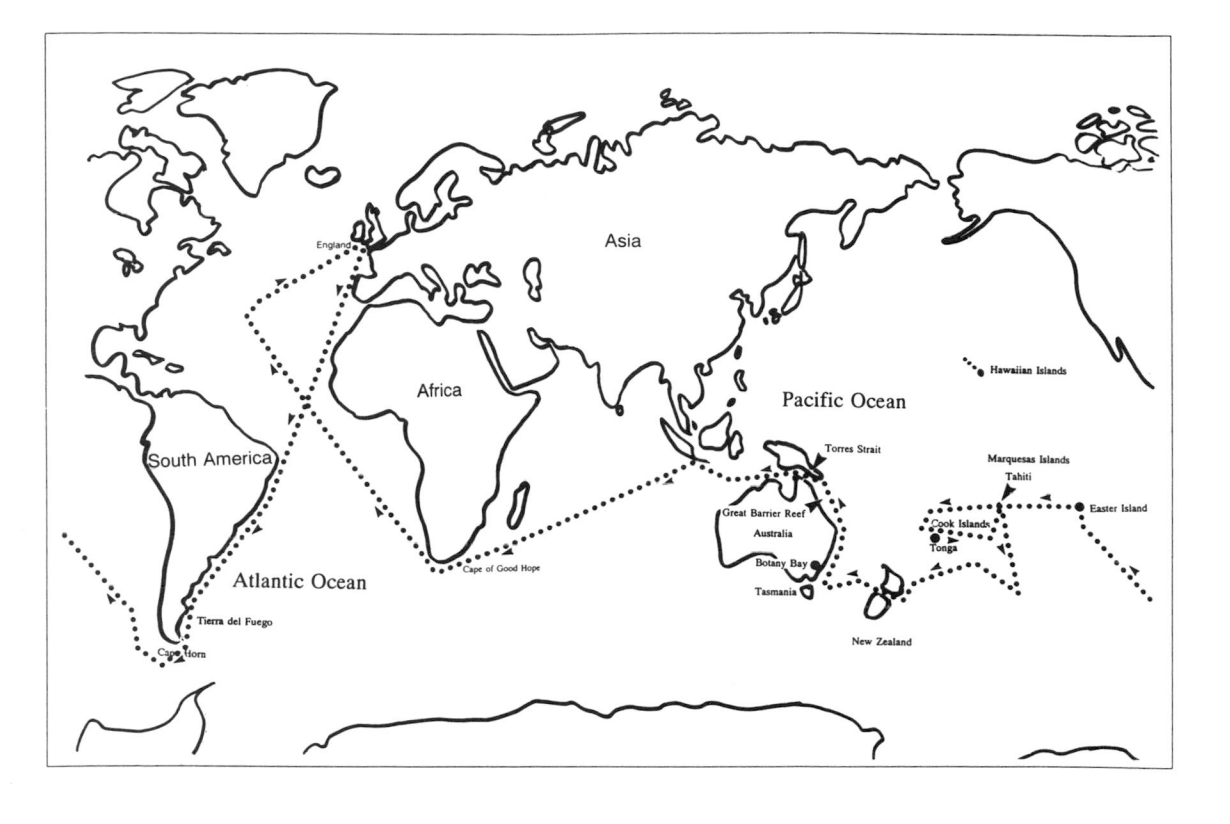

The ship was completely refitted and renamed the *Endeavour;* provisioned for 18 months, it carried 94 men, 11 of whom were civilians. Among these was a wealthy young man, **Joseph Banks** (see entry), a naturalist who was later to become president of the Royal Society. Banks had contributed a large sum to the cost of the voyage, and he brought with him two botanists, an astronomer, an artist, and four servants. Several members of the rest of the crew had sailed with the *Dolphin,* the ship **Samuel Wallis** (see combined Philip Carteret-Samuel Wallis entry) commanded when he discovered Tahiti the previous year.

On his first voyage, 1768-71, Cook attempted to find Terra Australis, the great southern continent.

Sets record by reaching southernmost point

The *Endeavour* sailed from Plymouth, England, on August 26, 1768. Tahiti was the official destination, but Cook carried secret instructions authorizing him to continue south after completing his astronomical observations in the hope of discovering "a continent or land of great extent." If he found no land he was to sail southwest between latitudes 40° and 50° until he reached the eastern coast of "the land discovered by Tasman now called New Zealand." He could then return by either Cape Horn or the Cape of Good Hope.

Cook made the outward voyage by way of Cape Horn, at the southern tip of South America. Although the Southern Hemisphere was in midsummer, the hills of Tierra del Fuego were covered with snow. In fact, two of Banks's servants froze to death when Banks took a party ashore to collect specimens and they were unable to return to the ship before nightfall. After passing the Horn, Cook sailed the *Endeavour* farther south than anyone had ever sailed before. The powerful roll of the sea from the west convinced him there was no great continent in that direction for many hundreds of miles. He knew he would have to sail west in order to make sure, but he did not do so at the time. Instead, since he needed to reach Tahiti to make his astronomical observations, he turned north.

Finds Tahiti

Locating a small island in the middle of the Pacific was not an easy task, and Cook had only the measurements of one previous navigator to guide him. Estimates of longitude were often inaccurate in the days before the chronometer, a highly accurate instrument for keeping time, came into general use. Calculations of latitude were more reliable, so the only way of finding Tahiti was to locate its latitude a few hundred miles to the east and to sail westward along that latitude until the land came into sight. That is what Cook did, and he sighted the peaks of the islands on April 11, 1769. As the ship approached the good anchorage of Matavai Bay, hundreds of Tahitians rowed out in their canoes to greet Cook's party, carrying peace offerings and crying "Taio! Taio!" ("Comrade! Comrade").

Tahiti proved to be a paradise for the naturalists, who occupied the three months they spent there collecting samples of the local plants and animals. The artist made sketches of the samples as well as of the landscape and the islanders. Cook had instructed everyone under his command to treat the population "with every imaginable humanity," and these orders were carried out—unlike many expeditions that followed.

After scientists observed the transit of Venus and charted the coast of the island, the *Endeavour* sailed from Tahiti. Cook took with him an islander named Tupia who proved invaluable as a pilot and interpreter. On Tupia's advice Cook visited other neighboring islands and, following his instructions, sailed to the south. Cook pursued a zigzag course but saw no sign of land until, on October 6, 1769, the ship touched on the east coast of New Zealand's North Island. The *Endeavour* thus became the first European ship to reach that site since the voyage of **Abel Tasman** (see entry), the Dutch navigator, over a century before. Banks believed they had found the southern continent but Cook was unconvinced.

Encounters Maoris

The truth could be established only by a careful survey of the coast, which had to wait until fresh water was loaded onto the *Endeavour*. Cook dropped anchor in a protected bay and for two days watched the coast. On the third day he sent a boat ashore but the Maoris, the native inhabitants of New Zealand, drove it away. A second attempt met with no more success and a third led to a struggle in which Cook had to order his men to fire. The Maoris fought with great courage, but four of their men were killed. Cook was very upset by his first attempts at friendship having ended so badly.

Farther north Cook found friendlier tribes of Maoris, and as the slow, meticulous work of circumnavigating the two islands proceeded, he and the Maoris came to admire one another greatly. Cook pronounced the quality of their boats to be excellent and noted the expert construction of their fortified villages. He also respected their courage. "All their actions and behavior toward us," he wrote, "tended to prove that they are a brave, open, warlike people and void of treachery." So great was his admiration that he returned to New Zealand on each subsequent voyage he made to the Pacific, using Queen Charlotte Sound on the north tip of South Island as his base of operations. On their part, the Maoris were still handing down the story of Cook's humanity and gentle bearing toward them a hundred years later.

Endeavour damaged by reefs

The *Endeavour* completed its 2,500 mile voyage in less than six months. Cook then turned for home, choosing the route around the Cape of Good Hope as being safer than the Horn for a ship that had already been at sea for 18 months. On April 19, 1770, the southeast corner of Australia was sighted. Sailing north for ten days along the coast, surveying as he went, Cook at last found an anchorage at Botany Bay. Unlike the Maoris, the Aborigines on Botany Bay avoided all contact with the European sailors. Tupia had been able to speak to the Maoris, whose ancestors had sailed from Tahiti, but he could not speak to the Aborigines.

Continuing northward, the *Endeavour* was soon within the treacherous area of the Great Barrier Reef—1,250 miles of coral ridges capable of ripping a ship to pieces. For a week the ship crawled forward a few yards at a time while boats ahead took soundings and men high in the rigging tried to spot the dark shadows of hazardous reefs in the water. After navigating almost 1,000 miles in this manner, the bottom of the ship scraped across a pinnacle of coral and the sea gushed in. For a night and a day the *Endeavour* was stuck on the reef; only the flat-bottomed hull stopped it from turning over. Pumps were manned constantly but still there was water four feet deep in the ship's bottom when it was lifted on the tide.

The crew had to "fother" the vessel—an intricate procedure by which a sail, filled with oakum (hemp soaked in tar), wool, rope ends, and dung, is passed under the ship and pulled tight in the hope that the suction of the water will draw the refuse as a plug into the leak. The ship then slowly made its way to the mouth of a river a few miles to the north, where Cooktown now stands. When the *Endeavour* was finally beached, the crew discovered that it was not the fothering but an immense piece of coral stuck like a plug in the largest of the holes that had saved the ship. It took two months to make the *Endeavour* seaworthy again.

Finally escapes reefs

Cook then decided to find a passage through the seemingly endless reef to the open sea, but the strong current and unpredictable winds threatened to carry the ship back onto the reef. A few days later the threat became greater when the wind died and the ship, unable to anchor in the deep water outside the reef and unable to move without wind against a strong tide, was only one yard from a wall of coral. Fortunately a puff of wind carried it back out to sea for a moment. Seeing an opening in the reef, Cook managed to sail through the narrow gap to comparative safety inside the reef. He noted in his journal, "It is but a few days ago that I rejoiced at having got without the reef; but that was nothing ... to what I now felt at being safe at an anchor within it."

Returns to England

Cook captained the *Endeavour* painstakingly northward to the Torres Strait and passed through it on August 21 and 22, 1770, the first to do so since Luis Vaez de Torres, the Spanish explorer, discovered the strait in 1606. After a lengthy stay for repairs at Batavia, the ship sailed for the Cape of Good Hope and home. Cook reached England on July 12, 1771, not quite three years after he had left. Cook had made a notable achievement: because he had taken food with a high vitamin C content such as lemon juice and sauerkraut on the voyage, none of the men in his party died from scurvy; however, dysentery and malaria contracted in Batavia killed a third of the crew.

In spite of the doubt that the voyage cast on the existence of a southern continent, there were still scientists in England determined to believe in it. They felt Cook had deliberately avoided the regions in which it must lie. Cook proposed that he lead another expedition, this time with two ships, in order "to put an end to all diversity of opinion about a matter so curious and important." The admiralty promoted him to commander and provided him with the 462-ton *Resolution* and the 340-ton *Adventure,* two more converted Whitby colliers. The hulls were covered with an extra skin of planking as protection against

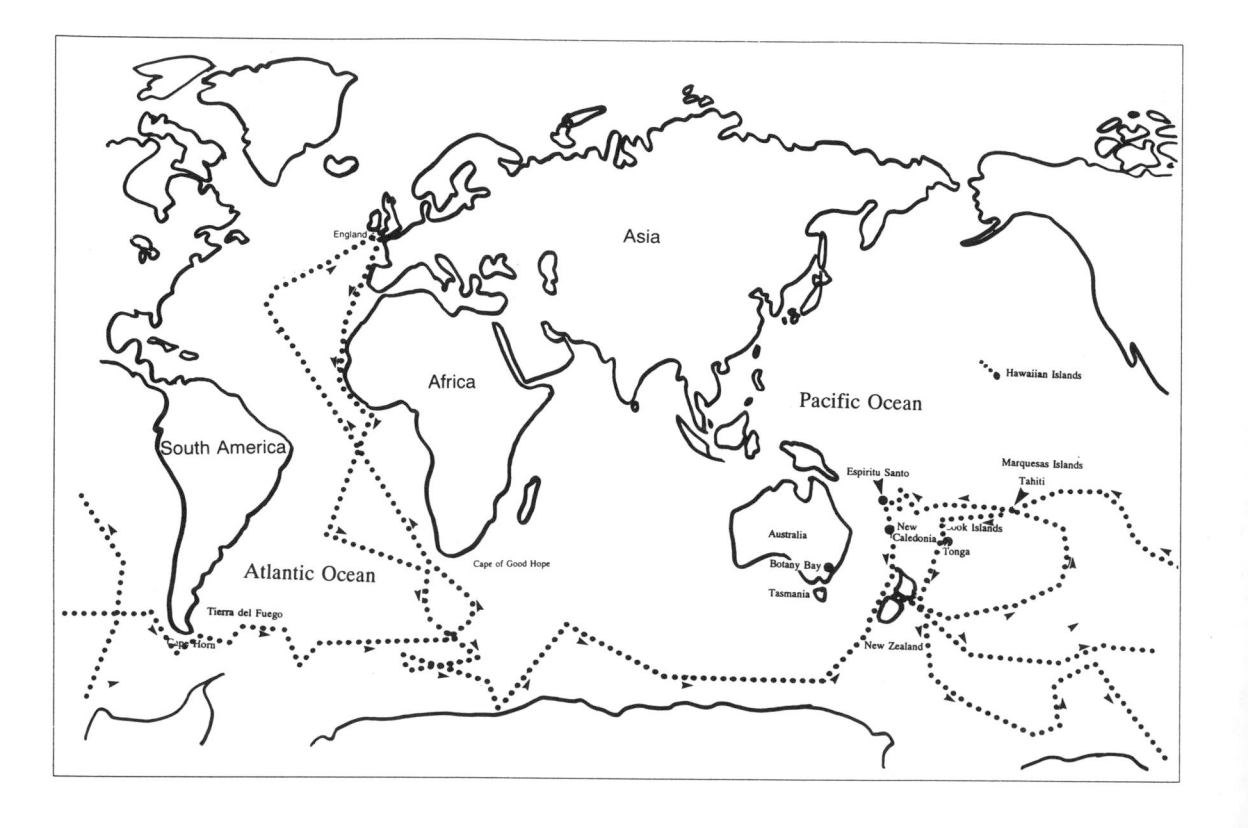

Map labels: England, Asia, Africa, Hawaiian Islands, Pacific Ocean, South America, Espiritu Santo, Marquesas Islands, Tahiti, New Caledonia, Cook Islands, Tonga, Australia, Atlantic Ocean, Botany Bay, Cape of Good Hope, Tasmania, Tierra del Fuego, Cape Horn, New Zealand

Cook's second expedition, 1772-75, confirmed a southern continent did not exist.

borer worms in warm seas; the space between the two skins was packed with tar and oakum to repel the worms. Banks had intended to rejoin Cook on this second voyage, but he angrily withdrew when Cook refused to accommodate his 15-member party of scientists, artists, secretaries, and servants.

Renews search for southern continent

The *Resolution* and the *Adventure* sailed from Plymouth on July 13, 1772, reaching the Cape of Good Hope in October. From there they sailed south into the freezing storm belt that surrounded Antarctica. Soon the ships were having to make their way through a sea littered with ice floes and icebergs, some so enormous that sailors called them ice islands. On January 17, 1773, Cook wrote: "At ¼ past 11 o'clock we crossed the Antarctic Circle, and are undoubtedly the first and only ship that ever crossed that line." On February 8, the two ships lost each other in a fog, and on March 16 Cook turned northeast in the face of impenetrable ice. One hundred and seventeen days after leaving the Cape and having sailed 11,000 miles—much of it where no other ship had been—Cook brought the *Resolution* into Dusky Sound on the coast of New Zealand's South Island. Some weeks later they found the *Adventure* safely moored in Queen Charlotte Sound.

Cook's party passed the southern winter visiting Pacific islands, including Tahiti, where they received the customary warm welcome. In September they sailed for New Zealand and on the way there the two ships were separated, this time for good. Cook left a message in a bottle for the captain of the *Adventure* and departed to explore the Pacific between New Zealand and Cape Horn.

Confirms that no continent exists

Battling through the ice, on January 30, 1774, they reached latitude 71° 10', the farthest point south yet attained and only some 1,250 miles from the South Pole. By then Cook was certain that no continent existed in those latitudes. "I will not say that it was impossible to get farther to the South," he wrote, "but the attempting of it would have been a dangerous and rash enterprise and what I believe no man in my situation would have thought of." A 16-year-old midshipman, **George Vancouver** (see entry), later to win fame for his exploration of the west coast of Canada, clung to the bowsprit of the ship, determined to be the one to reach farthest south. He yelled out, "I am the farthest south man in the world!" Vancouver kept this record for 49 years, until the explorations of the British navigator James Weddell.

Charts Pacific islands

It would have been simple for Cook, having achieved his mission, to head for home. However, with the support of his officers and men, he decided to turn north and search for more islands. During the next six months Cook's party visited Easter Island, the Marquesas, Tahiti again, and Espiritu Santo in Vanuatu. Cook charted the islands of the Vanuatu Archipelago and the island of New Caledonia, which he was the first European to see. Returning to Queen Charlotte Sound, he found his message had been removed but he could not learn from the local islanders what had happened to the *Adventure*. As it turned out, the ship had returned to England. A month later Cook set off on a final attempt to find land between New Zealand and Cape Horn. None was sighted. The expedition spent Christmas in a cove off Tierra del Fuego, celebrating with goose pie and Madeira wine and entertaining the local people. On December 28 they rounded the Horn into the South Atlantic, having definitely discounted the myth of a southern continent. A relieved Cook wrote: "I was sick of these high latitudes where nothing is to be found but ice and thick fogs."

Received as hero in England

Upon his return to England in late July 1775, Cook was recognized as a hero. In addition to being awarded several honors, Cook was given a land appointment that allowed him time to work on his papers and records. He now had some time to spend with his wife. He had married Elizabeth Batts in 1762 but had spent most of his days since then at sea while his wife lived alone in a small house in the river town of Greenwich outside London. They eventually had six children but only one survived to adulthood.

In 1776 the British admiralty decided to commission another voyage to the Pacific. This time the goal was to determine whether it was possible to find the Northwest Passage around North America by sailing from the west to the east. Once again Cook was put in charge of the expedition even though he was still in poor health as a result of the rigors of his previous voyage. The *Resolution* was refitted and a second ship, the *Discovery,* was commissioned. However, they were not in the best possible condition because the American Revolution was straining British naval resources. The members of the crew included George Vancouver and William Bligh, who was later to become famous because of the book *Mutiny on the Bounty* and its accompanying film adaptation.

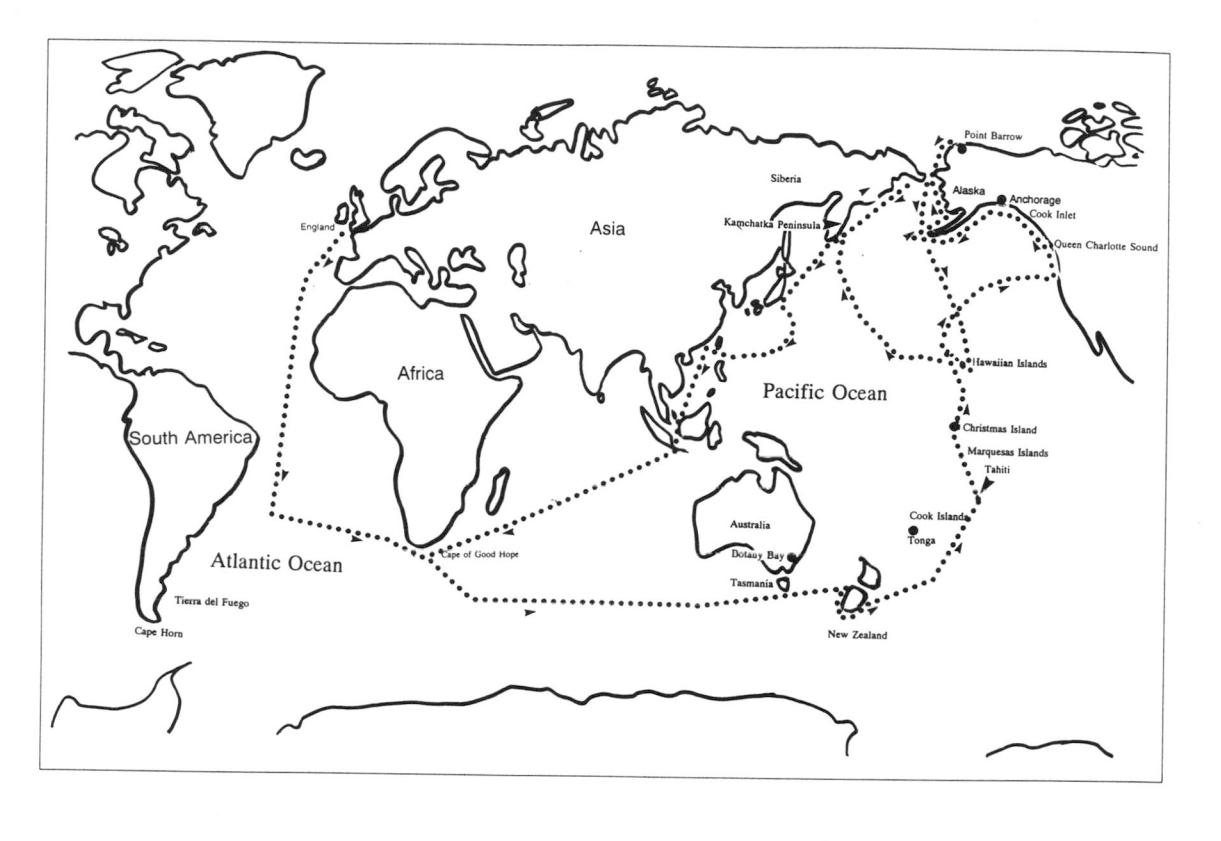

The following labels appear on the map:

Point Barrow
Siberia
Alaska
Anchorage
Cook Inlet
Kamchatka Peninsula
Asia
Queen Charlotte Sound
England
Africa
Pacific Ocean
Hawaiian Islands
Christmas Island
Marquesas Islands
Tahiti
South America
Cook Islands
Tonga
Australia
Atlantic Ocean
Botany Bay
Cape of Good Hope
Tasmania
Tierra del Fuego
Cape Horn
New Zealand

Searches for Northwest Passage

Cook embarked from England on July 12, 1776, sailing around the Cape of Good Hope and then south into the Indian Ocean to explore Prince Edward and Kerguelen islands. He went to New Zealand by way of Tasmania, then north to the Cook Islands, Tonga, and Tahiti. In Tahiti, where he was suffering greatly from rheumatism, a group of Tahitian women demonstrated their traditional techniques of massage therapy, which greatly reduced the pain. From Tahiti Cook continued north toward Alaska, where he was to investigate possible routes east. On December 25, 1777, he passed by Christmas Island. On January 18, 1778, he made his most significant discoveries—the Hawaiian Islands, which he named the Sandwich Islands, after the head of the British admiralty.

Explores Alaska for route

Once he reached Alaska, Cook tried various routes to see

During his final voyage, 1776-80, Cook searched for the Northwest Passage.

if they connected with a passageway around America. The most promising was Cook Inlet, which is a large bay where the city of Anchorage now stands. Like most of his other investigations, however, this route inevitably led nowhere. Cook sailed through the Aleutian chain as far north as 70° 44', near Point Barrow on the north coast of Alaska. He found no way around either North America or Siberia.

Lives among Hawaiian islanders

Cook took his party to Hawaii to spend the winter. On the morning of January 17, 1779, they stepped ashore at Kealakekua Bay on the west coast of the "Big Island" of Hawaii. About 1,500 canoes had surrounded the two ships as the islanders had come out to welcome them. The Hawaiians thought Cook was the reincarnation of Lono, the god of harvests and happiness. Although unaware of this, Cook treated the chiefs and priests with his usual solemnity and consideration.

For a few weeks all went well, but even so, when Cook announced his decision to depart there was undisguised relief on the part of the chiefs. Entertaining a god and his retinue had proved to be exhausting and expensive. Cook was forced to return to Kealakekua a week after his departure, however, because a mast on the *Resolution* had been damaged in a storm. This time relations with the islanders were not so good. When one of the seamen died and was buried on shore, the islanders were astonished to learn that Lono's followers were mortal.

Killed by Hawaiians

During the night of February 13, 1779, the cutter of the *Discovery* was stolen. The next morning Cook went ashore, escorted by the king of Kealakekua and some of his marines, to announce his intention of taking on board and holding as hostage a tribal chief until the cutter was found. A crowd of islanders began to throw stones. Although Cook gave orders not to shoot, a crewman opened fire. The islanders fell on Cook, stabbing him in the back and clubbing him to death. His dismembered body was taken back to the village as the surviving marines made their way to the ship. A few days later Cook's remains were brought to the ship by the villagers. Following Cook's death the two English ships sailed north during the spring and summer of 1779 to the Kamchatka Peninsula and the coast of Siberia. They reached England on October 4, 1780.

Francisco Vásquez de Coronado

Born c. 1510,
Salamanca, Spain
Died September 22, 1554,
Mexico City, Mexico

Spanish nobleman and explorer Francisco Vásquez de Coronado led the first European expedition into what is now the southwestern United States and discovered numerous geographical landmarks, including the Grand Canyon.

Francisco Vásquez de Coronado, a Spanish nobleman and explorer, led the first European expedition into what is now the southwestern United States. Though the expedition did not accomplish its mission—to find gold—it did discover numerous geographical landmarks, including the Grand Canyon.

Coronado went to Mexico (then the viceroyalty of New Spain) as a member of a group led by Antonio de Mendoza, the colony's first viceroy. After helping to put down an uprising in the king's mines, Coronado was named governor of New Galicia, a province on the western coast of Mexico. As governor, he oversaw Spanish explorations on the province's northern frontier.

Coronado was soon enlisted to help two explorers—**Estevanico** (see entry), a Moroccan slave, and Fray Marcos

Coronado extensively explored the American Southwest,
a territory previously unknown to Europeans. ▶

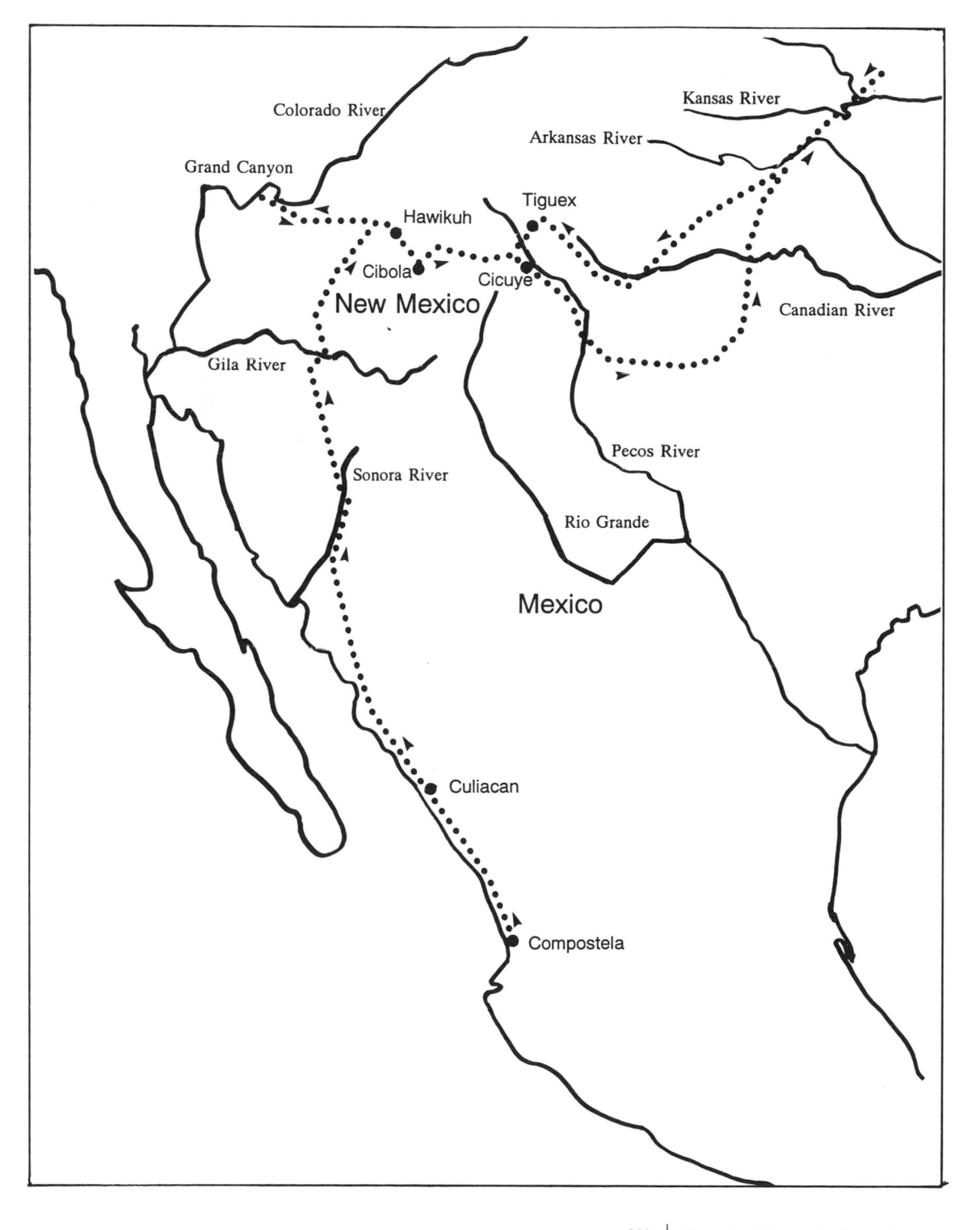

de Niza, a Franciscan friar—prepare for a journey to the north to verify reports of the fabulous "Seven Cities of Cibola." Estevanico had heard stories about the cities when he was in a party led by **Álvar Núñez Cabeza de Vaca** (see entry), a Spaniard who explored the southern region of what is now the United States.

The Seven Cities of Cíbola

Five and a half months after Estevanico and Fray Marcos left for Cíbola, Fray Marcos returned alone. He reported that Estevanico had been killed at the Zuni pueblo (village) of Hawikuh (in what is now western New Mexico) and that he himself had seen the large and very rich city of Cíbola from a distance. Impressed by this report, Coronado traveled with Fray Marcos to Mexico City, where they delivered the news to the viceroy.

Since Mendoza had long been interested in exploring the area north of Mexico, the friar's stories spurred him into action. Mendoza decided to launch an expedition with Coronado as its leader. In order to carry out this important mission, Coronado assembled a force of about 300 Spaniards and 1,000 Native Americans at Compostela, a town on Mexico's western coast. Before they set out, Mendoza traveled to Compostela to review the expedition in person. To support Coronado from the sea, the viceroy also sent two ships up the Gulf of California under the command of Hernando de Alarcón. The ships, which lost contact with Coronado, traveled 200 miles up the Colorado River.

The search for Cibola

In the early spring of 1540, Coronado journeyed with his army to the town of Culiacán, the present-day capital of the Mexican state of Sinalao. With an advance force of about 100 Spaniards, a number of Native Americans, and four friars, he proceeded up the Yaqui River valley. One of his first acts was to found the town of San Gerónimo and to put a man named Melchor Días in charge. Días later ventured up the Colorado River to try to find Alarcón and his ships but had no success.

Crossing the Colorado near present-day Yuma, Arizona, Días traveled four days in what is now California. He became the first European to reach this area.

Meanwhile, Coronado and his men had crossed the Gila River and entered the region of the Colorado Plateau, reaching Hawikuh in July. Coronado and his men had no difficulty capturing the town, but once inside they realized it did not come close to matching Fray Marcos's glowing description. The Spaniards were furious with the friar. A soldier with the expedition wrote, "Such were the curses that some hurled at Fray Marcos that I pray God may protect him from them." Fray Marcos was sent back to Mexico in disgrace.

Discovery of the Grand Canyon

Coronado sent Pedro de Tovar and Fray Juan de Padilla to explore the area to the northwest, where they found ancient Hopi villages in what is now northern Arizona. The Hopis told them about a great river to the west, so in August Garcia Lopez de Cárdenas led a small group of Spaniards in search of this river. While exploring they came upon a magnificent canyon; from its edge they viewed the Colorado River flowing far below. Cárdenas and his party were thus the first Europeans to see the Grand Canyon. After three days of unsuccessful attempts to climb down the cliffs to the river, they were forced to turn back.

Coronado had also sent an exploring party east under the command of Hector de Alvarado. Alvarado reached the pueblo of Acoma, perched high on a rock, where the inhabitants gave the Spaniards food. After a short rest they continued on to Tiguex in the Rio Grande Valley north of present-day Albuquerque, New Mexico. Alvarado reported back to Coronado that the people of Tiguex had an abundance of food, so Coronado decided to make his winter headquarters there.

The "Tiguex War"

During the winter of 1540-41 the Spaniards' demands for supplies and their disagreements over women led to hostilities between them and the Tiguex people. After capturing one pueblo, the Spanish burned 200 of their captives alive. Several Spaniards were also killed during various engagements in the "Tiguex War." Coronado was wounded several times.

In the meantime, Alvarado had traveled east to Cicuye on the Pecos River, where he had captured a Plains tribesman (perhaps a Pawnee), whom the Spanish named "the Turk." The Turk told stories of a land to the east, called "Quivira," that was ruled by a powerful king. The Turk claimed that abundant gold could be found there. Intrigued by the Turk's stories, Coronado left Cicuye to find Quivira. He went east into the Great Plains, where he and his men saw enormous herds of buffalo. But when they saw that the Plains tribes had no gold—that, in fact, they had very few material possessions at all—the Spanish realized that they had been tricked once again. Coronado sent his main force back to the Rio Grande with large supplies of buffalo meat. In a last effort to find wealth, he took a small party of men north and then east. But his attempts were futile. As a soldier wrote, "Neither gold nor silver nor any trace of either was found." By this time the Spaniards had probably reached the area that is now central Kansas. Finally, the Turk confessed that he had lied in order to draw the Spanish soldiers into the interior. He was subsequently strangled to death, although Coronado reportedly opposed his execution.

Illness and last years

Coronado returned to Tiguex in October 1542. Shortly thereafter he was injured in a riding accident. Since he had been in poor health for some time, the Spaniards were ready to return to Mexico. They left Tiguex in April and arrived in Mexico City in the late autumn. The viceroy was angry that the expedition had not discovered any treasure. Gradually coming to realize that Coronado had done the best he could, Mendoza reappointed him governor of New Galicia in 1544.

At about the same time, a Spanish royal judge began a formal investigation into accusations that Coronado was guilty of brutality to the Native Americans. Although the investigation resulted in Coronado losing his post as governor, he was eventually cleared of all charges. He then became an official in the municipal government of Mexico City; in 1547 he testified in favor of Mendoza during an investigation of the viceroy's rule. In reward for his service to the king of Spain, Coronado was given a land grant in 1549. His health continued to decline, however, and he died in Mexico City five years later.

Hernán Cortés

Born 1485,
Medellín, Spain

Died December 2, 1547,
Castilleja de la Cuesta, Spain

Hernán Cortés was a Spanish conquistador who conquered Mexico and sponsored several exploring expeditions in the Americas.

Hernán Cortés gained an advantage when the Spanish accidentally introduced smallpox to the Mexican people. Cortés's artillery, the fact that the Aztec King, Montezuma, believed Cortés was a god, and, finally, the smallpox epidemic itself (which killed the native people in great numbers) permitted Cortés to subdue the Aztecs and build a Spanish city at their capital. After his conquest of the Aztecs he sponsored several explorations in the Americas. Ironically, Cortés's accomplishments were not rewarded as he would have liked, and he spent the last years of his life petitioning the Spanish king for recognition.

Goes to Hispaniola

Born in the Spanish town of Medellín to a family of minor nobility, Cortés was sent at the age of 14 to study law at the University of Salamanca. In 1504 his family raised the money to send him to the new Spanish colony of Santo Domingo in the Caribbean. Located on the island of Hispaniola, the colony was first visited by **Christopher Columbus** (see entry) only 12 years earlier. When he arrived, Cortés was given a small land grant and named the public notary in the town of Azua, about 50 miles west of Santo Domingo. He spent the next seven years on the island.

Becomes mayor of Santiago

In 1511 the governor of Santo Domingo sent a Spaniard named Diego Velázquez to conquer the nearby island of Cuba. Cortés was engaged as Velázquez's secretary. In a foreshadowing of future conflicts between the two men, Cortés and Velázquez quarreled, and Cortés was held in prison temporarily. Eventually they made peace and Cortés was appointed mayor of the town of Santiago in eastern Cuba. At that time he also married Catalina Xuárez, the sister of a friend of Velázquez. Cortés became prosperous by mining gold and raising livestock.

In 1517 Velázquez sponsored a voyage by Francisco Hernandez de Cordoba to the Yucatán Peninsula on the American mainland, in what is today eastern Mexico. The Spanish were met by armed Maya warriors and suffered heavy casualties. They brought back reports of a highly civilized people. Intrigued, Velázquez soon sent his nephew, Juan de Grijalba, to the Yucatán with a larger expedition to investigate further. Grijalba landed on the island of Cozumel at the eastern end of the Yucatán and then sailed west along the coast to a place about 50 miles from the modern city of Veracruz. There he was met by emissaries sent by Montezuma. Grijalba sent one of his lieutenants, Pedro de Alvarado, back to Cuba to give a report and to deliver gold the Spanish had found.

During Grijalba's absence, Velázquez had recruited Cortés to lead the next expedition to the mainland. As reports came back from Mexico, Cortés had no trouble recruiting his countrymen to join the venture. At his headquarters in Santiago he assembled a large company of men and one Spanish woman and a great quantity of supplies. Velázquez began to wonder about Cortés's intentions when he learned of the preparations the explorer was making. He did not have time to act, however, before Cortés departed in February 1518.

Seizes Tabasco

After leaving Santiago, Cortés sailed along the south coast of Cuba to the port of Trinidad where he enlisted Alvarado and additional soldiers. His total force consisted of about 550 soldiers, 100 sailors, 14 cannon, and 16 horses. Following Grijalba's lead, he went first to Cozumel. In Cozumel he learned about two castaways from a Spanish ship that had been wrecked on the coast of the Yucatán in 1511. He was able to locate one of the men, Jeronimo de Aguilar, who had learned to speak Maya and could act as an interpreter.

The Spaniards then sailed along the coast to Tabasco. When the local inhabitants resisted Cortés's demand for supplies, he seized their town. After six days, the Native Americans from the area massed in a large army and tried to push the Europeans off their shores, but they were defeated by the European artillery and cavalry. As part of the reparations they were forced to pay to the Spanish, the Tabascoans turned over a number of slaves, including a young woman named Malinche, whom the Spaniards called Marina. She was from a high-ranking family nearby and spoke Nahuatl, the language of the Aztecs. She served as translator from Nahuatl into Maya for Aguilar. She later became Cortés's mistress and, oftentimes, his spy.

Founds Veracruz

Cortés and his army made their second landing farther west, near the present-day city of Veracruz. He anchored there on Good Friday and was met by a contingent of the local dignitaries on Easter Sunday 1519. He also received his first emissary from Montezuma. It was here that Cortés learned about the Aztec god Quetzalcoatl. According to Aztec legend, Quetzalcoatl was expected to return to the people from over the sea. Unfortunately for the Aztecs, Montezuma thought Cortés was Quetzalcoatl. The Aztec ruler was worried about some recent grim omens that, according to his astrologers, predicted the fall of the Aztec dynasty. Because of these omens, Montezuma forbade the Spaniards to come to the capital of the Aztec Empire, Tenochtitlán, which is now Mexico City.

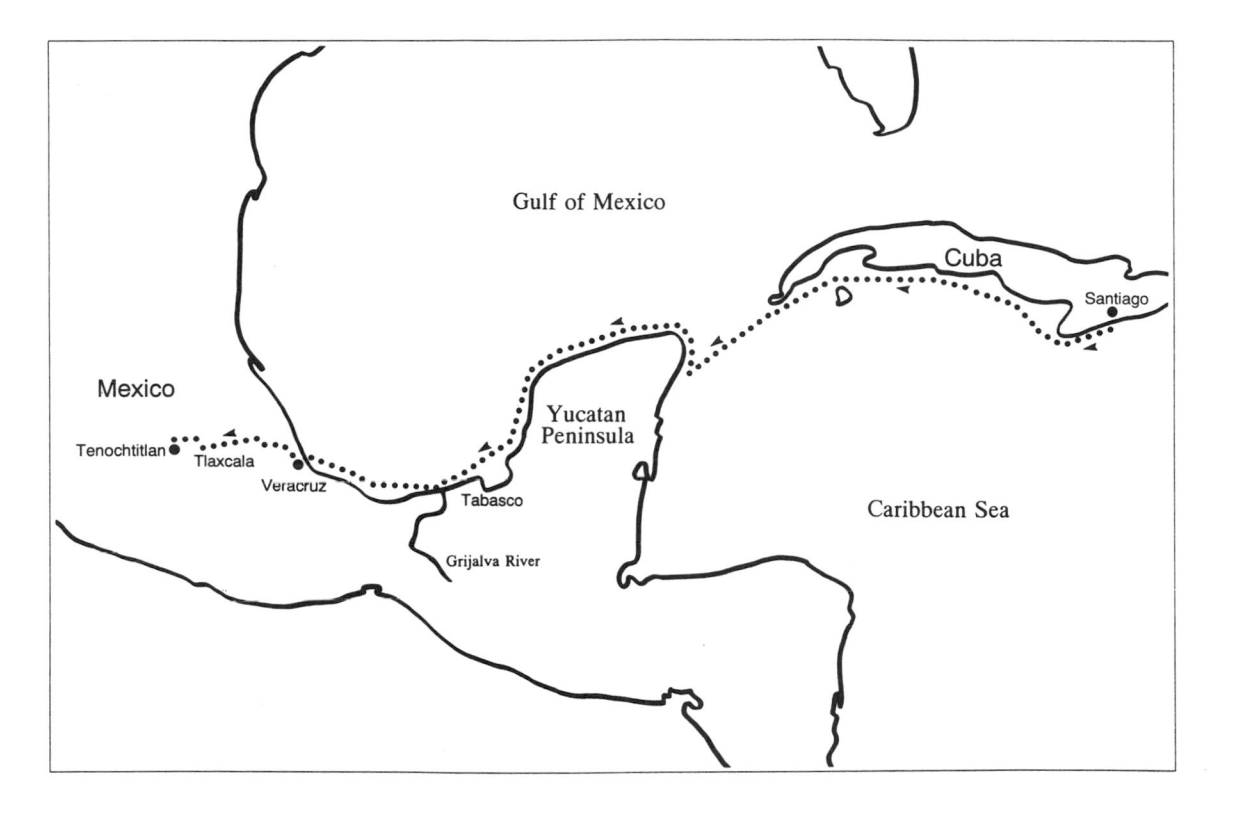

Meanwhile, needing a base camp, Cortés built the town of Villa Rica de la Vera Cruz, which became known as Veracruz. His competition with Velázquez resumed when he received word that Velázquez had been named commander of mainland settlements founded on the mainland of Mexico. To bypass Velázquez's authority, Cortés loaded a ship with all the treasures he had taken and sent it to Spain. In so doing, he put himself under the direct rule of King Charles V of Spain rather than Velázquez. As a further assurance of his power locally, Cortés had the rest of his ships destroyed, thus preventing Velázquez sympathizers from returning to Cuba.

When Cortés took the capital city of Tenochtitlán on August 13, 1521, after a seven-month battle, he had conquered the Aztec empire.

Makes famous march to Tenochtitlán

Determined to visit Tenochtitlán, Cortés left Veracruz on August 15, 1519. He was accompanied by 300 foot soldiers and 15 cavalry. His route led them onto the plateau of Mexico via Jalapa, Xocotla, and Tlaxcala. Cortés succeeded in forming an alliance with the independent state of Tlaxcala, and 6,000 Tlaxcalan volunteers went with him on his march to Tenochtitlán. As he pushed on through Mexico, Cortés received more emissaries from Montezuma, who brought valuable gifts while simultaneously trying to keep the Spanish force from advancing. But the gifts only made Cortés all the more eager to reach Tenochtitlán.

At Cholula, Cortés narrowly escaped a plot to destroy his army when Marina found out about the conspiracy in time to save the Spaniards. Cortés retaliated by gathering 6,000 Cholulan warriors in the main square and mowing them down with gunfire. Leaving Cholula, the Spanish force climbed the snowy pass between the spectacular volcanoes of Popocatépetl and Iztaccíhuatl to look down upon the Valley of Mexico. There lay the great city of Tenochtitlán, which they reached in November 1519.

Takes Montezuma captive

At first the Spanish were welcomed by Montezuma, but the Europeans knew they were in a dangerous position. Cortés decided he would be safer if he took Montezuma hostage, so he had the Aztec king held prisoner in the Spanish living quarters. Apparently believing that Cortés was the god Quetzalcoatl and that he had to obey him, Montezuma gave the Spaniards valuable gifts, including large quantities of gold. While Cortés held Montezuma in captivity, he took advantage of the dissension he saw among the Aztecs and ruled them through the king. However, in April 1520 the Spaniards upset the Aztecs by taking over one of their temples and turning it into a shrine to the Virgin Mary. Relaying to Cortés what the Aztec gods had told him, Montezuma advised the Spaniard to leave the city if he wanted to live.

In early May Cortés heard that Velázquez had sent Pánfilo de Narváez to Mexico to arrest him. Cortés decided to leave Tenochtitlán and return to the coast. He left Alvarado behind with a small force. Returning to Veracruz, Cortés overcame Narváez in a battle and convinced most of the defeated soldiers to join him.

When Cortés went back to Tenochtitlán, he found that Alvarado had made the population angry by attacking an unarmed and peaceful religious procession. In order to calm the people, Cortés forced Montezuma to appear before them, but the angry crowd stoned their king to death.

Retreats from Tenochtitlán

Fearful for their lives, Cortés and his men left Tenochtitlán in the middle of the night on June 30, 1520. As the Spaniards marched over the causeway that led out of the city, they were attacked and at least 450 of them were killed. The Spanish afterwards referred to this event as the Noche Triste, or Sorrowful Night. At the town of Otumba the Spanish were able to overcome an Aztec army; they then retreated to Tlaxcala where they found that their allies were still loyal. They recuperated in Tlaxcala for several months.

Returns to conquer the Aztecs

In the meantime smallpox, a disease introduced in the New World by the Europeans, had broken out and decimated the Aztec population. Montezuma's successor died during the epidemic and was replaced by the war chief Cuauhtémoc. Spanish reinforcements continued to arrive from Cuba. At the end of December 1520 Cortés left Tlaxcala and returned to the Valley of Mexico. He captured the small towns around Tenochtitlán and cut off supplies of water and food. Thousands of Aztecs died from hunger and disease. Several pitched battles took place, with the Spaniards gradually advancing on the city.

After seven months Cortés had taken the central square and controlled most of the city. Cuauhtémoc surrendered on August 13, 1521. He was later tortured to reveal where the Spanish could find supposedly hidden treasure. Cortés immediately started on the task of rebuilding Tenochtitlán into the Spanish city of Mexico, which became present-day Mexico City. Having taken over the Aztec capital, Cortés had effectively conquered the people of Mexico.

Becomes governor of New Spain

On October 22, 1522, Charles V rewarded Cortés's exploits by appointing him governor and captain general of New Spain, as the newly conquered region was called. In addition to his responsibilities as governor, Cortés remained committed to exploring the new country. In particular, he was interested in searching for the Northwest Passage, a water route between the Atlantic and Pacific oceans, which had thus far eluded explorers. Cortés sent several expeditions to explore both coasts of New Spain. In October 1524 Cortés himself traveled south to Honduras to track down a rebellious lieutenant. He took Cuauhtémoc with him as insurance against an uprising during his absence. When Cortés was informed that the Aztec leader was plotting against him on the trip to Honduras, Cortés had him hanged.

Loses power in New Spain

Cortés was away from Mexico for a year and nine months. When he returned he found that the government was being taken over more and more by royal officials sent from Spain. Unhappy with this turn of events, Cortés left for Spain in 1528 to try to convince the king to name him viceroy of New Spain, thereby making him the highest authority in the new land. Cortés was received with great honors and given the title of Marqués del Valle de Oaxaca, with extensive rights over a large section of central Mexico. But he made no headway with his efforts to be given real power. Upon his return to Mexico in July 1530 his position continued to deteriorate. In 1535 Antonio de Mendoza arrived to take the position of New Spain's first viceroy.

Explores Pacific Coast

As part of his reward from Charles V, Cortés had been put in charge of exploration in the South Sea (Pacific Ocean) and promised a share of any riches that were found there. In 1534 he sent out an expedition that sailed across the Gulf of California and landed in La Paz Bay in Baja California, where a pearl fishery was discovered. Deciding to personally look into this new possibility of wealth, Cortés set sail from the port of Sinaloa on April 18, 1535, with three ships and about 170 men. On May 3 he landed in La Paz Bay, claiming the country for Spain; however, it turned out to be poor desert land that yielded no food or water. Cortés stayed in the area for a year, but he finally gave up on the possibility of finding any riches and returned to Mexico.

Cortés continued to have mixed success with his exploration efforts. In 1539 he sponsored a successful voyage by Francisco de Ulloa, who sailed around the tip of Baja California and up its west coast. In so doing, de Ulloa discovered that Baja was a peninsula and not an island. In 1540 Cortés hoped to be given responsibility for the expedition planned by Spain to find the mythical "Seven Cities of Cíbola." Instead, Viceroy Mendoza gave the expedition to **Francisco Vásquez de Coronado** (see entry).

Tries to regain favor in Spain

Dissatisfied with his position, Cortés traveled back to Spain to visit the king again the same year. Charles V was not in the country at the time, however, so Cortés was unable to present his petition personally. Cortés's standing continued to decline. In October 1541 he and two of his sons, one of whom had been born to Marina, took part in a Spanish expedition against the city of Algiers in North Africa. The Spanish fleet was destroyed in a violent storm. Cortés escaped, but his pride was wounded when he was not asked to take part in any war councils thereafter.

Cortés lived in Spain for the rest of his life. He spent his time writing letters to the king asking for the honors he felt were his due. The Spanish *conquistador* died a disappointed man, convinced his accomplishments for Spain had never been sufficiently recognized.

Jacques Cousteau

Born June 11, 1910,
Saint-André-de-Cubzac, France

Probably the world´s most noted underwater explorer, Jacques Cousteau invented the aqualung breathing apparatus and designed the first underwater research stations.

Jacques-Yves Cousteau's name is virtually synonymous with exploration of the earth's oceans and rivers. A leading expert in oceanography, he has used documentaries, television programs, and books to educate the public on the diversity of sea life and the importance of the world's oceans. It was in 1944, while diving off the coast of Toulon in the Mediterranean Sea, that Cousteau became mesmerized by the beauty of reefs and the sea's underwater habitats.

Using his winning personality and celebrity status, Cousteau has also spoken out on conservation issues, suggesting that so-called industrial progress has placed civilization in jeopardy. He argued, for example, that nations that dumped radioactive waste and mustard and nerve gases underwater were endangering the planet's safety.

Early interest in photography

Cousteau's childhood interests in photography and

inventions formed the basis for his adult successes. He was born on June 11, 1910, in his parents' ancestral home in Saint-André-de-Cubzac, a small village in the south of France. Cousteau quickly became familiar with the culture outside village life. Because his father was a lawyer who represented American businessmen in Europe and the United States, he spent his youth in Paris and then New York City.

Cousteau's first love was photography. At the age of 13 he purchased one of the first home movie cameras sold in France and started to make his own films. An indifferent student, he was expelled from a Paris secondary school, or lycée, for throwing rocks at the school windows.

Career in the French navy

After his parents sent him to a boarding school in Alsace, his grades improved; he was then admitted to the French Naval Academy in 1930, graduating second in his class with a degree in engineering (1932). Upon graduation, Cousteau joined a naval voyage around the world that included a stop in Los Angeles, where he filmed movie stars Mary Pickford and Douglas Fairbanks greeting the French officers. He served with the navy for a while in Shanghai, China, before returning to Europe via the trans-Siberian railroad.

Cousteau entered the pilot training program at the French navy's aviation school. He had made his first solo flight and was close to graduation when an accident dashed his hopes for a flying career. While he was driving at night on a deserted mountain road, his car spun out of control and crashed. Cousteau was seriously hurt; his right arm was paralyzed. Forced to drop out of aviation school, Cousteau underwent several years of physical therapy before he regained full use of his arm.

After he had sufficiently recovered, Cousteau was assigned to the cruiser *Dupleix,* which was stationed at Toulon, a French port on the Mediterranean. In Toulon a fellow officer suggested to Cousteau that he take up swimming to help rehabilitate his arm. This suggestion redirected Cousteau's life in ways neither man could then see. In the summer of 1936 he began to spend all his free time at the beach. He started using goggles as a way of seeing underwater and adapted his camera so he could film fish.

Invention of the aqualung

Cousteau began to think about the problem of breathing underwater. Since the first deep-sea dives in the 1870s, the only way to supply oxygen was from an air line leading from the boat, which greatly restricted the diver's underwater mobility. After much hard work, Cousteau eventually developed a breathing device he called the aqualung. The aqualung consists of an air canister of compressed air, a regulator that supplies a constant flow of oxygen (at the same pressure as the water the diver is in), and a mouthpiece that enables the diver to breathe.

Cousteau's opportunity to develop the aqualung came after the Germans invaded France in 1940. Cousteau stayed in Toulon, where the French navy was interned, and there in 1942-43 he worked on the aqualung. He had the good fortune of having an uncle who was a director in a French company that produced compressed air and other industrial gases. The U.S. Navy later renamed Cousteau's aqualung "scuba" for "self-contained underwater breathing apparatus." His invention revolutionized underwater exploration. In 1937 Cousteau married his first wife, Simone Melchior, who later became his partner on most of his sea voyages.

At the end of World War II, Cousteau convinced the French navy that his new invention could be put to an immediate practical use. He organized diving crews to remove the mines blocking southern French ports. Cousteau remained in the French navy until 1956 and continued experimentation with underwater photography. He improved his equipment in order to make increasingly deeper dives. He developed an underwater camera that could operate up to 600 meters (1,970 feet) below the water's surface, making some of the first photographs and films of life undersea.

Underwater sea explorations

In 1951 Cousteau commissioned the first of his famous

exploring ships, the *Calypso,* and began to investigate the world's great bodies of water, beginning with the Red Sea. Two years later Cousteau published a book that included many startling photographs. The English edition, *The Silent World,* sold some 500,000 copies in the first year, launching Cousteau's career as an author. His more than two dozen books on undersea life, which have been translated into several languages, cover such topics as whales, squid, octopuses, and sharks. Among the numerous titles are the 20-volume *Ocean World* and *The Cousteau Almanac of the Environment: An Inventory of Life on a Water Planet.* Perhaps no other writer has done more to inform the public on the role of water in world ecology.

In 1955 Cousteau made a film, *The World of Silence,* with French director Louis Malle. It won international film awards, including the first of Cousteau's three Oscars for best documentary. In 1957 Cousteau was appointed director of the Oceanographic Museum of Monaco. This position allowed him to deploy the *Calypso* in several new scientific explorations.

Cousteau climbing into his diving saucer on board the Calypso *docked in New York Harbor, August 1959.*

Looking for ways to actually live beneath the sea, Cousteau developed a number of "Conshelf" stations, the first underwater living environments where divers lived and worked for weeks at a time. Cousteau's underwater stations predated the U.S. Navy's Sealab experiments. In the first Conshelf project, occurring in 1962, two men stayed for a week in a small chamber 33 feet below the surface of the Mediterranean Sea. The next project, Conshelf 2, took place in 1963 in the Red Sea off the coast of Egypt and involved more complicated experiments. This time five men lived in a more complex underwater settlement for one month, again at a depth of 33 feet. Conshelf 3 followed in 1965, by which time Cousteau was thinking of setting up semipermanent stations, similar to a space station, where people could live indefinitely.

Environmental spokesman and educator

Beginning in 1960, when he opposed the French government's decision to dump nuclear waste in the Mediterranean, Cousteau became a spokesman for environmental causes. He used his fame as an underwater explorer to lobby for greater awareness of the environmental dangers faced by the world's oceans. He spoke with passion about his belief that the fate of the planet and the human species is being jeopardized by pollution and the lack of population control. According to Cousteau, whatever is dumped into the seas will remain there indefinitely, affecting the earth's ecological balance.

Cousteau effectively used television films to educate people around the world. In 1970 he produced 12 one-hour programs in a series titled *The Undersea Odyssey of the "Calypso,"* followed by six more programs in 1973. Cousteau produced in 1984 a series on the underwater exploration of the Amazon River and then, starting in 1985, 22 one-hour programs on the world's oceans. In all, Cousteau has made more than 100 documentaries and has won 10 Emmys.

Revered in France as a wise old prophet, Cousteau has been the recipient of numerous awards in that country and elsewhere. The U.S. government awarded Cousteau the Medal of Freedom in 1985, and he was elected to the prestigious Académie Française in 1988.

Pero da Covilhã

Born 1450,
Covilhã, Portugal

Died 1545,
Abyssinia (Ethiopia)

When he traveled to Abyssinia, or modern-day Ethiopia, Pero da Covilhã's mission was to find the mythical Christian king Prester John. Instead, Covilhã wound up in comfortable captivity and spent the rest of his life in Abyssinia.

Has early career as diplomat and spy

Covilhã was born in Portugal, in a village that bore his family name. As a youth, he went to Spain and served seven years in the household of the duke of Medina Sidonia in Andalusia. He then returned to Portugal and became a member of the court of King Alfonso. Because he could speak Spanish, Covilhã was sent back to Spain to spy on rebel Portuguese who lived there. He later went to North Africa where he served as both a diplomat and a commercial agent in Morocco. As a result of this experience he became fluent in Arabic.

Pero da Covilhã was a Portuguese nobleman who discovered that it was possible to reach India by sailing around Africa. Fluent in several languages, he was the first Westerner to visit Abyssinia, which is now Ethiopia.

Given important mission by the king

In 1481 Alfonso's son, John II, succeeded to the throne; he revived voyages of exploration for which Portugal had been famous during the reign of John I (1385-1433), the most glorious period in Portugal's history. John II called Covilhã back to Portugal and introduced him to Afonso de Paiva, a man from the Canary Islands off the northwest coast of Africa. The king entrusted Covilhã and de Paiva with an important mission: John II wanted them to find Prester John, a mythical Christian king living somewhere in the East. Although looking for the land of Prester John was the main object of their journey, they had another tall order to fill: John II wanted them to find out:

> what were the principal markets for the spice and particularly the pepper trade in India; and what were the different channels by which this was conveyed to Europe; whence came the gold and silver, the medium of this trade; and above all they were to inform themselves distinctly, whether it was possible to arrive in India by sailing round the Southern promontory of Africa.

The journey was planned with the help of Jose Vizinho and the king's physician, Master Rodrigo, both of whom had been present when the king turned down **Christopher Columbus**'s (see entry) request for Portuguese help in making his famous voyage.

Accompanied by de Paiva, Covilhã was to make his journey to the east coast of Africa by traveling overland from the north. About the same time, King John sent another Portuguese, **Bartolomeu Dias,** on a voyage by sea that was to lead him around the Cape of Good Hope at the southern tip of Africa. The geographical information supplied by Dias and Covilhã would enable the Portuguese explorer **Vasco da Gama** (see separate entries) to make his epic voyage around Africa to India a few years later.

Sails to the East

On May 7, 1487, Covilhã and de Paiva received their

final instructions from John, who gave them 400 gold cruzados to pay for the expedition. The cruzado was a coin made from solid gold earned in trade with the west coast of Africa. Covilhã and de Paiva departed from the town of Santarém in central Portugal, equipped with a "map for navigating, taken from the map of the world ... and a letter of credence for all the countries and provinces of the world."

Covilhã and de Paiva headed for the Spanish port of Barcelona and from there went to Naples, Italy. On the Greek island of Rhodes they disguised themselves as Muslim merchants and bought a supply of honey to sell in Egypt. Unfortunately, in Alexandria, Egypt, they fell ill with fever, and the local governor impounded their honey. After they recovered they bought a fresh supply of goods and pushed on to Cairo, Egypt. In 1488 they met a group of pilgrims from Morocco who were traveling to Mecca on the Arabian Peninsula. With the pilgrims they sailed for two months over the Red Sea to the port of Aden at the entrance to the Indian Ocean.

Leaves de Paiva and seeks India via Africa

At Aden the two Portuguese travelers separated. De Paiva would go to Abyssinia to look for Prester John while Covilhã pursued information about the spice trade and the possibility of reaching India by sailing around Africa. Covilhã first went across the Indian Ocean to Cannanore, a port on the Malabar Coast of southwest India. His next stop was Calicut, which was the center for the Indian spice trade. At Goa, 300 miles to the north, Covilhã took a ship to Hormuz on the south coast of Persia. Hormuz was the principal port of the Persian Gulf at that time. He then journeyed down the coasts of Arabia and Africa to Sofala, an important Arab port in what is now Mozambique.

Sent on search for Prester John

The trip to Sofala convinced Covilhã that Africa could be circumnavigated. He returned to Cairo in 1490 with this valuable information, stopping at the ports of Kilwa, Mombasa, and

Malindi along the way. When he reached Cairo, he learned that de Paiva had died without finding Prester John. Covilhã was preparing to return to Portugal to deliver his information when he met two Portuguese, Rabbi Abraham de Beja and Joseph de Lamego. They had been searching for him to deliver letters they were carrying from John II. They themselves had been sent to learn about trade in the port of Hormuz. When they learned that Covilhã had already been to Hormuz, Lamego agreed to carry Covilhã's reports back to Portugal.

Apparently the letters Covilhã received instructed him to concentrate on the search for Prester John. He sailed to Aden and Hormuz, then to Jidda on the west coast of Arabia. Next he visited the Muslim holy cities of Mecca and Medina in Arabia. He went back to Sinai and found a ship sailing down the Red Sea that took him to the port of Zeila in what is now Somalia.

Imprisoned in Abyssinia

When Covilhã reached Zeila, he learned that Emperor Iskander of Abyssinia was nearby, engaged in a war with a Muslim king. Covilhã was able to meet the emperor and accompanied him back to his stronghold at Shewa in the Ethiopian highlands. The emperor took a liking to Covilhã and treated him well. He told the Portuguese that some time in the future "he would send him to his country with much honor." Before long, however, Iskander was killed in battle and Covilhã's circumstances changed dramatically. He found himself kept more or less as a prisoner at the Abyssinian court.

On one occasion Covilhã was given permission to leave. Laden with gifts from the Abyssinians, he started for home accompanied by a large band of retainers. Unfortunately, the members of his escort party became involved in a scuffle with local residents along the way. Displeased, the new emperor recalled the whole party back to his court at Tegulet. Covilhã was forced to settle down in Abyssinia. He married a noblewoman and was given an official position and valuable lands. He was not permitted to leave the country, but he was allowed to write to the king of Portugal to explain that he was being detained.

Stays in Abyssinia

Covilhã's letters to John II aroused immense interest about Africa in Europe. The king sent a Portuguese named Fernao Gomez to try to help Covilhã, supported by the fleet of Afonso de Albuquerque. Gomez reached Abyssinia in 1508 but, like Covilhã, once he arrived he was not allowed to leave. In 1520 John II sent an official mission to Abyssinia under Rodrigo da Lima. Da Lima found both Covilhã and Gomez still living there.

Da Lima was impressed with the knowledge Covilhã had obtained on his journeys. According to the report written about the da Lima mission, Covilhã was "a man who knows all the languages that can be spoken, both of Christians, Moors and Gentiles, and who knows all the things for which he was sent; moreover, he gives an account of them as if they were present before him."

When the da Lima expedition left Abyssinia in 1526 they took an Ethiopian envoy with them back to Portugal. Although relations between the two countries had apparently improved, Covilhã remained in Abyssinia. It is not known whether Covilhã's permanent residence there was by choice, or because he was never allowed to leave. For whatever reason, the Portuguese explorer stayed in his adopted country for the rest of his life.

Charles Darwin

*Born February 12, 1809,
Shrewsbury, England*

*Died April 19, 1882,
Kent, England*

Charles Darwin made one trip around the world aboard the H.M.S. Beagle, gathering data on which to base his theory of evolution, known as Darwinism.

Charles Darwin's biological theories overturned traditional beliefs, resulting in a revolution in thinking about the origin of life. Today, Darwin remains an intellectual giant who disputed the idea that each species was individually created as described in the Book of *Genesis,* replacing it with his own theory of evolution widely accepted by scientists.

Shows early interest in science

Charles Robert Darwin was born in Shrewsbury, England, on February 12, 1809; his mother was Susannah Wedgwood, the daughter of Josiah Wedgwood, the founder of the famous pottery firm; his father, Robert Waring Darwin, was a physician and the son of Erasmus Darwin, a physician, poet, and botanist who codified his own ideas on organic life. Darwin's mother died when he was a child, and his older sisters provided his early education; he benefited from the attention shown him by the large Darwin and Wedgwood families. At an early age, he began collecting specimens and conducting scientific experiments.

In 1817 he was sent to a day school but did not do well; a year later he attended the Shrewsbury School, directed by Dr. Samuel Butler, where he studied the classics, which he did not especially like. Darwin went to Edinburgh University to study medicine but he left school because attending operations on unanesthetized patients deeply troubled him. While there he befriended the zoologist Robert Grant and the geologist Robert Jameson; both men contributed to Darwin's developing interest in marine animals and the history of the earth. Darwin's father next sent him to Cambridge to prepare for a career in the Church of England as a clergyman. There he met Professor John Henslow, a botanist, who became his mentor and stirred in Darwin a passion for natural history. Reading **Alexander von Humboldt**'s (see entry) book on his experiences collecting scientific data in South America further inspired Darwin.

Joins expedition to South America

Darwin earned a bachelor of arts degree from Cambridge in June 1831 and then traveled to North Wales to learn geologic fieldwork from Adam Sedgwick, a Cambridge professor. After graduation, Henslow recommended Darwin for the position of unpaid naturalist on board the H.M.S. *Beagle* under the command of Captain Robert FitzRoy. The expedition had been chartered to establish a number of chronometric, or time-keeping, stations and to survey the southern coasts of South America, including Patagonia, Tierra del Fuego, Chile, and Peru, as well as several Pacific islands. Darwin's father initially opposed the trip because it was dangerous and would delay his son's entry into the church, but Josiah Wedgwood II convinced his brother-in-law to grant permission.

The *Beagle,* a ten-gun sloop-brig that weighed 235 tons and measured 90 feet long and 24 feet in the beam, left Plymouth, England, on December 27, 1831. Although Darwin had no formal scientific training, over the course of the five-year trip he turned himself into an expert scientist. He and FitzRoy shared FitzRoy's cabin with the understanding that

FitzRoy would prefer to be alone occasionally. FitzRoy believed in the literal interpretation of the Bible and desired to bring Christianity to native peoples. On board the *Beagle* were three men and one woman FitzRoy had taken to England from Tierra del Fuego previously and was now bringing back to their native land to spread Christianity. An aristocrat and perfectionist who demanded the same from his crew, FitzRoy was a man of great mood swings who would show silence or anger when displeased. He was also capable of kindness toward Darwin and others. As Darwin amassed data to question divine creation, he and FitzRoy disagreed.

Begins formulating evolution theory

Since Darwin was often seasick, his solution was to spend as much time ashore as possible and travel overland to meet the *Beagle* at another port. He was an adventurous man who often showed courage in dangerous situations and enjoyed the exotic beauty of South America. His physical stamina and athletic ability were a match for the harsh conditions he often found. He taught himself the scientific method—he collected evidence meticulously and theorized correctly from it.

The *Beagle* sailed first to the Cape Verde Islands, remaining there for 23 days while FitzRoy fixed the islands' position and visited Sao Tiago, a volcanic island. At the urging of Henslow, his mentor at Cambridge, Darwin had brought the first volume of Charles Lyell's *Principles of Geology*. Darwin did not believe Lyell's theory that the earth's surface had changed over time through the continuing effects of earthquakes and erosion. When he inspected the white rock sticking out from the sea cliffs at Sao Tiago and saw how lava from a series of volcanic eruptions had shaped it, he knew Lyell was right: no one physical event had made the island's surface or the sea cliffs.

Because he was often seasick during the voyage around South America, Darwin spent as much time ashore as possible, traveling overland and meeting the Beagle *at its next port.* ▶

Galapagos
Islands

Brazil

Bahia

Rio de Janeiro

Pacific Ocean

Parana River

Santa Fe

Mercedes

Chile

Valparaiso

Uruguay

Montevideo

Concepcion

Rio de la Plata

Bahia
Blanca

Juan Fernandez Islands

Argentina

Valdivia

Atlantic Ocean

Chiloe Island

Patagonia

Santa Cruz River

Falkland Islands

Strait of Magellan
Mount Sarmiento
Navarin Island
Cape Horn

Tierra del Fuego
Beagle Channel

Collects evidence for theory

Reaching Rio de Janeiro on April 3, Darwin soon met Patrick Lennon, an Irishman who owned a coffee plantation 100 miles north of the city. Darwin found the trip an excellent introduction to the exotic life and beauty of South America. He noticed how nothing is safe in a jungle and how every creature adapts in order to survive. Along the way, Darwin began collecting evidence to send to Henslow; he wrote his mentor, "I never experienced such intense delight."

At the plantation, Lennon got into a quarrel with his manager and threatened to sell all the female slaves and their children. The two men drew guns, and Darwin and others stopped them. Darwin was taught to hate slavery and when he told FitzRoy of his experience, FitzRoy defended slavery. The two men argued loudly, and FitzRoy told Darwin to move out of the cabin. FitzRoy then apologized and Darwin accepted, placing the success of the voyage first.

For the next two months Darwin stayed in Rio, where he continued collecting spiders, butterflies, birds, and seashells while the *Beagle* returned to Bahia for coastal surveying. "I am becoming quite devoted to Natural History; you cannot imagine what a fine miserlike pleasure I enjoy when examining an animal differing widely from any known genus," he wrote. In one day he collected 68 species of a tiny beetle.

Party encounters local war

The *Beagle*'s next destination was the unknown lands of Patagonia and Tierra del Fuego. "I long to set foot where no man has trode before," Darwin wrote in anticipation of the experience. One night the crew witnessed Saint Elmo's fire, a luminous spray of electricity from protruding objects such as ships' masts and yardarms occurring in stormy weather. "Everything is in flames," Darwin wrote, "the sky with lightning, the water with luminous particles, and even the very masts are appointed with a blue flame." At the Buenos Aires port, an Argentinean ship fired at the *Beagle*, which retreated to Montevideo; the British frigate *Druid* was sent to Buenos Aires to demand an apology.

FitzRoy's courage bound him closer with his men. In Montevideo, a government minister asked the *Beagle* crew to guard the property of British merchants against black troops now in rebellion. Darwin armed himself with two pistols, but an incident was avoided. On August 19, the *Beagle* headed south to begin surveying the coast of Patagonia in southern Argentina. On September 7 the ship arrived at Bahia Blanca, 400 miles south of Buenos Aires, where soldiers at an Argentinean garrison were suspicious of the *Beagle*'s purpose, and Darwin's.

Finds prehistoric bones

At Punta Alta, Darwin found fossilized bones bigger than those of any living animal. His significant discovery—the bones of "numerous gigantic extinct Quadrupeds," including a Megalonyx and Scelidotherium—was a new addition to zoology. The bones were stacked upon the beach and were encrusted with seashells that, according to Darwin, formed "a perfect catacomb for monsters of extinct races." Darwin theorized that South America must have been an island and these creatures, which had lived in isolation, had died out when the two landmasses were connected.

In January 1833 high seas and bad weather forced the *Beagle* to take a month to round Cape Horn to reach Tierra del Fuego, a landmass surrounded by glaciers and snowcapped mountains. FitzRoy handled the *Beagle* successfully, anchoring the ship at the entrance of a channel named after the *Beagle*. Equipped with supplies from the London Missionary Society, the Fuegians returning with the expedition were setting up a camp for converting the natives to Christianity. After five days, FitzRoy decided to explore the Beagle Channel and leave his missionary party with the natives. When he returned in a week, disaster had struck. The Fuegians had ruined the camp and stolen the supplies. FitzRoy took the failure personally, wondering why his attempt to civilize the natives had been rejected. Darwin, on the other hand, felt that primitive races were best left alone to survive without the interference of outsiders; otherwise, they would inevitably die out.

Explores the pampas region

Because there was too much charting for one ship to handle in stormy weather, FitzRoy purchased an American sealing ship, which he renamed the *Adventure*. Darwin spent ten weeks in Maldonado, a small town at the mouth of the Río de la Plata, where he continued his collecting. The *Beagle* then took him to El Carmen in Patagonia, where Darwin was to begin an ambitious inland journey across the unexplored pampas, which was largely a no-man's-land. South American Indians living in the pampas made sporadic raids in resisting General Juan Manuel Rosas, who was conducting a war of extermination against them.

An Englishman living in El Carmen volunteered to be Darwin's guide, and six gauchos were hired for protection. Darwin was determined to investigate the flora and fauna of the pampas, but the adventure also appealed to him. He was struck by the variety of birds and other animals that the waterless plain supported. He was particularly fascinated by flocks of 20 to 30 rheas, a kind of ostrich; a rare smaller version, which Darwin caught, was sent back to England and was named after him—*rhea darwinii*.

Meets gauchos and desperados

Darwin immensely enjoyed the company of the gauchos, expert horsemen and hunters who used a weapon called a *bolas*. The *bolas*, which was made of two to three stones tied to leather thongs, was whirled around a gaucho's head and then thrown at an animal. The gauchos admired the stamina Darwin showed when he went mountain climbing. After crossing the Rio Colorado, Darwin's party came to General Rosas's camp. General Rosas explained his campaign against the Indians; Darwin was disturbed but helpless when Rosas's men started to shoot three prisoners who would not betray the whereabouts of their comrades.

The *Beagle* returned to Bahia Blanca on August 24, and Darwin relayed an account of his adventures to FitzRoy before beginning the next 400 miles of his trip to Buenos Aires. Darwin spent four months in Buenos Aires while waiting for the *Beagle*. He traveled to the port city of Santa Fe collecting more fossils. Then he ran a high fever (probably malaria) and was nursed for a week before abandoning his horse to return by ship to Buenos Aires. However, the captain would travel only a few miles at a time. In the village of Las Conchas, Darwin's way was blocked by armed men: a revolution was underway and no one could enter the city. Fearing he would miss the *Beagle,* Darwin finally found General Rosas's brother, who gave him permission to travel on at his own risk. He safely reached the home of friends and was able to escape two weeks later on a ship that maneuvered through the blockade to Montevideo.

Explores Rio Santa Cruz

The *Beagle* took on a year's provisions and left on December 7, 1833, passing by the Falkland Islands down to Tierra del Fuego through the Beagle Channel. Before entering the Pacific Ocean, the bottom of the *Beagle* scraped a rock at Port Desire; the vessel turned back to the mouth of the Rio Santa Cruz to be beached for repairs. Carpenters assured FitzRoy that the damage was minor.

The party acquired three whaleboats and began a three-week trip to explore the Santa Cruz. They saw signs of Native American life but did not actually encounter any people in the cold desert region of southern Patagonia. Darwin observed guanacos, South American animals that are related to the camel but have no hump; once he even saw a thousand guanacos in a herd. He also watched pumas and, in the Andean foothills, condors that would swoop down and eat whatever the pumas had left. Darwin shot a condor with an eight-foot wingspan.

When the wind and tide failed, the crew pulled the boats from shore using ropes with collars. Although the snow-covered tops of the Cordillera Mountains broke into view, the explorers seemed not to be getting closer to them. The mountains were actually only 30 miles away when FitzRoy ordered the men to head back to the *Beagle.*

The ship was now "afloat, fresh painted and as gay as a frigate." The others were relieved, but Darwin expressed some disappointment: "Almost every one is discontented with this expedition, much hard work, and much time lost and scarcely anything seen or gained ... To me the cruise has been most satisfactory, from affording so excellent a section of the great tertiary formations of Patagonia." Again FitzRoy had to navigate the *Beagle* through the straits of Tierra del Fuego, dodging falling sheets of ice. "The sight of such a coast is enough to make a landsman dream for a week about shipwrecks, peril and death," Darwin wrote.

Climbs in Andes

At the end of May 1834 the *Beagle* entered the Strait of Magellan for the last time and exited into the Pacific Ocean. Because of stormy weather the ship was forced to put in on Chiloe Island; when the weather improved the party continued on to Valparaíso, the chief port of Chile, arriving on July 22, 1834. Darwin stayed as a guest in the home of a Shrewsbury acquaintance and spent time mountain climbing in the Andes. At 12,000 feet he discovered a bed of fossil seashells and white petrified pine trees covered in marine rock deposits. During his explorations he was able to conclude that South America was once submerged beneath the sea and then pushed up by earthquakes and volcanic eruptions. The *Beagle*'s departure was further delayed when FitzRoy suffered a nervous breakdown as a result of a misunderstanding with the British admiralty office over the purchase of the *Adventure*. Darwin used the time to return to the Andes, where he was bitten by the poisonous Benchuga bug.

Witnesses earthquake

On February 20, 1835, an earthquake struck the coast of Chile and destroyed the city of Concepción. Upon witnessing the earthquake, Darwin observed:

A bad earthquake at once destroys the oldest associations; the world, the very emblem of all that is solid, had moved beneath our feet like a crust over a fluid; one second of time has created in the mind a strange idea of insecurity, which hours of reflection would not have produced.

At Concepción, Darwin saw immense damage, which extended 400 miles up the coast and was made worse by volcano eruptions. He found that the earthquake had permanently raised the land; he saw evidence of such uplift from previous quakes as well.

Investigates formation of Andes

When the *Beagle* returned to Valparaíso in March 1835, Darwin arranged with FitzRoy to leave the ship and travel overland through the Andes by crossing the dangerous Los Patos, a mountain pass into Peru. Darwin found more evidence of the changing geological history of the earth—"It is an old story, but not the less wonderful, to hear of shells, which formerly were crawling about at the bottom of the sea, being now elevated nearly 14,000 feet above its level." Darwin theorized that the Andes had been formed by suboceanic volcanoes. He wrote three books on South American geology, and parts of the letters he wrote to Henslow were read before meetings of professional societies in London. While Darwin was away his reputation was being made.

Speculates about origins of life

Darwin rejoined his ship at the Peruvian port of Copiapó on July 5, 1835. In September the *Beagle* left for the Galápagos Islands, reaching Chatham Island eight days later. During a five-week stay Darwin wrote, "the natural history of this archipelago is very remarkable: it seems to be a little world within itself, the greater number of its inhabitants, both vegetable and animal, being found nowhere else."

Given the evidence before him, Darwin started to ask himself questions about the origin of life, such as existing species being similar to extinct species, one species replacing a different yet similar species, species on an oceanic island resembling species from a nearby continent, and species from the same environment being dissimilar to each other. For example, the various Galápagos islands had identical physical and climatic features yet the finches, including one species named after Darwin, had different physical attributes and eating habits (some ate seeds and some insects; each had an appropriate beak size).

Finds evidence of evolution

On its homeward trip the *Beagle* stopped for ten days in Tahiti, where Darwin hiked into the interior. The expedition spent Christmas 1835 at a mission station on the North Island of New Zealand. Darwin compared the New Zealand Maoris, who had been subject to more Western influence, unfavorably to the Tahitians. Stopping at Sydney, Australia, the *Beagle* let Darwin off and he took a 12-day riding trip to the town of Bathurst, traveling part of the time with a group of Aborigines.

The Beagle sailed via Tasmania and King George Sound in southwestern Australia to the Cocos Islands in the Indian Ocean, where Darwin investigated the formation of coral reefs, disproving Lyell's hypothesis that they had been formed on the rims of submarine volcanic craters. Atolls, or lagoon islands, Darwin knew, exist at sea level and the coral polyps must live in shallow water and warm temperatures. But what if the coral below 120 feet was dead and the ocean floor gradually sank while the coral polyp pushed new reefs to the surface? Darwin, with FitzRoy, tested his theory at the Keeling atoll and discovered the bottom was sandy—he was right. Darwin concluded the process took millions of years and resulted in three types of coral formations—atolls, barrier reefs, and fringing reefs.

Returns to England

The *Beagle* continued on to Mauritius, an island in the Indian Ocean. In Cape Town Darwin had dinner with the famous astronomer Sir John Herschel; in St. Helena he slept near Napoleon's tomb; and on Ascension Island he was

informed by letters from England that some of his reports had been praised by the Royal Geological Society in London. After making last ports of call in Bahia, Brazil, and the Azores, the *Beagle* reached Falmouth, England, on October 2, 1836. Darwin left immediately for Shrewsbury, "having lived on board the little vessel very nearly five years."

Upon returning to England, Darwin wrote: "Animals, our fellow brethren in pain, disease, death, suffering and famine—our slaves in the most laborious works, our companions in our amusements—they may partake of our origin in one common ancestor—we may be all netted together." In 1837 he wrote the following entry in his journal:

In July opened first notebook on Transmutation of Species. Had been greatly struck from about the month of previous March on character of South American fossils, and species on Galapagos Archipelago. These facts (especially the latter) are the origin of all my views.

As a result of the five-year Beagle *voyage,* Darwin had a lifetime of data upon which to base his revolutionary theories.

Alfred Russell Wallace

Alfred Wallace (1823-1913) was a British naturalist who made two important scientific expeditions to South America and Indonesia and formulated the modern theory of evolution at the same time as Charles Darwin. He became interested in the natural sciences and started studying astronomy, agriculture, and botany on his own. When he took a job as a schoolmaster in the city of Leicester in 1844, he met Henry Walter Bates, another amateur student of biology. They went on several trips together collecting specimens, and in 1848 they decided to go to the port city of Belém, Brazil, near the mouth of the Amazon River, where they spent a year collecting specimens. From 1850 to 1852 Wallace traveled alone in Venezuela, Colombia, and Brazil. On the return voyage to England Wallace's ship was destroyed by fire. After being stranded for ten days in a lifeboat with several other survivors, Wallace was rescued; however, the notes and specimens he had taken with him on the voyage were lost.

Once he was back in England, Wallace spent his time writing about his discoveries and attending scientific meetings, where he met Darwin. In 1854 Wallace traveled to the East Indies, which today is Malaysia and Indonesia, where he continued his investigation of the multiplication of species. He spent the following eight years visiting every major island in the archipelago. While in Southeast Asia he made several major discoveries. Among them was the "Wallace Line," an imaginary boundary between the islands of Bali and Lombok: east of the line the plants and animals are like those of Asia, west of it they resemble Australian and New Guinea species.

In 1858 Wallace published his first book about evolution. That same year, while he was ill with fever on the island of Ternate in eastern Indonesia, he had a sudden brainstorm: species evolved by the process of natural selection. This meant that haphazard genetic changes are perpetuated if they help a species adapt to its natural environment. Knowing that Darwin was working on the same idea, Wallace wrote him a letter describing his own theories. As a result, in July 1858 Darwin presented a paper listing himself and Wallace as coauthors to the Linnaean Society in London. It was the world's introduction to the modern theory of evolution. Greatly admiring Darwin's *Origin of Species,* Wallace wrote *Contributions to the Theory of Natural Selection* in 1870. He continued to write about many subjects during the remaining years of his long life, including the islands in the Malay Archipelago, socialism, space travel, geographical distribution of species, vaccination, and human evolution.

After reading *Essay on the Principle of Population* by Thomas Malthus, Darwin recognized that animals must die if their number is greater than the available food supply. This is the principle of natural selection.

Writes about theory of evolution

As a result of the *Beagle* voyage, Darwin had a lifetime of data upon which to base his theory. He never went abroad again. It is important to note that he had not yet reached 30 years of age. His most important work, *The Origin of Species,* was published in 1859; all copies sold in one day. Using comparative anatomy as evidence, in this book Darwin formulated the theory of evolution that has guided scientists ever since: In the struggle for survival, successive generations of a species pass on to their offspring the characteristics that enable the species to survive. Darwin named this process natural selection. Other scientists were thinking along similar lines. Darwin's friend Alfred Russell Wallace was working toward the same conclusion independently on the basis of research he did in Brazil and the East Indies, thus forcing Darwin to publish his own theory.

Marries and has a family

Following his return to England, Darwin lived for a while as a bachelor in London. On November 11, 1838, he proposed to his cousin, Emma Wedgwood; she accepted and they married on January 29, 1839, the same month Darwin was elected to the famed Royal Society. The Darwins first settled in London, but because of Darwin's poor health, the couple moved to Down House in the English county of Kent, 15 miles from London, where they spent the rest of their lives. They had ten children, three of whom died in childhood.

Since no organic cause could be found for Darwin's ill health, he was suspected of being a hypochondriac, a person who worries abnormally over personal health, often creating imaginary illnesses. A strong possibility is that he suffered from Chagas' disease: he was bitten by the Benchuca, the "black bug of the pampas," which is a carrier, and he had all the symptoms of the disease. Darwin died at the age of 73 at Down House on April 19, 1882. He received no honors from the British government during his lifetime because his ideas offended the Church of England; however, at the request of Parliament, he was accorded the honor of burial in Westminster Abbey.

Alexandra David-Neel

Born October 24, 1868,
Paris, France
Died September 8, 1969,
Digne, France

Alexandra David-Neel, a noted French authority on Buddhism, was the first European woman to travel to Lhasa, the capital of Tibet.

Alexandra David-Neel experienced life as a Buddhist first-hand, both as a scholar and as a visitor to monasteries. Widely traveled, she was the first European woman to travel to Lhasa, the capital of Tibet, which was closed to Westerners.

David-Neel was born in the Paris suburb of Saint-Mandé on October 24, 1868. Her father was a French journalist and her mother was from Belgium. Because her parents had an unhappy marriage she spent a lonely childhood. She ran away from home several times, and she immersed herself in books about Eastern religions and philosophy. Because of her interest in non-Christian religions, she traveled to India when she was in her early twenties. She was unable to afford a lengthy stay abroad, however, and soon returned to France. In 1894 she began singing with an opera company under the stage name of Mademoiselle Myrial, traveling to French colonies in Indochina, to Greece, and to Tunis in northern Africa.

Buddhism

An ancient Asian religion that is still widely practiced today, Buddhism was founded in India in the fifth or sixth century B.C. by Siddhartha Gautama, who was known as the Buddha. The Buddha taught the practice of meditation as a way to achieve a state of perfection wherein a person is free of all desire. The Buddha's philosophy was based on "four noble truths": life is suffering; suffering is caused by earthly desire; suffering can be ended through transcendence of worldly concerns to a state called Nirvana; and an "eight-fold noble path" leads to Nirvana. This path requires "right views, right resolve, right speech, right action, right livelihood, right effort, right mindfulness, and right concentration."

Throughout the centuries Buddhist schools and monasteries were established in Ceylon, Tibet, China, Korea, and Japan. Tibetan Buddhism, which Alexandra David-Neel followed, has a long, complex history that is closely linked with religious and political developments in Asia during the seventh through the seventeenth centuries. In 1641 the Dalai Lama, the head lama, or monk, of Tibetan Buddhism, was proclaimed the temporal, or secular, leader of Tibet; the Panchen Lama was chosen as spiritual leader. Both are known as grand lamas, who receive their status through divine reincarnation: when a grand lama dies his spirit passes to an infant who has just been born. After the Tibetan revolt against China in 1959, the Dalai Lama went into exile in India; the Chinese then appointed the Panchen Lama as ruler of Tibet.

Although Buddhism had become extinct in India by the thirteenth century A.D., it continues to thrive in Asia. Modern Western culture has been significantly influenced by the religion in its various forms, particularly Tibetan Buddhism and Zen Buddhism, which teaches "sudden enlightenment" through meditation.

Visits Dalai Lama

In Tunis she met and married a French engineer, Philippe-François Neel, adopting the name David-Neel. Her husband was able to finance her travels, with the result that they spent most of their married life apart. After her marriage, David-Neel returned to Paris. She began to study Oriental religions and to lecture on comparative religion. In 1910 the French Ministry of Education sent her to India to continue her research. The next year, she learned that the Dalai Lama, the spiritual and political leader of Tibet, had fled his country because of a Chinese invasion and was staying in Bhutan, a country between India and Tibet. She went to visit him there and was the first European woman admitted into his presence. David-Neel made another visit to say goodbye to the Dalai Lama when he was preparing to return to the Tibetan capital of Lhasa in 1912.

Lives as Buddhist in Sikkim

From Bhutan David-Neel traveled to the nearby kingdom of Sikkim, where she began studying the Tibetan language. She lived at the monastery of Podang. A 15-year-old Sikkimese student lama, Yongden, who was appointed as her companion, would remain with her for the rest of his life. In order to experience the life of a Buddhist nun, David-Neel went to a remote cave in Sikkim, where she spent the winter of 1914-15 meditating. Yongden and other servants, who lived a short distance from the cave, brought her one meal a day.

At the end of winter David-Neel left Sikkim and traveled a short distance into Tibet, which was forbidden to Westerners. She visited the monastery of Tashilumpo, now called Jihk'a-tse, which is the residence of the Panchen Lama, the second-ranking Tibetan lama. Because of her unauthorized visit to Tibet, David-Neel was directed to leave Sikkim, and she returned to India. Accompanied by Yongden, she nonetheless made two short trips into Tibet during the summers of 1915 and 1916; she also traveled to Burma, Japan, and China.

Attempts to enter Lhasa

In northern China David-Neel stayed in a Buddhist monastery for two years translating Tibetan texts. During the winter of 1922-23 she and Yongden traveled across the Gobi Desert in southern Mongolia. They tried to enter Tibet from the north, with David-Neel wearing a disguise. When her disguise was discovered she was escorted out of the country. In the summer of 1923 David-Neel and Yongden tried to get to Lhasa once more. They crossed the border into the southeastern part of Tibet with a group of Buddhist pilgrims. Dressed as a Tibetan woman, David-Neel posed as Yongden's mother. This time her disguise was a success.

Admitted into Lhasa

Yongden's status as a lama enabled them to travel freely. At a leisurely pace they journeyed through the Tibetan countryside, stopping to visit monasteries and areas of natural beauty. Once Yongden sprained his ankle and David-Neel had to carry him for a while. Another time they got lost and were nearly attacked by robbers before they frightened them away by shooting a gun.

They reached Lhasa during the Buddhist New Year in early 1924. Still in her disguise, David-Neel roamed throughout the city and even toured the Potala, the mighty palace of the Dalai Lama. Leaving Lhasa, she and Yongden traveled to a Catholic mission at Podang in the Himalayas on the Indian side of the border. While she was at the mission she wrote to her husband, who had heard no news of her for two years.

Returns to France

In May 1925, David-Neel and Yongden went to France, where she wrote about her experiences as the first European woman to have traveled to Lhasa. Her articles were serialized in a magazine and then made into a book, which was a great success. David-Neel used the proceeds from the book to buy a house in the south of France, in the town of Digne. She named the house Samten Dzong, which means Fortress of Meditation. She also convinced her husband to legally adopt Yongden. David-Neel and Yongden lived together in the house in Digne for the next several years while her husband stayed in North Africa.

In 1936 David-Neel and Yongden made a trip back to China. By that time the country was in turmoil because of civil war and the Japanese invasion. The two travelers took refuge in a monastery on the Tibetan border and stayed there for six years, until the end of World War II. While she was at the monastery David-Neel received word of her husband's death in 1941.

At the end of the war, David-Neel and Yongden returned to Digne, where they remained for the rest of their lives. Yongden died in 1955. David-Neel lived until she was nearly 100 years old, having enjoyed a truly unique career that allowed her to pursue her lifelong interest in Buddhism.

Bartolomeu Dias

Born c. 1450,
Portugal

Died 1500,
Off the Cape of Good Hope, Africa

Bartolomeu Dias's pioneering voyage around the southern tip of Africa, which came to be called the Cape of Good Hope, opened a sea route from Europe to India. This was an important advance for trade in the fifteenth century. Ironically, Dias himself perished in a storm off the Cape of Good Hope several years after he discovered it.

The voyages of explorer Diogo Cão in 1485 had taken Portuguese ships far down the western coast of Africa to Cape Cross, almost to the southern tip of the continent. King John II of Portugal, who was attempting to revive his country's leadership in voyages of exploration, decided to send a new expedition to determine if it was possible to sail all the way around Africa. For commander of the voyage he chose Bartolomeu Dias, a knight of the royal household. Dias was descended from an old seafaring family and had led many trading voyages to Guinea on the west coast of Africa.

Bartolomeu Dias was the first European to sail around the Cape of Good Hope at the southern tip of Africa.

Attempts voyage around Africa

Dias's expedition included two small sailing ships and a supply ship. The solution to the problem of provisions for long-distance journeys, the supply ship would anchor on a coastline along the way to wait for the other ships in a fleet; on the return trip, these ships would be able to take on new provisions from the supply ship.

The expedition left Lisbon, Portugal, in August 1487. By December, it had reached Walvis Bay, in what is now Namibia, without much difficulty. South of the bay the ships encountered strong head winds, which drove them out to sea, away from the sight of land. They were driven south for 13 days before they were able to turn and head eastward to regain the shore. But after sailing for some time they still did not sight any land.

Sights land

Dias realized that the wind must have carried the ships beyond the southern tip of Africa and that in order to regain the continent they would have to head north. Accordingly they turned northward, and on February 3, 1488, they sighted land. Since the shoreline ran in a northeastward direction, Dias concluded that they had indeed rounded the southern cape of the continent.

The Portuguese found themselves in a bay from which they could see African herdsmen with their cows. For this reason, Dias named the place Bahia dos Vaqueiros, or Cowboy Bay. This body of water, which lies off the south coast of South Africa, is now known as Mossel Bay. Although his crew objected to going farther into unknown territory, Dias insisted on continuing eastward up the coast. But when the ships reached the Great Fish River, where the south African coast starts heading north, his anxious crew forced him to turn back.

Discovers Cape of Good Hope

On the way back to Portugal in May 1488, Dias followed the shoreline of the continent so that he could see the great cape that is the southern tip. He decided to call it Cabo Tormentoso, or Cape of Storms, which is indeed an accurate name—and a prophetic one, as it turned out. Continuing the voyage home, Dias stopped on the coast of Angola to take on provisions from the supply ship anchored there. He reached Lisbon in December 1488, after an absence of 17 months and 17 days.

The Cape of Storms was later renamed the Cape of Good Hope, although historians are not certain about the origin of the name. According to one authority, John II wanted a name that represented the hope of reaching India by sea; another suggests that Dias originally named it Cabo da Bõa Esperança—the Cape of Good Hope.

Portuguese seek India route

Dias continued to serve the king in nautical affairs. On March 4, 1493, he was sent out in a rowboat to talk to the captain of a Spanish ship that had just anchored in Lisbon harbor. The captain was **Christopher Columbus** (see entry), who told Dias about the new land he had found on the other side of the Atlantic. Columbus's discovery did not interest the Portuguese; they were more excited about the possibilities opened up by Dias's expedition around the Cape. They now knew it was possible to sail around Africa to get to India, an important advance for trade between Europe and India. As a result of Dias's discovery, the new king, Manuel I, commissioned **Vasco da Gama** (see entry) to lead an expedition to follow up on Dias's earlier voyage by sailing all the way to India.

Sails with Cabral

Upon the successful return of da Gama, Manuel I immediately prepared a major expedition to continue explorations. The commander was a young nobleman, Pedro Cabral; Dias captained one of the 13 ships in the fleet. Leaving Lisbon on March 9, 1500, Cabral sailed much farther west than da Gama alone had ventured. On April 22 the Cabral party was rewarded by the sight of the coast of a previously unknown land—Brazil.

The expedition turned east and recrossed the Atlantic. On the way around the Cape of Good Hope, they ran into bad weather. During the storm, three of the ships sank, including the one commanded by Dias. The Portuguese explorer drowned along with his crew off the south African coast, which he had been the first to navigate.

Francis Drake

Born c. 1540,
Devonshire, England

Died January 28, 1596,
At sea, off Portobelo, Panama

Sir Francis Drake was one of the world's greatest seamen. He was known for his religious fervor and his audacity, courage, and patriotism. Even his avowed enemies envied his abilities. The first Englishman to sail around the world, Drake also played an important role in defeating the Spanish Armada. He is credited with establishing England as the world's major maritime power during his time, an advantage that propelled the country into an unparalleled era of expansion and prosperity.

Drake rose from obscurity to become a national hero. He was born in Devonshire on an estate belonging to Lord Francis Russell. His father was a small farmer and a passionately religious Protestant minister. The elder Drake's views, along with local religious unrest, had a profound effect in shaping the young boy's character. Drake grew to detest Catholicism and particularly the Catholic country of Spain.

Religion played an important role in all facets of European life in the sixteenth century. People lived, died, and were

Sir Francis Drake, an English seaman and pirate, was the captain of the second ship ever to sail around the world. He also led the English in defeating the Spanish Armada.

judged by the Church. England, however, had broken away from the Roman Catholic church in the 1530s, when King Henry VIII divorced his first wife, Catherine of Aragon, against the wishes of the pope and then established the Church of England. The struggle had left much of England bitterly divided. When a Catholic rebellion spread to Devonshire, the Drake family fled to Kent.

Career as a seaman

Drake was the eldest of 12 sons. Although the family had few material possessions, Drake's father was literate and taught his son to read and write. Drake began his life on the sea at age 13, when he became an apprentice to the captain of a small boat that transported freight back and forth across the English Channel and to ports on the North Sea. When the captain died, he left his boat to Drake. Navigating through treacherous currents and enduring the harshness of winter storms were excellent training for Drake's later assignments.

Having learned his trade, Drake turned to distant relatives John and William Hawkins, prosperous shipbuilders who were conducting trade in the New World. Drake joined the Hawkins fleet at age 23 and made several voyages to the West Indies. The Spanish, England's old Catholic enemy, treated the English as pirates, impounding their cargoes, sinking their ships, and killing as many seamen as possible. Drake vowed revenge. His brilliant seamanship soon came to the attention of Queen Elizabeth I, a ruler who had ambitious plans for England's future.

Assignment as a privateer

Determined to stem the tide of wealth that was pouring into Spain from the New World, Elizabeth made Drake a privateer. He could now legally plunder Spanish lands. In 1572 Drake provisioned two small ships, the *Pasha* and the *Swan,* with a total of only 72 men and set sail for Central America. He attacked the poorly defended Spanish city of Nombre de Dios in Panama, knowing it was a storage site for much of the

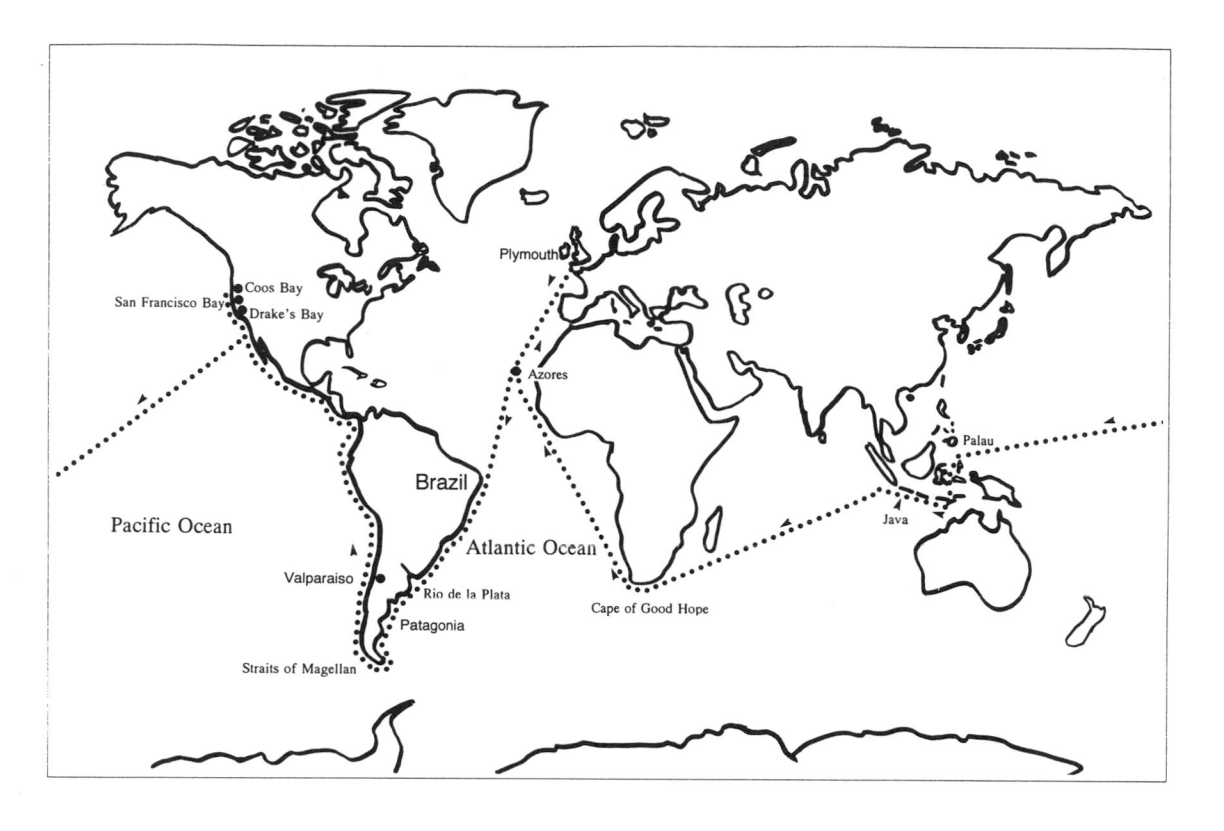

treasure bound from the New World for Spain. Taking the town by surprise, he nearly succeeded in capturing the entire Spanish treasure fleet. He then burned the town of Portobelo and destroyed most of the ships there. During this trip Drake crossed the Isthmus of Panama and for the first time saw the Pacific Ocean. Inspired, he prayed that God would allow him to sail an English ship in that sea.

When he returned to England, his ship laden with gold, Queen Elizabeth was secretly delighted, but a truce had been temporarily declared between England and Spain, so the triumph could not be officially acknowledged. Drake received a portion of the bounty, and, though his fortune and his reputation had been made, he had also become an enemy of King Philip II of Spain.

Voyage to the Pacific Ocean

Drake began the adventure of his life on November 15,

Drake embarked on his trip around the world (1577-80) when he was commissioned by Queen Elizabeth I to cross the Strait of Magellan and explore the unknown lands beyond.

1577, when he was commissioned by Queen Elizabeth to cross the treacherous Strait of Magellan, at the tip of South America, and explore the unknown lands beyond for potential trade and profit. Setting out with five small ships and fewer than 200 men, he reached the Brazilian coast. He rechristened his flagship, naming it the *Golden Hind*. He also dealt with a mutiny, which had been festering since the expedition left Plymouth, by reluctantly executing its leader, Thomas Doughty. Drake then consolidated his cargo, abandoning two of the smaller vessels, and prepared to go where no Englishman had ever ventured.

Because navigation and knowledge of the area's geography were primitive or nonexistent, the Strait of Magellan had taken a heavy toll on Spanish ships. The Spanish had therefore avoided the strait and used a more northerly route, reaching the Pacific through the Isthmus of Panama. Drake's seamanship prevailed, however, as he crossed the 300-mile waterway in a record 14 days. Once through the strait, his fleet was beset by fierce storms. One boat sank, and another turned back to England. The *Golden Hind* sailed on alone, its voyage unhindered as it inched northward along the coast of South America. Drake captured rich prizes in the Spanish port of Valparaíso and intercepted a treasure ship loaded with gold and silver from Peru.

Arrival at the Spice Islands

Continuing his journey up the coast of North America, he anchored at Coos Bay, in the area that is now Oregon. He traveled north again and became the first European to sight the western coast of modern-day Canada. Intense cold, however, prevented him from going farther up the coast to search for a sea passage across North America.

The next leg of Drake's exploration proved to be easier. In July 1579 he headed west across the Pacific Ocean, and after 68 days he was the first European to sight the South Pacific island of Palau. After landing in the Philippines, he made a profitable stop in the Moluccas, or the fabled Spice Islands. Welcomed by the sultan, Drake added six tons of cloves to his vessel already overflowing with gold, jewels, coins, and other treasure. After an anxious episode of running aground on a reef, Drake crossed the Indian Ocean and came around the tip of Africa via the Cape of Good Hope.

New social status and wealth

On September 26, 1580, two years after sailing through the Strait of Magellan, Drake brought his ship back to Plymouth Harbor. The *Golden Hind* was the first English ship to sail around the world. Spain protested Drake's piracy, but Queen Elizabeth knighted him and showed her regard by boarding the *Golden Hind*. In 1581 Drake became the mayor of Plymouth, a position he filled with distinction. His new social status and wealth required a suitable setting, so he bought an estate, Buckland Abbey, near Plymouth. Two years after the death in 1583 of Mary, his wife of many years, Drake married a young heiress, Mary Sydenhem. One of his great disappointments was that he had been childless in his first marriage, but he remained childless in his second marriage as well.

It is thought that Philip II of Spain constantly worried about Drake's activities. He had reason to worry, as in 1585 Drake assumed the command of 25 ships that carried out punishing raids, first on Santiago in the Cape Verde Islands and then on Cartagena in Colombia, St. Augustine in Florida, and San Domingo in modern-day Cuba. These losses nearly broke Spain, which had already been made vulnerable by the country's worsening economic conditions. It was probably then that Spanish seaman began to think Drake had supernatural powers.

Defeat of the Spanish Armada

In 1586 Spain began to prepare a fleet of warships, known as the Invincible Armada, that would finally defeat England. Philip II planned to seize the British throne from Elizabeth I and return the English to the Roman Catholic fold. But preparations for the armada, which ultimately was to consist of 130 ships carrying 30,000 men, suffered a severe setback in 1587, when a fleet of 30 English ships under Drake's command launched a surprise attack in Cádiz harbor. There the Spanish were keeping ships and supplies, all intended for the armada, but within 36 hours of the attack they were destroyed. Drake, who excelled in the unexpected, called this rout on Spain's own territory "singeing the King of Spain's beard."

In July 1588, however, a refurbished Spanish Armada appeared in the English Channel. Drake was appointed vice-admiral of the British fleet that set out to meet the Spanish. After a long battle, the Spanish fleet retreated to the French harbor of Calais. Showing another stroke of genius, Drake sent fire ships into the harbor. Driven by a brisk wind, the fire ships destroyed everything they touched, and the Spanish fleet went up in flames. This was Drake's last great victory. Poems and songs were composed in his honor, and his popularity spread around the world.

Toward the end of his life, Drake conducted two unsuccessful voyages, but they did not diminish his brilliant career. While attempting an attack on Spanish colonies in the West Indies in 1596, he died of fever and was buried at sea off the coast of Panama. Having remained true to himself and to his ideals, Drake had not been changed by wealth and fame. He was a remarkably fair and just man who inspired his country to greatness.

Paul Du Chaillu

Born c. 1831,
Paris, France

Died April 30, 1903,
St. Petersburg, Russia

P aul Belloni Du Chaillu was a colorful American explorer with a love of adventure and a gift for storytelling. Traveling mainly on his own in Africa, he was the first Westerner to see and photograph gorillas and the first to report on the tribal life of Pygmies. A major mountain range in Gabon, Africa, is named for him.

Du Chaillu was always mysterious about his origins, variously claiming to have been born in Paris, New York, and New Orleans. Du Chaillu was the son of a French trader and his part-African mistress. His father set up a trading post on the coast of Gabon in West Africa in 1845; Paul joined him in 1848 and became interested in learning the native language and exploring the interior. According to some stories, Du Chaillu was rescued by American missionaries when his canoe was overturned, and they painted such a glowing picture of their country that he decided to travel there in 1852. In the United States, he studied natural science and became an American citizen.

Paul Du Chaillu was an American of French origin who made three trips to Gabon in West Africa; he was the first Westerner to write about the gorilla.

Explores tropical forest

Du Chaillu wanted to return to Gabon and explore the dense tropical forest in the interior. In 1855 he convinced the Philadelphia Academy of Natural Sciences to support an expedition; he spent the next four years in Gabon, traveling throughout the country alone with only modest supplies.

In his book about his experiences, *Explorations and Adventures in Equatorial Africa,* he wrote:

> I travelled—always on foot and unaccompanied by other white men—about 8,000 miles. I shot, stuffed and brought home over 2,000 birds, of which more than 60 are new species, and I killed upwards of 1,000 quadrupeds, of which 200 were stuffed and brought home, with more than 80 skeletons ... I suffered 50 attacks of the African fever, taking, to cure myself, more than fourteen ounces of quinine. Of famine, long-continued exposures to the tropical rains, and attacks of ferocious ants and venomous flies, it is not worthwhile to speak.

Du Chaillu traveled up the Ogooúe River, a route followed by many African explorers, as far as the site of Lambaréné, the place where Dr. Albert Schweitzer would later build his famous hospital. A mountain range that was named for Du Chaillu in south central Gabon rises to more than 3,000 feet between the Ngounié and the Ogooúe rivers. It forms the country's main watershed and contains the highest peak in Gabon.

Criticizes slave trade

Du Chaillu was a perceptive observer of the slave trade, the chief industry of Gabon, and reported on the terrible effect that it was having on the African people. Du Chaillu described one camp as "an immense enclosure defended by a wall of 12 foot high stakes that contained a large number of barracks surrounded by trees under which slept enough people to make up a large African village."

Writes about gorillas

In the Ntem highlands Du Chaillu stayed with members of the Fan tribe, who hunted gorillas and elephants as sources of food. Du Chaillu went on a number of these hunting expeditions, and described one in which the gorilla won the contest. He later wrote that one of his African friends, in a confrontation with a gorilla:

> stood his ground, and as quickly as he could reloaded his gun. Just as he raised it to fire the gorilla dashed it out of his hands, the gun going off in the fall, and then in an instant, and with a terrible roar, the animal gave him a tremendous blow with an immense open paw, frightfully lacerating the abdomen, and with this single blow laying bare part of the intestines. As he sank, bleeding, to the ground, the monster seized the gun, and the poor hunter thought he would have his brains dashed out with it. But the gorilla seemed to have looked upon this also as an enemy, and in his rage flattened the barrel between his strong jaws.

During his time in Gabon, Du Chaillu killed several gorillas.

Returning to the United States in June 1859, he wrote about his discoveries, including detailed information about the gorillas. Unfortunately, the two live baby gorillas he had brought with him died en route. His book contained so many amazing tales that, even though they were true, many people refused to believe him. His stories about the gorillas were particularly fantastic; the gorillas seemed to be almost mythical creatures, more like unicorns than actual animals. During a lecture he gave at the London Ethnological Society in July 1861, he was practically accused of being a liar, and he and his adversary almost came to blows.

Photographs gorillas

Determined to prove that he was telling the truth, Du Chaillu returned to Gabon in 1863 with a larger expedition. He encountered difficulties, however, and lost his scientific instruments; the party was also attacked by members of the

Ashango tribe. Du Chaillu had learned photography before leaving for Africa, and the photos he took and the specimens he collected convinced the skeptics. His reputation was restored by the book he wrote about his experiences, *A Journey in Ashango Land,* in which he also gave the first reports by a Westerner of life in a Pygmy tribe. He appeared before the Royal Geographical Society in London and was endorsed for membership.

Writes children's books

Du Chaillu had made his last trip to Africa. He retired to the Marlborough Hotel in New York City, where he spent most of his time writing children's books under the pseudonym Uncle Paul. Many of the books were based on his experiences in Africa. He also traveled frequently; in 1871 he made a trip to Scandinavia, then wrote a book about his experiences there. During a trip to Russia in 1901 he became ill; he died in St. Petersburg on April 30, 1903.

Jules-Sébastien-César Dumont d'Urville

Born May 23, 1790,
Condé-sur-Noireau, France

Died May 8, 1842,
Near Meudon, France

French knowledge of the Antarctic and South Pacific was greatly aided by Jules-Sébastien-César Dumont d'Urville. He began his career as a naval officer by helping the French government to acquire one of the most beautiful examples of classical Greek art, the *Venus de Milo*. His later discoveries led to extensive revisions of existing charts and maps and redesignation of island groups.

Buys *Venus de Milo* for France

Dumont d'Urville was born in the village of Condé in Calvados in Normandy. He entered the French navy in 1807 and studied at the naval base of Toulon on the Mediterranean, where he graduated at the head of his class in 1811. During a charting mission from 1819 to 1820 in the Aegean Sea off the coast of Greece, Dumont d'Urville's ship stopped at the island of Milos. While on Milos, Dumont d'Urville recognized the *Venus de Milo* and began negotiations to purchase the statue

Jules-Sébastien-César Dumont d'Urville was a French naval officer who made a number of important scientific expeditions to the Pacific Ocean; he was also the first Frenchman to explore Antarctica.

for France. This was considered such an important find that he was awarded the French Legion of Honor medal and promoted by King Charles X. The *Venus de Milo* may still be seen today in the Louvre Museum in Paris. Dumont d'Urville was also married around this time.

In August 1822, Dumont d'Urville began his first voyage of exploration, which took him around the world and lasted for three years. As an officer aboard the *Coqville* on the Duperrey expedition, which explored the Gilbert and Caroline islands in the central Pacific, he collected specimens of unknown plants and insects. When the ship returned to Toulon on May 22, 1825, Dumont d'Urville had acquired an extensive collection that he used as a basis for a number of scientific articles and a book.

Finds remains of expedition

On his return Dumont d'Urville proposed to make an expedition to study the South Pacific islands and search for traces of a voyage led by the **Jean François de Galaup, Comte de La Pérouse** (see entry), a French explorer who had been lost in that area since 1788. The trip began on April 25, 1826, on the *Astrolabe*. Dumont d'Urville ran into some good luck in Sydney, Australia: an English captain brought back reports of finding the remains of La Pérouse's ships on the island of Vanikoro in the Santa Cruz Islands, now part of the Republic of the Solomon Islands.

Dumont d'Urville reached Vanikoro on the *Astrolabe* in 1828. Later describing what he found, he wrote: "lying at the bottom of the sea, three or four fathoms below the surface, our men saw anchors, cannons, shot and a huge quantity of lead plates." Further exploration verified that these were indeed the remains of the La Pérouse expedition. He learned the rest of the story of the wreck from the islanders: about 30 of the men had succeeded in getting ashore but had been massacred; others, who were better armed, had managed to stay alive for seven months, after which they had sailed for the north. They were never heard from again.

Gathers largest scientific collection

During his voyage Dumont d'Urville charted various islands in the island groups of Melanesia and charted the New Zealand coast, including Cook Strait, which separates North Island from South Island. He brought back 1,600 plant specimens, 900 rocks, and 500 insects as well as a number of drawings. The expedition amassed the largest collection of scientific material that had so far been brought to Europe. Because of Dumont d'Urville's findings, existing charts were extensively revised and the islands of the South Pacific were regrouped as Melanesia, Micronesia, Polynesia, and Malaysia.

Receives no recognition for work

When he returned to France on March 25, 1829, Dumont d'Urville did not receive the recognition he expected. Some belittled the extent of his scientific work, and he was criticized for the death rate on his ship—29 crew members were lost. He took a desk job in Toulon where he wrote two books about his expedition that restored his reputation. In 1835 his only daughter was killed in a cholera epidemic; his older son had died ten years earlier.

By 1836 Dumont d'Urville was eager to make another expedition to the South Pacific, but the French king, Louis-Philippe, had become more interested in Antarctica. He wanted the French to explore beyond the territory that had just been discovered by James Weddell, an Englishman. Although Dumont d'Urville was partially crippled with gout, he agreed to seek the new destination. On September 7, 1837, he sailed from Toulon with the *Astrolabe* and another vessel, the *Zelée,* both of which were unequipped for Arctic exploration.

Explores Antarctica

After charting the Strait of Magellan in early December, Dumont d'Urville docked the ships for repairs. Heading south in January, his party soon encountered their first ice packs. Because the ice was very heavy that year they were not able to go far. The ships were forced to turn north, considerably short of the point Weddell had reached in 1823. Dumont d'Urville rested the party in the South Orkney Islands and tried again in February.

The *Astrolabe* and the *Zelée* entered an inlet in the ice and were soon iced in. The fleet was trapped for a week; then after freeing the ships the party landed on Weddell Island before continuing westward. Dumont d'Urville sighted the northern part of the Graham Peninsula, which he named Louis Philippe Land, and the islands of d'Urville and Joinville, which he called Joinville Land. Although both of these areas had been sighted before, Dumont d'Urville produced valuable cartographic work in the Falkland Islands, the South Orkney Islands, and the South Shetlands Islands.

Scurvy takes crewmen

Because of a scurvy epidemic (caused by lack of vitamin C), Dumont d'Urville sailed north to take on provisions at Valparaíso, Chile. He then headed for the Pacific, which had been his original destination. From May 1838 until December 1839 the two French ships crisscrossed the Pacific, visiting Tahiti, Tonga, Fiji, Vanuatu, the Solomons, the Caroline Islands, the Dutch East Indies, and New Guinea. By the time the exploring party reached Hobart, Tasmania, in Australia in December 1839, many of the men aboard both the *Astrolabe* and the *Zelée* were ill from fever and dysentery. More than 20 men died.

In Hobart Dumont d'Urville heard about the attempt by the British explorer James Clark Ross to find the South Magnetic Pole; Dumont d'Urville decided to find it himself. Once again the ships headed into the Antarctic. In mid-January Dumont d'Urville's ships were close to the Arctic Circle, and one morning the members of his party awoke to find themselves in a calm sea facing a coastline of vertical ice cliffs that were at least 120 feet high. Behind them, rising from 3,000 to 4,000 feet, lay a vast land completely covered with ice and snow. Dumont d'Urville named this forbidding terrain Adélie Land after his wife; it later came to be known as the Adélie

Coast. He was not able to find a gap in the ice where he could go ashore.

On January 29, 1840, while in a fogbound sea, the Frenchmen sighted another ship approaching. As it hoisted the American colors, they saw it was the *Porpoise,* one of the ships of Charles Wilkes's Antarctic expedition, the first great maritime exploration by the United States. The two ships passed without exchanging signals or any other greeting. The next day Dumont d'Urville, sighting the icepack they had encountered at the beginning of their journey into the ice-bound land, turned north toward Hobart.

Receives overdue recognition

On his way back to Europe from Hobart, Dumont d'Urville explored the Loyalty Islands off New Caledonia and the Louisiade Archipelago off the southeast coast of New Guinea. He reached Toulon on November 6, 1840. In spite of criticism once again about the number of men lost on his voyage, he was promoted to admiral and awarded a gold medal by the French Geographical Society. While Dumont d'Urville was working on the account of the expedition, he, his wife, and their only remaining son were killed in a train wreck in Versailles, France, on May 8, 1842.

Amelia Earhart

Born 1897,
Atchison, Kansas
Disappeared June 1937,
Over the Pacific Ocean

Amelia Earhart, an American aircraft pilot, was the first woman to fly solo across the Atlantic Ocean. She also set numerous other flying records. She disappeared mysteriously during an attempted flight around the world.

Admired for her achievements in aviation and for her adventurous nature, Amelia Earhart became a well-known personality during the 1920s and 1930s. She loved daredevil stunts, such as jumping off a metal tower with a parachute and piloting a one-person submarine. Her brief career was filled with record-setting flights, drama, and excitement.

Earhart was drawn to challenges, and perhaps this is what made her a good pilot. She also enjoyed the "beauty" of flying. Writing about a flight she took from Hawaii, she said, "After midnight the moon set and I was alone with the stars. I have often said that the lure of flying is the lure of beauty, and I need no other flights to convince me that the reason flyers fly, whether they know it or not, is the aesthetic appeal of flying."

Early interest in flying

Amelia Mary Earhart was born in Atchison, Kansas, where she lived with her sister and grandparents until she was

12. Her father was a lawyer employed by a railroad company, and during her teens she and her family lived in various cities where her father was working.

At the age of 20 Earhart went to visit her sister, who had moved to Toronto, Ontario. The year was 1918, and servicemen wounded in World War I could be seen on the streets of the city. World War I was the first war in which airplanes were used, and it was during this time that Earhart first visited an airfield. She decided then that she wanted to learn to fly. Like many young women of the time, she volunteered to work as a nurse's aide at a local military hospital. After the war, she took a medical course at Columbia University in New York City.

Earhart eventually returned to her family, then living in Los Angeles, and at an air show one day she persuaded her father to spend ten dollars to send her up on a joyride. Her love of flying was confirmed, and she immediately set about arranging to take lessons. With money she earned driving a sand and gravel truck, she hired Neta Snook—the first woman instructor to graduate from the Curtiss School of Aviation—to teach her. After only two and one half hours of instruction, she decided to buy her own plane. A job sorting mail at the local telephone company and a loan from her mother enabled Earhart to buy a small experimental plane for $2,000.

Record-setting flights

Shortly after she began flying, Earhart started setting records. Her first was a new altitude record of 14,000 feet. Soon another pilot broke this record, but the determined Earhart immediately tried to set a new one. Flying without instruments, she ran into dense fog at 12,000 feet. The flight came close to ending in a crash, but she managed to land safely, though without having met her record-breaking goal.

When Earhart's parents divorced in 1924, she bought a yellow roadster to drive her mother to the East Coast. In order to pay for the car, she sold her plane to a young man. As she stood watching the plane take off, the man immediately crashed and was killed. In Boston Earhart resumed her medical studies for a short while and then became a social worker in a settlement house. Because of her work and small salary, Earhart had little time or money for flying, but she still took every opportunity she could find to pursue it.

Earhart's career took a dramatic turn in 1928, when she received an unexpected invitation from a committee headed by the publisher and publicist George Palmer Putnam in New York City. The committee was in the process of selecting the first woman to travel, as a passenger, on a plane across the Atlantic Ocean. Earhart was interviewed and chosen. On June 3, 1928, she and a male pilot and navigator took off in the *Friendship,* the same plane American explorer **Richard Evelyn Byrd** (see entry) had flown across the North Pole. Encountering fog, however, the plane was forced to land in Newfoundland and wait there for two weeks.

The second attempt at flying across the Atlantic was successful; 20 hours and 40 minutes after takeoff, the *Friendship* landed in a bay in Wales, where Earhart and the crew were greeted with great enthusiasm. Although she had been only a passenger, Earhart received international attention because she was the first woman to have flown across the Atlantic.

Instant celebrity

On her return to the United States, Earhart suddenly found that she was considered a spokesperson for women aviators. With Putnam as her manager, she presented lectures throughout the United States, and she also wrote a column on aviation for *Cosmopolitan* magazine. Her name was used to market numerous products, including her own design of traveling clothes, as well as Amelia Earhart luggage, which continued to be sold even in the 1990s. Earhart began to be known not only for her flying accomplishments but also for her adventurous spirit.

Earhart's career as an aviator grew as she continued to set new records. On a trip from New York to Los Angeles to visit her father, she became the first woman to fly solo both ways across the country. In 1929 the Lockheed Company presented Earhart with a brand-new Vega, a new type of single-wing plane that was also flown by two other famous female pilots, **Amy Johnson** and **Beryl Markham** (see separate entries). Flying the Vega, Earhart participated in the first Women's Air Derby across the United States. In 1930 she set a new speed record for women. Later she made a tour of the United States in an autogiro, a forerunner of the helicopter, in which she set an altitude record. Earhart also became the first person to fly from Hawaii to the American mainland, and in 1935 she set a speed record on a solo flight from Los Angeles to Mexico City and another from Mexico City to New York.

In 1931 Earhart married Putnam, her publicist. Her fame grew as her husband continued to use his talent to make her one of the best-known personalities in the United States. As a celebrity, she had new and interesting experiences. For example, she took First Lady Eleanor Roosevelt on a flight over Washington, D.C., and then escorted her around the White House grounds in a race car.

Transatlantic flight

One of Earhart's most celebrated accomplishments was her solo flight across the Atlantic in 1932. She wanted to earn the fame she felt she had not deserved after her Atlantic flight as a passenger four years earlier. She took off from Harbor Grace, Newfoundland, on a spring evening. For the first few hours the flight went well, but before long Earhart began to have difficulties. The plane ran into a violent electrical storm, the altimeter failed, and ice collected on the wings. As the plane went into a tailspin, it descended 3,000 feet before regaining stability, only to have the engine catch on fire.

Exhausted by these problems, Earhart decided to land in Ireland rather than continue on to Paris as she had planned. She touched down in a pasture outside Londonderry, Northern Ireland, 14 hours and 56 minutes after she had left Newfoundland. Once again she became a celebrity, and this time she felt she had earned it. Earhart's flight won her fame throughout Europe, and when she returned to New York, she was greeted with an extravagant ticker-tape parade.

Final flight

Five years later Earhart began to make plans for what was to be her final flight. Her new goal was to fly around the world at or near the equator, something never before attempted. Purdue University purchased a new twin-engine Lockheed Electra specially modified for the flight, presenting it to Earhart on her thirty-ninth birthday. In the early morning hours of March 17, 1937, she took off from San Francisco for Hawaii, where her flight was to begin, setting yet another record by reaching Hawaii in just under 16 hours. As Earhart was leaving Hawaii, however, her heavily laden plane crashed on takeoff. It took $50,000 and five weeks of work to repair the Electra.

Because of the delay, Earhart decided to reverse the planned course of her flight. By flying from west to east, she could take advantage of changed weather patterns and air currents. She also replaced the original navigator with Fred Noonan. Beginning in Miami, Florida, they took off on June 1, 1937, and headed for Brazil. From there they flew across the Atlantic to Africa and then across the Red Sea to Arabia, Karachi (in Pakistan), Calcutta (in India), and Burma. A month later they reached New Guinea, an island north of Australia. The next part of their trip was the most dangerous because they had to land on Howland Island, a speck of land only two miles long located in the middle of the Pacific Ocean. The size of the island would make it easy to miss.

An unsolved mystery

Earhart and Noonan never reached Howland Island, and neither they nor their plane were ever found. It is possible that they simply missed the island, ran out of fuel, and crashed into the ocean. Another theory holds that part of Earhart's mission was to spy on the Japanese-held islands in the Pacific. According to this premise, the Japanese were aware of her mission and intercepted her plane, taking her captive; in fact, a recent biography of Earhart claims that evidence supports this conclusion and therefore solves the mystery of her disappearance.

Most experts have remained unconvinced, however, saying there is no real proof of the fate of Earhart because her plane has never been found. In 1992 investigators on Nikumaroro—a small atoll, or coral island, south of Howland—discovered a shoe and a metal plate that might have been left by Earhart and Noonan. But to this day no one knows for certain what happened to these pioneering aviators.

Lincoln Ellsworth

Born May 12, 1880,
Chicago, Illinois

Died May 26, 1951,
New York, New York

Lincoln Ellsworth was an American aviator who took part in several flying expeditions over the Arctic; he was the first person to fly across Antarctica.

Lincoln Ellsworth was a wealthy adventurer who became fascinated with polar air exploration. Flying in crafts that would be considered primitive by today's standards, he was a new breed of explorer who had to deal with shifting winds, snow and ice, and several other difficulties. Crash landings and lost equipment were common hazards. Ellsworth participated in the first trans-Arctic air crossing and, in a supreme act of courage, led the first trans-Antarctic air crossing. Unconcerned with legalities, Ellsworth claimed over 300,000 square miles of territory for the United States. Although these acquisitions were never officially recognized, he named a good part of the land for his father, calling it Ellsworth Land.

Begins career as naturalist

Ellsworth was born in Chicago on May 12, 1880. His father was a wealthy mining engineer. Ellsworth also became an engineer and spent the early part of his career working and prospecting for gold in Canada and Alaska. From 1914 to 1917 he worked as a naturalist collecting specimens for the United States Biological Survey. As a good luck charm Ellsworth wore an ammunition belt once owned by his hero, Wyatt Earp, the Texas border marshal. When World War I broke out he went to France as a volunteer pilot even though he was overage. During the war he met the famous Norwegian Arctic explorer **Roald Amundsen** (see entry) in Paris, and he began to think seriously about the possibilities of polar exploration.

Joins polar expeditions

In the early 1920s Ellsworth led a topographic survey for Johns Hopkins University that extended from the Amazon Basin to the Pacific shores of Peru. On his return to New York he again met Amundsen. They agreed to undertake in 1925 an expedition to the North Pole that would use two amphibian planes, and Ellsworth asked his father to help finance the venture. While preparations were being made for the flight Ellsworth helped rescue two men who had crash-landed in Norway, a feat for which he was awarded a medal by the King of Norway. During the actual expedition the party made a crash landing without a functioning radio; they were given up for lost. It took the explorers 30 days of intense effort to carve out a takeoff field on the rough polar ice surface. After crowding all six of the party into one plane, they reached Spitsbergen off the coast of Norway.

Ellsworth and the Norwegian government jointly financed the second polar expedition led by Amundsen. Ellsworth was also a member of the party aboard the dirigible, or rigid airship, the *Norge,* which was designed and piloted by the Italian Umberto Nobile, when it flew over the North Pole on May 12, 1926. Their 3,393-mile journey from Spitsbergen to Alaska captured the attention of people all over the world.

Supports other expeditions

Following the success of the *Norge,* Ellsworth became involved in efforts by **Hubert Wilkins** (see entry) to sail a submarine under the North Pole. Once again, he provided money for the project, but this time he did not participate in the expedition; the venture was unsuccessful. In 1931 Ellsworth made an 800-mile canoe trip through central Labrador. During that same year he accepted a German invitation to fly in the giant dirigible the *Graf Zeppelin* along the Arctic coast of Siberia to Franz Josef Land and Northern Land. The airship left Leningrad, Russia, on July 26 and returned on July 31, completing a trip of 5,000 miles. The expedition resolved several questions about Arctic geography, including the discovery that two islands drawn on maps did not exist.

Heads own expedition

Up to this time Ellsworth had helped finance several expeditions but had never actually led one of his own. He was inspired by **Richard Evelyn Byrd** (see entry), who had flown over the South Pole four years earlier. Ellsworth decided he would be the first person to fly across the continent of Antarctica, calling it the last great adventure. He purchased a plane and hired Bernt Balchen, the pilot who had flown with Byrd. Leaving New Zealand in December 1933, they arrived at the supply base that Byrd had named Little America II in January 1934. One night the ice under the plane began to break up, and by the next morning the plane had sunk.

Refusing to give up, Ellsworth went back to the United States, bought a new plane, and returned with Balchen to Antarctica. Hubert Wilkins accompanied them to handle logistics on the ground. This time Ellsworth proposed tackling the problem from the other direction—approaching Little America II from Deception Island off the Graham Peninsula. After initial test flights Ellsworth and Balchen left Deception Island on January 3, 1935. They had been airborne for only an hour when Balchen suddenly turned back, claiming the weather was too bad to continue. The attempt had to be abandoned once again, and Ellsworth realized the weather would never meet Balchen's specifications.

Continues attempts to cross Antarctica

In November 1935 Ellsworth returned to Antarctica with

a new pilot, a Canadian named Herbert Hollick-Kenyon, in a Northrop monoplane, the *Polar Star.* Flying from Dundee Island southwest of Joinville Island, on November 25, 1935, they made their first attempt to cross Antarctica. During the flight they discovered a new range of mountains, which Ellsworth named the Eternity Mountains; however, they were forced to turn back after 11 hours by bad weather. They tried a second time on November 22, landing four times along the way to rest and check their position; each time they were forced to wait for clearer skies. As they prepared to leave after the fourth landing, it took them two days to dig the plane out from under the snow.

Makes first flight across Antarctica

The *Polar Star* was finally airborne again, only to run out of fuel. On December 5 Ellsworth and Hollick-Kenyon were forced to land at a point about 60 miles from the Ross Sea. They walked 10 days to reach Little America II on the Bay of Whales. The anticipated 14-hour flight had actually taken 22 days, but Ellsworth had accomplished his mission: they had made the first flight over Antarctica from the Weddell Sea to the Ross Sea; the area they covered is now called Ellsworth Land. Since the base was not occupied, the explorers had to wait nearly a month, until January 14, to be picked up by a British ship. By then Ellsworth was very ill with a gangrenous left leg and frostbite.

Claims territory for U.S.

Ellsworth returned to Antarctica once more in 1939, making a flight of 305 miles into the interior and claiming much of the previously unseen territory, which he named the American Highlands, for the United States. Throughout his exploring career Ellsworth wrote several books, the last of which, *Beyond Horizons,* was published in 1938, the year before his final trip. Ellsworth died in New York City in 1951. Although Ellsworth had claimed more than 300,000 square miles of Antarctic terrain for his country, the United States has never asserted territorial claims. In fact, during the International Geophysical Year, the United States was instrumental in negotiating the 1959 Antarctic Treaty, which designated the continent an international region that is to be used only for peaceful scientific purposes.

Erik the Red

Born c. 950,
Stavanger, Norway

Died c. 1004,
Greenland

E rik the Red was a Norse explorer whose most important voyage began as the result of a violent feud. He was banished from his home in Iceland for three years as punishment for killing two men. During this exile, he became the first European to land on Greenland. He later established Norse colonies that endured in Greenland for the next 500 years.

Erik's travels began early in life. He was born in southwestern Norway near the town of Stavanger. His father became involved in a feud with another family and killed a man. In those days, such a crime was punished with exile in Iceland, which had first been settled by the Norwegians in the 870s. Erik's family moved to a remote part of western Iceland.

Feud and banishment

After he was grown and married, Erik himself became involved in a blood feud. In the year 982, he killed two of his enemy's sons. As punishment, he was banished from the coun-

Erik the Red was a Norseman from Iceland who was the first European to land on and settle Greenland.

try to live overseas for a period of three years. Erik had heard about the voyages of a man named Gunnbjörn Ulfsson, who had discovered a group of small islands west of Iceland. Ulfsson said that he had seen a much larger land beyond them.

Since Erik was now forced to leave the country, he decided to make the best of the situation and announced that he was going to sail in search of Ulfsson's land. With a crew of hired men, he sailed due west from the Icelandic peninsula called Snaefellsnes. Erik sighted Gunnbjörn's Skerries, probably the islands off the coast near the modern town of Angmagssalik in eastern Greenland. Then he landed on the shore of this vast new country at a place he named Midjökull (Middle Glacier).

Discovery of Greenland

Because of the pattern of ocean currents, eastern Greenland has a much harsher climate than western Greenland, and Erik did not stay long where he first landed. He sailed south down the coast and around the southern tip of Greenland in search of a more pleasant environment. He landed along the southwest coast at an area that was to become known as the Eastern Settlement (Eystribygd, in the region of what is now Julianehåb or Qaqortoq). He spent the winter on an island he named Erik's Island.

In the spring of 983, Erik sailed up a nearby fjord that he also named after himself. During the following winter he stayed on the southern tip of Greenland, and then he sailed up the east coast in the spring of 984. He returned once again to Erik's Island to spend the following winter. By this time, the term of Erik's banishment from Iceland was complete. He sailed around the southern tip of Greenland and returned safely to his native land in the summer of 985.

Colonization of Greenland

It was not long, however, before the blood feud between Erik and his neighbors started again. As a result, Erik began to promote the colonization of his newly found land. He wanted people to move overseas with him, and he called the new country "Greenland" because he thought the name would attract settlers. Greenland must have sounded appealing, because Erik left Iceland in 986 with 14 ships carrying 400 to 500 people as well as domestic animals and household goods.

Erik settled at a place he named Brattahlid (now a trading station called Qagssiarssuk) at the head of Erik's Fjord, which became the center of the Eastern Settlement. The Western Settlement (around present-day Godthåb or Nuuk) was about 180 miles farther up the coast. There was another, smaller settlement between the Eastern and Western Settlements.

Son's explorations

Erik had three sons—Leif, Thorvald, and Thorsteinn—and a daughter named Freydis. One of his sons, **Leif Eriksson** (see entry), became a famous explorer in his own right. In the year 999, Leif pioneered the first direct route to Norway from Greenland, bypassing Iceland. When Leif voyaged to Vinland in 1001 or 1002, Erik wanted to go with him but fell off his horse on the way to the ship, injuring his leg. Because of this mishap, Erik was unable to accompany Leif on his most famous voyage: Vinland was the name the Norse used for the area of North America, possibly Nova Scotia, that Leif was first to visit.

Greenland after Erik

Erik and Leif had a disagreement after one of Leif's voyages. While in Norway, Leif converted to Christianity. He later brought the first Christian missionary to Greenland. Erik believed in the Viking religion and was not pleased with his son's role in bringing Christianity to Greenland. Erik died sometime during the winter of 1003-04. Ironically, although he never accepted Christianity, he was buried on the grounds of what became the Christian cathedral at Brattahlid.

The Norse Greenland settlements prospered for a while, but later they were afflicted by a change in the climate. The weather grew much colder and was no longer suitable for European farming practices. More ice began to form in the ocean, and this made travel back and forth to Iceland more difficult. The last recorded voyage between Iceland and Greenland was made in 1410, although it is likely that there were some later trips. The settlers faced other difficulties. The Inuit, or indigenous people, advancing from the north, are thought to have destroyed the Western Settlement around 1350. The last Norsemen in the Eastern settlement probably disappeared sometime in the early sixteenth century. By the time English navigator and explorer Martin Frobisher saw the coast of Greenland in 1576, the colonies that Erik the Red established had disappeared.

Estevanico

Born c. 1500,
Azemmour, Morocco

Died 1539,
Hawikuh (a Zuni pueblo in New Mexico)

Estevanico was a Moroccan slave who, along with Spanish explorers, traveled from Florida along the Gulf of Mexico and into the southwestern United States. He was captured by Native Americans and escaped to become a successful "medicine man." After an epic overland journey he finally reached the Spanish outpost of Mexico City. He was the first Westerner to reach some areas of the southwestern states. He preceded **Francisco Vásquez de Coronado** (see entry) in visiting the "Seven Cities of Cíbola," seven pueblos in northern Mexico about which there had been mythical stories, where he was killed by Zuni warriors.

Taken to Spain as a slave

At the beginning of the sixteenth century, when Estevanico was born, the Arabs of Morocco were in constant warfare with their Spanish and Portuguese neighbors to the north. At some point during one of these conflicts, Estevanico was cap-

Estevanico, often called "the Black," was a Moroccan slave who accompanied Cabeza de Vaca on his odyssey through the southwestern United States.

tured and sold as a slave in Spain. The Spanish often referred to him as Estevanico the Black. Estevanico may well have been descended in part from black Africans, since for many years the Arabs and Berbers—native Caucasian people—of North Africa had contacts with blacks who lived south of the Sahara Desert.

Estevanico came into the possession of Andrés Dorantes de Carranca, a Spanish nobleman who took Estevanico with him and joined the expedition to North America led by Pánfilo de Narváez. Another Spaniard, **Álvar Núñez Cabeza de Vaca** (see entry), who would later become one of the most famous explorers of North America, also took part in this voyage.

Goes to North America

The Spanish ships landed on the Florida coast in April 1528. Disregarding the advice of his captains, Narváez abandoned his ships and marched into the interior on May 1 in search of gold. The history of his trek comes from the report that Cabeza de Vaca made after his return to Spain. Narváez's expedition was attacked by Native Americans near the site of present-day Tallahassee, Florida. The Spaniards went from there to a bay on the Gulf of Mexico and constructed five boats, with which they hoped to sail along the coastline to a Spanish outpost in Mexico. They set sail on September 22, 1528; Estevanico was in the boat commanded by Dorantes.

In November the small fleet was hit by violent storms. Dorantes's boat and the one captained by Cabeza de Vaca were wrecked, possibly on Galveston Island or Mustang Island, off the coast of Texas. The survivors spent the winter on the island; by the spring of 1529 only 15 men were still alive. Thirteen of them, including Estevanico, left Galveston to try to reach Mexico by walking overland. Cabeza de Vaca was too sick to travel and was left behind, presumably to die.

Captured in Texas

The party led by Dorantes headed west and south. Several men died along the way; the rest, including Dorantes and

Estevanico, were captured by Native Americans at San Antonio Bay on the Texas coast. They were harshly treated by their captors, and by the autumn of 1530 only Dorantes, Estevanico, and Alonzo de Castillo were still alive. Dorantes managed to escape, traveling inland to a village of the Mariame tribe, where his life was easier although he was held in captivity. In the spring of 1532 Estevanico and Castillo also escaped and joined Dorantes at the Mariame village.

Meets Cabeza de Vaca

During the winter of the following year Estevanico and the others were surprised to encounter Cabeza de Vaca; he had not only survived but had been working as a trader among the various Native American tribes. The four Europeans were not allowed to stay together, but they planned to meet and then make their escape in the autumn at the annual Native American festival to celebrate the harvest of prickly pears. In September 1534 the four men managed to flee from a site near the present-day city of San Antonio. They encountered a camp of the Avavares tribe, where they were warmly welcomed as medicine men with special powers, probably because of their foreign appearance.

Becomes known as medicine man

Estevanico, Cabeza de Vaca, Dorantes, and de Castillo performed healing rituals for the Native Americans. Estevanico was especially noted for his ability to learn other languages and to use sign language. When the four men left the Avavares in the spring of 1535, they found that their reputation as healers had preceded them and they were welcomed wherever they went. As they traveled farther west, they saw evidence of many different cultures. Visiting the Pueblo tribes of the area that is now New Mexico, they saw metal bells and medicine gourds the Pueblos had made. Estevanico kept one of the gourds to use in his healing rituals.

When they reached the Rio Grande at the end of 1535, Castillo and Estevanico headed upstream. They came upon the permanent towns or pueblos of the Jumano tribe. When

Cabeza de Vaca and Dorantes joined Castillo and Estevanico, they found Estevanico surrounded by Native Americans, who treated him like a god.

Learns about Seven Cities of Cíbola

As they traveled toward Mexico, the men heard tales of a group of wealthy cities in the interior, called the Seven Cities of Cíbola. The Spanish search for wealth in these mythical cities would later have fateful consequences for Estevanico. From the Rio Grande, Estevanico and the three Spaniards traveled into what is now the Mexican state of Chihuahua. As they moved south, they began to see more and more evidence of contact with Europeans; they met a party of Spaniards in March 1536. They reached Tenochtitlán (present-day Mexico City) the following July, more than eight years after they had landed on the Florida coast.

Scouts trail to cities

Viceroy Antonio Mendoza welcomed the three Spaniards and Estevanico in Mexico, treating them to generous hospitality. Eventually Dorantes sold or gave Estevanico to Mendoza. Intrigued by the tales Cabeza de Vaca told of wealthy cities to the north, the viceroy commissioned an expedition to find the Seven Cities of Cíbola. He accepted the offer of a Spanish friar, Fray Marcos de Niza, to lead the exploring party, and he appointed Estevanico to be the friar's guide.

Estevanico and Fray Marcos began their journey on March 7, 1539. Two weeks later Fray Marcos decided to camp while Estevanico went ahead to scout the trail. After four days Native American messengers returned to Fray Marcos to report that Estevanico had heard news that he was within 30 days' march from Cíbola and he wanted Fray Marcos to join him.

Fray Marcos immediately started northward, but Estevanico did not wait for him. As the friar entered each new village, he found a message from Estevanico saying that he had continued on. Fray Marcos chased after him for weeks but was unable to catch up.

Estevanico headed through the vast desert region of the Mexican state of Sonora and the area that is now southern Arizona. He was the first Westerner to enter the area of Arizona and New Mexico. In May he reached the Zuni pueblo of Hawikuh, which was supposedly the first of the Seven Cities of Cíbola.

Killed by Zunis

Wherever he traveled, Estevanico was in the habit of sending his medicine gourd ahead of him with Native American messengers to announce his arrival. Usually this token assured him a welcome. At Hawikuh, however, the reception was not so warm as he had expected. When he displayed his "magic" gourd, the Zuni chief threw it down in anger. Then the chief took all of Estevanico's possessions and put him in a house on the edge of the town without food or water. The next morning Estevanico was attacked by warriors and killed.

When they were later asked why they had killed Estevanico, the Zuni said that Estevanico had claimed that there was a huge army coming behind him with many weapons. Meeting in council, the chiefs had decided he was a spy and that the safest course of action was to kill him. After Estevanico was dead, his body was cut into pieces and distributed among the chiefs. Several of Estevanico's Native American escorts escaped the Zuni village. When they found Fray Marcos they gave him the news of Estevanico's death.

Marcos finds Estevanico's belongings

Later, in his report to Mendoza, Fray Marcos said that he traveled north until he could see Hawikuh, or Cibola, but that he did not enter the pueblo. In his report he claimed it was a rich place, even grander than Mexico City. Since Hawikuh is in fact only a small pueblo, it seems likely Fray Marcos lied about seeing the town.

Fray Marcos's report inspired Mendoza to send out another expedition led by Francisco Vásquez de Coronado. When Coronado's party reached the small village of Hawikuh, the only traces of Estevanico they found were his green dinner plates, his greyhound dogs, and his metal bells. All of these items were now in the possession of the Zuni chief.

Explorer 1

Launched January 31, 1958
Reentered Earth's atmosphere March 31, 1970

S purred by the launch of the Soviet Union's *Sputnik* satellite, the United States pursued two space programs simultaneously. The original project would produce *Vanguard 1*, but this satellite went into orbit several weeks after the success of *Explorer 1*.

Explorer 1 was the first United States satellite to orbit Earth.

U.S. space program initiated

Plans to send the first American satellite into space were announced on July 29, 1955, when "the launching of small unmanned Earth-circling satellites" was approved by President Dwight D. Eisenhower. The launch was to be part of the United States contribution to the International Geophysical Year (IGY) in 1958. (The IGY was a worldwide project in which scientists from 67 nations worked together to study the composition of the Sun as well as phenomena of Earth, such as the Northern Lights and deep ocean currents.) The first satellite development program, the *Vanguard* project, was

Van Allen radiation belts

The existence of the Van Allen radiation belts was confirmed by detectors designed by James A. Van Allen and placed aboard *Explorer 1*. The two belts extend 400 to 40,000 miles above Earth in the magnetosphere, which is outside Earth's atmosphere; sometimes they are considered a single band of varying intensity. The belts consist of charged particles, or protons and electrons, that circulate along Earth's magnetic lines of force. These lines extend from above the equator to the North Pole, down to the South Pole, then back to the equator.

Scientists speculate that the charged particles are a result of solar flares, or sudden outbursts of temperature from small areas of the Sun's surface. The particles are carried by the solar wind into Earth's atmosphere, where they are trapped and cause such light spectacles as the Aurora Borealis at the North and South poles. The belts can also be hazardous when they dip into the atmosphere above the Atlantic Ocean to create a condition called the Atlantic Anomaly, which is dangerous to satellites that are orbiting Earth.

plagued by problems from the beginning. It would eventually be upstaged by both the Soviets and by another American satellite, *Explorer 1*.

Vanguard project developed

Project Vanguard was conducted by the U.S. Navy as a continuation of its earlier *Viking* program. Rather than work with an existing military rocket as the carrier vehicle for the new satellite, the United States decided to develop its small experimental weather rockets for the purpose. The decision to use these smaller rockets is hard to explain, but it was probably the result of political pressures rather than practical engineering issues.

Jupiter rocket rejected

The existing rocket, the Army's *Jupiter-C* rocket, was a promising possibility for use as a carrier vehicle. The *Jupiter* had been successfully fired on September 20, 1956, hurling a payload 3,400 miles across the Atlantic at a maximum altitude of 600 miles. Developed by famed German rocket scientist Wernher von Braun, *Jupiter* seemed to be the logical rocket to use; however, it was passed over.

Von Braun resented the decision not to use his rocket for the *Vanguard* project and continued experiments with his design at the Army Ballistic Missile Station in Huntsville, Alabama. Fearing he might conduct his own tests, the Defense Department warned von Braun not to use the *Jupiter* to launch any satellites.

Vanguard fails

Project *Vanguard* was officially inaugurated on September 9, 1955, soon after Eisenhower's speech. The final design of the *Vanguard* missile was approved in March 1956, and production began immediately. The first *Vanguard* was successfully launched from Cape Canaveral on October 23, 1957. It had a 4,000-pound payload and a 109-mile-high, 335-mile-long trajectory. Although this was an impressive start, it did not match the performance of the *Jupiter.*

The next two *Vanguards* produced were supposed to put an actual satellite into orbit; however, each of them exploded on launch, in December 1957 and February 1958, respectively. British newspapers nicknamed the flights "Kaputnik" and "Flopnik."

Vanguard TV-4 ("TV" stood for "test vehicle") succeeded in putting a 3.25-pound satellite (the smallest ever) into orbit on March 17, 1958, with two radio transmitters aboard. It was immediately named *Vanguard 1*. By then, however, it was too late to be a "first": *Sputnik 1,* the Soviet satellite, had been sent into orbit on October 14, 1957, five months earlier.

New program started

The U.S. government had been startled at being upstaged by the Soviets in the arena of space exploration. The Eisenhower administration told von Braun to ignore its recent orders and to design a satellite as quickly as possible. Fortunately, von Braun had the instrument design ready and waiting. He had developed a launch vehicle named *Juno 1,* a 4-stage rocket that was virtually indistinguishable from the 3-stage *Jupiter C.*

The secretary of the army said that once orders were received it would be possible to launch a satellite using the *Juno 1* in four months. A government commission endorsed this plan on October 25, 1957, and the secretary of defense gave the order on November 8. A few days later the target launch date was moved up to January 30, 1958, less than three months after the order to prepare the *Juno.*

Explorer 1 launched

Of the six *Juno* rockets that were then built on an unusually accelerated schedule, three launched satellites. The first was *Explorer 1,* launched on January 31, 1958—only one day later than the revised schedule. In orbit several weeks before *Vanguard 1, Explorer 1* was thus the first United States satellite. Eighty inches long and 6 inches in diameter, it weighed a mere 31 pounds; 18 pounds of its weight consisted of scientific instruments.

The first three satellites in the United States space program—*Explorer 1, Vanguard 1,* and *Explorer 2* (launched in March 1958)—were all much smaller than the *Sputniks*. However, they did have the advantage of containing carefully engineered miniaturized instruments that were able to gather large quantities of data. The most interesting information they recorded initially was that Earth is surrounded by a large zone of radiation called the Van Allen radiation belts. After 12 years in orbit, *Explorer 1* reentered Earth's atmosphere and disintegrated on March 31, 1970.

Edward John Eyre

Born August 5, 1815,
Yorkshire, England

Died November 30, 1901,
Near Tavistock, Devon, England

E dward John Eyre was born the son of a clergyman in Yorkshire, England. He immigrated to Australia at the age of 17, arriving in Sydney on March 20, 1833; he used the money he had brought to Australia to buy a sheep ranch. In 1834, after having problems with diseased sheep, he became a pioneer "overlander," a person who takes livestock overland from settled areas to the outback. Eyre made profitable trips moving animals from Sydney to Melbourne, from Melbourne to Adelaide, and from Sydney to Adelaide.

Edward Eyre was an English adventurer who was the first person to explore central Australia; he also made the first overland trip across Australia.

Makes important discoveries

In 1838 Eyre settled in Adelaide; still working as an overlander, he used the city as a base for exploring the interior. Embarking on his first trip in May 1839, he traveled north of Spencer Gulf, a large body of water on the south coast of Australia. There he discovered a mountain range that was later named Flinders Ranges and a large interior lake, eventually called Lake Terrens, which was usually dry. Later in the same year he went to the west side of Spencer Gulf and explored the Eyre Peninsula, which was named after him.

In January 1840, Eyre took a shipment of cattle from Albany on the south coast of western Australia to the Swan River on the west coast, near the site of the modern-day city of Perth. This trip inspired Eyre to form an ambitious scheme—to find an overland route where cattle could be driven from Adelaide to the west coast of Australia. Receiving financial support from the colonists in South Australia, he set out with a party of eight men from the head of Spencer Gulf in June 1840. At first he went north but could not find a way through the dried-up lake beds that make up this part of Australia. He did, however, go far enough to discover the largest of the lakes, which became known as Lake Eyre.

Makes dangerous desert crossing

From Lake Eyre the party headed due west, reaching a place called Streaky Bay on the west side of the Eyre Peninsula in November 1840. Ahead of them stretched an enormous desert, the Nullarbor Plain. "Nullarbor," which means "no trees," aptly describes the situation Eyre would encounter after he foolishly decided to cross the desert by a series of forced marches. To carry out his plan he sent back all of the members of the exploring party except his assistant, John Baxter, and three Aborigines. Eyre wrote in his journal that he was determined "either to accomplish the object I have in view, or perish in the attempt."

Throughout the trip Eyre and his companions were plagued by a scarcity of water and blowing sand that slowed them down. On March 12, 1841, they passed the last water hole at a place that is now called Eucla on the border of Western and South Australia. The only reason they survived was that the Aborigines knew how to get water out of the roots of trees from wells dug in the sand. By the middle of April they were short of food; to make matters worse, the southern winter was starting and the nights were turning very cold. No longer willing to endure the hardship, two of the Aborigines killed Baxter and left with the remaining provisions.

Completes journey across Australia

Although Eyre's only remaining companion was an Aborigine boy named Wylie, he decided to press on. His decision was fortunately rewarded by a rainfall that relieved their parched thirst. Since he and Wylie had no food, however, he had to kill one of his two horses so they would not starve. On June 2, they reached Esperance Bay on the south coast of Western Australia, where they met a French whaling ship at anchor. After resting on the boat for several days, Eyre insisted on completing the journey overland, finally reaching Albany in July 1841.

Eyre and Wylie had made the first trip across Australia. Yet instead of finding a way to drive livestock overland, Eyre had proved just the opposite—there was no practical way of doing so. On his return to Adelaide, Eyre was appointed magistrate for a large unsettled part of the colony of South Australia; he also wrote a history of his explorations.

Holds colonial government positions

After Eyre returned to England in 1844 he was appointed to a number of positions in the colonies: in 1846 he was named lieutenant governor of New Zealand; in 1854, lieutenant governor of St. Vincent in the West Indies; and in 1860, governor of the Leeward Islands in the Caribbean. In 1862 he received his most important post as governor of Jamaica, one of the "jewels in the crown" of Great Britain's empire. This was to be a temporary assignment during the absence of Jamaica's regular governor, William Darling.

Suppresses uprising

In October 1865, during Eyre's tenure as governor in Jamaica, a rebellion by the black native majority broke out in Morant Bay. Eyre used harsh measures to suppress the revolt, executing more than 400 people, flogging and torturing even more, and burning 1,000 houses. Among the protesters who were court-martialed and hanged was Eyre's political enemy, George Gordon, a member of the local legislature. Eyre declared martial law and suspended Jamaica's constitution. When news of his conduct was reported in England, a heated debate erupted: was he a hero who had saved Jamaica for the Crown, or was he not only incompetent but a murderer as well?

Censured and recalled

In 1866 Eyre was censured and recalled to England. Important literary figures such as Thomas Carlyle and Alfred Tennyson supported him, while others, such as Herbert Spencer and John Stuart Mill, demanded that he be tried for murder. After a series of attempts to bring Eyre to trial, a grand jury did not return an indictment against him. In 1868, citing "unnecessary rigour" as Eyre's principal wrongdoing, a royal commission cleared him of charges in connection with the incident. His legal fees were eventually paid by the government and he was awarded a small pension; he was not asked to serve again in any official capacity. Eyre retired to a country manor in Devon, England, where he lived until his death on November 30, 1901.

Matthew Flinders

Born March 16, 1774,
Lincolnshire, England
Died July 19, 1814,
England

Matthew Flinders was inspired to go to sea as a young boy when he read *Robinson Crusoe*, Daniel Defoe's classic novel about the adventures of a shipwrecked sailor. His real-life career as a navigator and chart-maker turned out to be just as dramatic as any novel: he was shipwrecked, taken prisoner, and survived a 700-mile voyage in a small boat across an open sea. Flinders served under some of the great heroes of English sea lore before charting the south coast of Australia, sailing around the continent of Australia, and proving that Tasmania was an island.

Joins navy at age 15

Flinders was born on March 16, 1774, in Lincolnshire, England. After entering the navy at the age of 15 he served as midshipman on a ship commanded by Captain William Bligh that sailed to Tahiti; he also fought with Admiral Horatio Nelson's forces against the French. He was then sent to the colony of New South Wales in Australia.

Matthew Flinders, an English navigator, was the first person to sail around Australia; he also established that Tasmania is an island and was the first to chart the southern coast of Australia.

In 1795 he served as a junior officer aboard the *Reliance,* where he befriended George Bass, the ship's surgeon. Both men were amateur exploring enthusiasts, so when they sailed into Sydney harbor they decided to explore the dangerous coast of Australia. For this purpose they bought an 8-foot boat they named the *Tom Thumb.* Soon after their arrival in Sydney they ventured south to Botany Bay and rowed up the Georges River. When the *Reliance* made a brief excursion to Norfolk Island in 1796, the two British officers made another trip south. This time they explored Lake Illiwarra, a large lagoon on the coast south of Sydney where the city of Wollongong is now located.

Confirms Tasmania is an island

In 1798 Flinders was promoted to the rank of lieutenant. During February of that year, when he was entrusted with the task of rescuing some stranded sailors, he explored the Furneaux Islands north of Tasmania and made a second trip to Norfolk Island. In the meantime his friend Bass had traveled south to Tasmania and had come back with the theory that it was an island, not a part of the mainland. Flinders and Bass confirmed the theory when they traveled south on a boat called the *Norfolk* from October 7, 1798, to January 12, 1799. They sailed westward through the strait that separates Tasmania from the mainland and then went completely around Tasmania in a counterclockwise direction. The strait was named Bass Strait, marking the surgeon's last exploring trip. Following their return, Flinders made a trip north to what is now Queensland.

Explores southern coast of Australia

In March 1800, Flinders returned to England on the *Reliance.* While he was there he wrote an account of his explorations with Bass. He also married a young woman from his native Lincolnshire and requested permission to take her back with him to Australia; permission was denied. On the recommendations of **Joseph Banks** (see entry), the famous naturalist and president of the Royal Society, Flinders was given a new assignment: the task of surveying the southern coast of Australia. He would not see his wife again for nine years.

On July 18, 1801, Flinders left England as captain of the 334-ton sloop the *Investigator*. Accompanying him was **John Franklin,** his nephew by marriage, who would later head major expeditions to the Canadian Arctic. They first sighted land at Cape Leeuwin in extreme southwestern Australia on December 6, 1801. The *Investigator* then sailed to King George Sound, which had been discovered by **George Vancouver** (see separate entries) and was the site of the town of Albany. Following the coast of the Great Australian Bight, a bay on the Indian Ocean, Flinders sailed eastward. On February 20, 1802, he reached Spencer Gulf, a large indentation in the south coast that extends far into the interior of Australia. This was an important discovery because no one had any idea what the interior was like, and Flinders thought it possible that this great bay might cut all the way into the middle of the continent or even divide it into separate islands.

Seeks passageway into interior

The possibility of finding a passageway into the interior of Australia was an exciting one. Flinders noted in his journal that he had the "prospect of making an interesting discovery." However, he was quickly disappointed: the gulf rapidly narrows and stretches only 200 miles or so into what is now the state of South Australia. As was Flinders's practice as he proceeded along the coast, he named the main geographical features after Royal Navy colleagues and supporters and he chose place-names from his home in Lincolnshire.

When Flinders reached the upper end of Spencer Gulf he took the ship's boat to explore the shoreline. Accompanying him were William Westall, a landscape draftsman; Ferdinand Bauer, a painter of plant and animal specimens; and Robert Brown, a biologist who would collect specimens of nearly 4,000 species during the course of the expedition. The party went ashore north of the modern town of Port Augusta; during their explorations they climbed to the top of Mount Brown in the Flinders Ranges.

Discovers Kangaroo Island

Sailing south out of Spencer Gulf, Flinders sighted a large island across the Investigator Strait. While the island had no human inhabitants, it supported a large population of whales, seals, and kangaroos; in fact it would later become the center of Australia's fisheries industry. Flinders's party was able to hunt enough kangaroos to furnish meat for the expedition for four months. In honor of their food supply Flinders named the island Kangaroo Island. The party then sailed into Gulf St. Vincent, where the city of Adelaide is now located; once again Flinders was not able to find a route to the interior.

On April 8, Flinders sighted the sails of a ship that belonged to a rival French expedition commanded by Nicolas Baudin. Carrying out a mission similar to Flinders's, Baudin had been working his way westward along the south coast. Despite the tensions between England and France, Flinders and Baudin had a friendly breakfast meeting. Flinders named the spot where they met Encounter Bay. The two expeditions then continued on their separate ways: Flinders to Sydney and Baudin to Kangaroo Island and then west to Spencer Gulf.

Circumnavigates Australia

On April 16, 1802, Flinders reached the site of modern-day Melbourne, which had actually been seen by another British captain some ten weeks earlier. He entered Sydney Harbor on May 9. Remarkably for that era, no one on board was sick with scurvy when they arrived. Flinders stayed in Sydney for a while before setting out again on the *Investigator* on July 22, 1802. He hoped to complete James Cook's nautical chart of the east coast of Australia. Unlike Cook, Flinders was able to find a passage through the Great Barrier Reef at the northern end of the coast, and he sailed through the Torres Strait between Australia and New Guinea to the Gulf of Carpentaria.

At this point the *Investigator* was leaking badly, and it turned out that many of the timbers were rotten. Since the ship could not fight its way back against the wind down the east coast, Flinders decided to travel west all the way around Australia. This last-minute detour proved to have historic results: when Flinders returned to Sydney on June 9, 1803, he became the first person to circumnavigate Australia.

The *Investigator* was beyond repair, so Flinders set sail as a passenger on the *Porpoise,* a captured Spanish vessel. Flinders had a greenhouse erected on the ship deck to hold his plant collection, which was being sent to the Royal Botanical Gardens at Kew, England. Seven days out of Sydney, the *Porpoise* hit a reef and sank. Flinders undertook a task that proved his navigational skills: he piloted the ship's small boat back to Sydney through 700 miles of open sea.

Taken prisoner by France

Flinders started out once again for England on a small ship, the *Cumberland.* When the ship began to leak in the Indian Ocean he was forced to land on the French island of Mauritius on December 17, 1803. Since hostilities between France and Great Britain had resulted in war, Flinders was taken prisoner. The French governor refused to recognize the authority of Flinders's letter of protection from the French emperor on the grounds that it applied only to the *Investigator.* In spite of efforts in England and orders from Paris, the governor held Flinders for six and a half years.

Health ruined during captivity

During his captivity Flinders worked on the journals of his expedition. Finally, just before Mauritius was captured by the British, he was released on June 14, 1810. When he reached England on October 23, 1810, his health was ruined. Flinders lived only long enough to see the account of his voyage published: *Voyage to Terra Australis* was issued on July 18, 1814; he died the following day at 40 years of age.

John Franklin

Born April 16, 1786,
Spilsby, Lincolnshire, England

Died June 11, 1847,
Near King William Island, British Arctic Islands

Sir John Franklin was a British naval officer put in charge of three expeditions to the Canadian Arctic, the first two of which were overland; he disappeared on the third.

Sir John Franklin's interest in geography and exploration began when as a teenager he went on a voyage to Australia with his uncle, the explorer **Matthew Flinders** (see entry). Franklin would later command three expeditions to the Arctic in search of the Northwest Passage. England honored him with a knighthood, but he also knew disgrace when he was relieved of the governorship of Tasmania. He died after his party became stranded in the Arctic during his third expedition.

Joins navy at early age

John Franklin was born in the village of Spilsby in Lincolnshire, England. At the age of 14 he entered the Royal Navy as a volunteer and fought in the Battle of Copenhagen during the Napoleonic Wars. Shortly thereafter, in 1801, he accompanied Matthew Flinders, who was his uncle by marriage, on an expedition aboard the *Investigator* to chart the

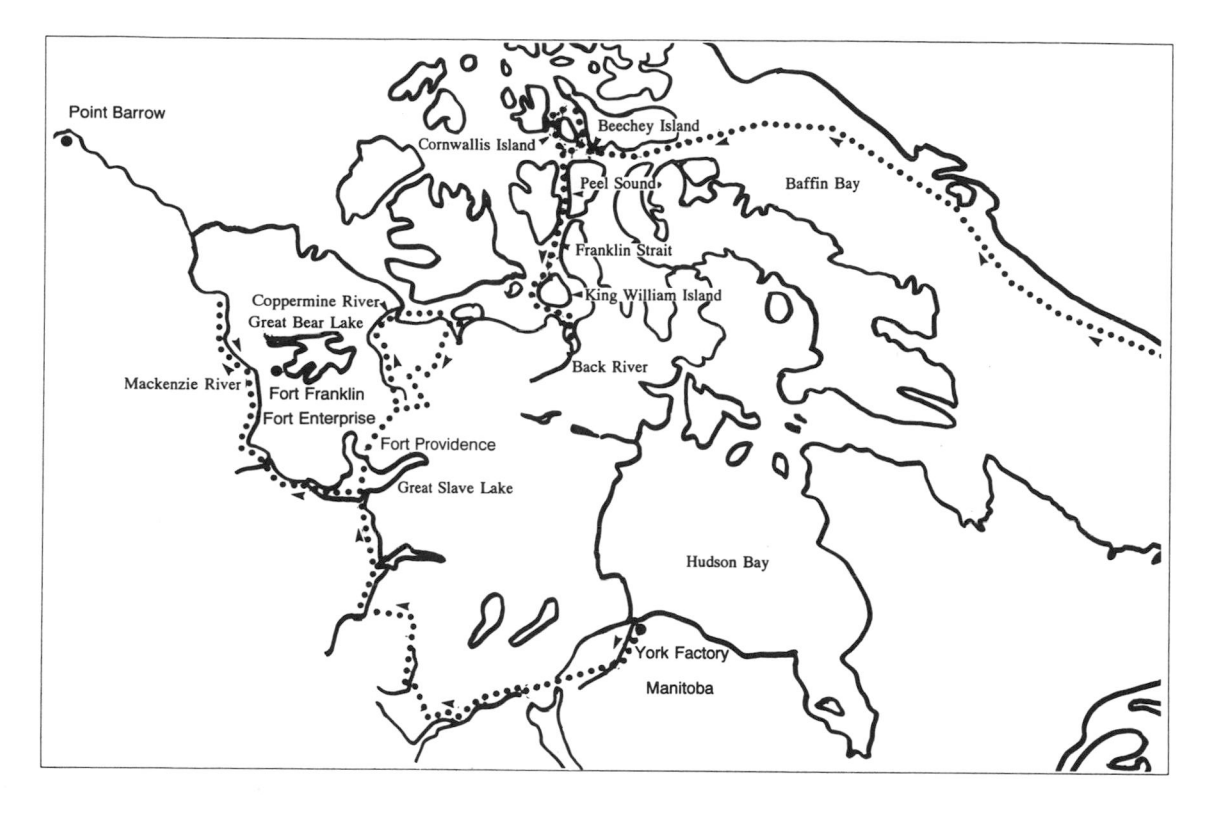

southern coast of Australia. When Franklin returned to England in 1804, he was reassigned to naval duty; he saw naval action in the Battle of Trafalgar and sailed off the coast of South America and in the North Sea. He was promoted to lieutenant in 1808 and then participated in the attack on New Orleans during the War of 1812 between Britain and the United States. At the end of the Napoleonic Wars Franklin was put on half-pay and waited for new assignments.

Franklin headed three important missions to the Canadian Arctic, in 1819-22, 1825-27, and 1845-47.

Leads Arctic expeditions

In 1818 Franklin was appointed second-in-command to Captain David Buchan on an expedition to the Arctic Ocean to try to find a passage from Spitsbergen, an area to the north of Norway, to northern Canada. Confirming the fact that no such passage exists, the expedition could not travel beyond Spitsbergen, where it was locked in ice for three weeks before returning to England.

Franklin was placed in command of the next venture, an overland expedition to explore the north coast of Canada from the Coppermine River to Hudson Bay. The party, which included Franklin, two midshipmen, two sailors, and a naturalist, left England on May 23, 1819, aboard a Hudson's Bay Company ship. They landed at York Factory in what is now Manitoba and traveled across with various fur-trading parties to the northwest. Entering unknown territory north of the Great Slave Lake in the summer of 1820, they built a base camp at Fort Enterprise on Winter Lake at the mouth of the Coppermine River.

Encounters hardship

On July 14, 1821, the explorers set out for the north coast with a party of trappers. Since the aid they had hoped the trappers would supply was inadequate, they were able to move only a short distance along the coast before winter set in and they were forced to return to Fort Enterprise. On the grueling return trip half of the trappers died of starvation and a British officer was killed by another trapper. The party had survived these hardships only to find, when they reached Fort Enterprise, that Native Americans had raided the fort and taken all of its supplies. One of the midshipmen, George Back, who would later become an important Arctic explorer in his own right, was able to keep everyone alive during the remainder of the expedition by bartering food from a friendly party of Native Americans. They stayed one more winter before returning to England.

Sets out for the north again

Although the expedition had been only moderately successful, Franklin was given a hero's welcome upon his return to England in 1822 and promoted to the rank of captain. Elected a member of the prestigious Royal Society, he soon began planning his next expedition. He also wrote an account of his adventures, which was published in 1823. He challenged the Canadian north again on February 16, 1825, this time traveling with his own team of canoeists and porters. His goal was to go beyond the delta of the Mackenzie River, which was explored by **Alexander Mackenzie** (see entry) in 1789.

Franklin's party descended the Mackenzie River until they reached the delta on June 22, 1826. They then split into two teams to explore the Arctic shoreline: two men headed east to the mouth of the Coppermine River and Franklin and Back started west to Port Barrow in Alaska. Franklin and Back completed only half of their journey; they were forced to turn back at Return Reef. Traveling to the mouth of the Coppermine River, they journeyed down the river to the western shore of Great Bear Lake, where they built Fort Franklin as a supply base. Three months later, in September 1827, Franklin and his party returned to England, this time without any loss of life.

Becomes governor of Tasmania

The next 16 years were a time of dramatic change for Franklin. He acquired a large public following and was made a knight in April 1828. Popularly dubbed "the Polar Knight," Franklin became a darling of English society. That same year he wrote an account of his Arctic experiences and he also remarried. His first wife having died after only two years of marriage, he married Jane Griffin in November 1828.

After Franklin was made governor of the island of Tasmania, off the coast of Australia in the South Pacific, Lady Jane became increasingly influential in his career. Arriving in Tasmania in January 1837, they ran into immediate trouble by showing an interest in the welfare of the island's convicts and the original inhabitants of Australia, the Aborigines. Franklin has been described as a kind and gentle soul, who in his career as a naval officer could not bear to watch the flogging of a disobedient seaman. Throughout the six years of his tenure he encountered increasing conflicts with the colonists and the Colonial Office. Unfairly blamed for an economic depression and victimized by a campaign of unfounded rumors, Franklin was censured and recalled in 1843.

Becomes an explorer again

Franklin turned to exploration as a way to clear his name. The admiralty put him in charge of an expedition to find the Northwest Passage. Even though he was now 58 years old, he approached the idea enthusiastically. The expedition sailed from London on May 19, 1845, provisioned for three years. It consisted of two ships, the *Erebus* and the *Terror,* and a party of 129 men. The expedition was last seen at the end of July 1845 by whalers in northern Baffin Bay.

Expedition is lost

It was only in 1848 that the admiralty began to worry about Franklin's fate. Urged on by Lady Jane Franklin, it sent out the first expedition to search for him in May 1848 under the command of Sir James Clark Ross. Several other expeditions followed, including those commanded by Horatio Austin, Sir John Ross, Richard Collinson, Sir **Robert McClure** (see entry), and Sir Edward Belcher. In April 1854, Dr. John Rae got the first news of Franklin's party from an Inuit he encountered while exploring the Boothia Peninsula. The remains of Franklin's expedition were finally found in 1859 by Francis McClintock in a private search sponsored by Franklin's widow.

Records found

Notes of the expedition that were found by McClintock provide a general picture of where Franklin went: he wintered at Beechey Island in 1845-46, then sailed around Cornwallis Island and through Peel Sound and Franklin Strait northwest of King William Island. The expedition wintered there in 1846-47; Franklin died of starvation in June 1847, ironically within sight of the Northwest Passage. Totally iced in, the rest of the party headed down the south coast on foot, trying to reach the mainland and the Back River, which they could use to travel south to Hudson Bay. With any luck, they would find trappers and traders along the way. All of the survivors of Franklin's expedition died during this overland march.

It had taken 11 years to solve the mystery of the fate of the expedition. Although Franklin died tragically, his name was cleared and he has become a legendary Arctic hero.

John Charles Frémont

Born January 21, 1813,
Savannah, Georgia

Died July 13, 1890,
New York, New York

John Charles Frémont, an American surveyor, was known as The Pathfinder for opening up large areas of the American West for exploration.

John Charles Frémont was an explorer, soldier, politician, and businessman whose talents were uniquely suited to his time, at least at the beginning of his career. He came of age when it was believed the United States was destined to occupy all of North America, and he is largely credited with opening the Far West to American settlement. A man of adventure, he helped to explore, survey, and map vast areas of the frontier. As a result of his father-in-law's political influence, Frémont's reports were widely publicized, firing the imagination of Americans eager to move westward. Known as "The Pathfinder" because he charted the best route to Oregon, Frémont experienced both success and failure during his lifetime. Some of his questionable decisions have made him a controversial figure in American history.

Frémont was the illegitimate son of an aristocratic Virginian named Anne Pryor—who had been childless and trapped for years in a loveless marriage—and her lover, a destitute French emigrant. When Pryor's husband learned of the affair, he was outraged; Pryor and her lover fled to Savannah, Georgia, where John was born on January 21, 1813. Frémont's father never became financially secure, so the family drifted from town to town. Only five years old when his father died, Frémont was raised by his mother in Charleston, South Carolina.

Career as a surveyor

In 1829 Frémont entered the College of Charleston, where he showed an aptitude for mathematics, but he did not graduate, possibly because of a romantic scandal. He then became an instructor of mathematics on a U.S. Navy ship while it traveled around South America. In the summer of 1836 he worked with a team that surveyed a proposed railway route between Charleston and Cincinnati, Ohio. Frémont liked this work so much he decided upon mapmaking and surveying as a career.

Commissioned in 1838 as a second lieutenant in the U.S. Army's Topographical Corps, Frémont joined the agency charged with surveying all the unmapped regions of the United States. He was soon assigned to assist a respected French scientist-explorer, Jean Nicholas Nicollet, in a mission to map the region between the upper Mississippi and Missouri rivers. Frémont was in his element; he loved the hardship and rugged beauty of the wilderness.

Upon his return Frémont found himself a frequent guest at the home of Senator Thomas Hart Benton of Missouri. He married Senator Benton's daughter, Jessie, on October 19, 1841. The Benton family was initially opposed to the marriage, but the senator soon became Frémont's most important sponsor. Intelligent and ambitious, as well as a talented writer, Jessie became invaluable to Frémont by helping him write the colorful reports that would make him a national hero. She also worked on his memoirs with him; in financially troubled times she even supported their family by submitting articles and sketches to periodicals.

Leader of expeditions to the West

In 1842 Frémont led his first expedition. His party surveyed a route settlers were using in their trek to Oregon, which extended from the Mississippi River to South Pass, Wyoming. Frémont used the famous mountain man Kit Carson as a guide. The two became friends, and Carson accompanied Frémont on many of his expeditions. Frémont also climbed Fremont Peak in the Wind River Range of Wyoming. His enthusiastic report on the mapping of the trail inspired more pioneers to try the journey west.

Frémont's next expedition, in 1843, had been ordered to push beyond South Pass, Wyoming, to Oregon. His party was heavily armed, carrying with them an unauthorized 12-pound cannon to use against unfriendly Native Americans. The cannon incident was the first of many conflicts Frémont was to have with the army. During this trip he surveyed the northern shores of the Great Salt Lake, and his report on the survey encouraged the Mormons under Brigham Young to settle there four years later. On this expedition Frémont also traveled north to the Snake River and then to the Columbia River, which he followed to its mouth on the Pacific at Fort Vancouver. Although he had been instructed to return by the Oregon Trail, Frémont could not resist the lure of California, which Kit Carson had described to him in vivid detail.

Role in "Bear Flag Revolt"

Warned by Native Americans that the Sierra Nevada were impassable in winter, Frémont decided to cross the mountains anyway with the help of a Native American guide. It was a treacherous trip. Suffering from cold and starvation, the party finally arrived at Sutter's Fort in California in March 1844. They obtained fresh supplies and then traveled east by way of the San Joaquin Valley, the old Spanish Trail, Muddy Pass, and the Arkansas River. After a delay of several months, their return to St. Louis caused a sensation. The expedition had been difficult and dangerous, but Frémont's reports fueled the expansionist ambitions of many powerful groups that were pushing for Mexico to cede California to the United States.

In 1845 Frémont was sent west again, leading a party of 60 men. This time the route was fairly direct. They crossed the Rocky Mountains, surveyed the southern end of the Great Salt Lake, and continued across the desert to Sutter's Fort. The Mexican government, suspicious of such a large group of armed Americans, ordered Frémont to leave. Frémont retreated to Oregon, where he received secret orders from Washington. No one has ever known the nature of those orders, but when Frémont returned to California in June 1846, he led a group of American settlers in what is called the "Bear Flag Revolt." When war was declared between Mexico and the United States on July 19, Frémont renamed his expedition the California Battalion and marched to Monterey. The war was quickly won by the United States.

Frémont's commander, Commodore Robert F. Stockton, was abruptly replaced by an old enemy of Frémont's, General Stephen W. Kearny. Stockton had made Frémont a lieutenant colonel and appointed him governor of California. When Frémont defied General Kearny's orders to give up his post, he was accused of disobedience and mutiny. Furious about being convicted and court-martialed, he resigned his commission in 1848.

Wealth and power

After leaving the army Frémont secured private backing and, in 1848, made another trip to survey a possible railroad route in which he and Senator Benton shared an interest. Unwisely, Frémont tried to lead his expedition across the Sangre de Cristo Mountains in Colorado in mid-December. The trip was a disaster; 11 men died, and Frémont was forced to retreat. Heading south, he finally arrived at Sutter's Fort to find that gold had been discovered. Since Frémont owned land in one of the goldfields at the foot of the Sierra Nevada, he suddenly found himself a rich man. With wealth came power, and in 1850 California elected him to the U.S. Senate.

In 1853 he led another private expedition in search of a southern railway route to the Pacific Ocean. By 1856 his exploits had made him a national hero, and he ran for president against James Buchanan as the first candidate of the newly formed Republican party. After his defeat he returned to California, making heavy investments in unprofitable mills and mining equipment.

Civil War commander

When the Civil War broke out in 1861, Frémont was made commander of the Department of the West. His ardent antislavery views brought him into conflict with authority once again. He arbitrarily declared martial law and issued an order freeing the slaves in Missouri. These actions were premature and embarrassing to President Abraham Lincoln, who relieved Frémont of his command.

He was given another command in Kentucky but found an able adversary in the southern general Thomas "Stonewall" Jackson. Frémont made several tactical errors, and Lincoln began to have second thoughts about Frémont's abilities. When the area was consolidated under another commander, a bitter Frémont again resigned from the army.

Unhappy final years

After the Civil War Frémont lost his remaining fortune in failed railroad-building projects. Turning cynical, he engaged in dishonest business deals. In 1878 Frémont was made governor of the Arizona Territory, a post he saw as an opportunity to revive his fortune. He consequently paid more attention to his business interests than to governing. He was asked to resign after serving five years because he used state money for personal expenses.

Frémont spent the last years of his life in New York, Washington, D.C., and Los Angeles. Jessie, who had always supported him and, it was rumored, even managed his military career, continued her writing. She was their only source of income. Just before his death on July 13, 1890, Frémont was awarded a pension by Congress. Although Frémont died a broken man, his reputation in shreds, he will always be remembered for his courage and determination in opening up the American West for settlement.

Vivian Fuchs

Born 1908,
Kent, England

Vivian Fuchs was born in the English county of Kent, the son of a farmer of German origin. He was educated at Cambridge University, where he studied geology. Between the years 1929 and 1938 he went on four geological expeditions to East Africa. During World War II he was a major in the British army and served in West Africa and Germany and received several medals for bravery.

Sir Vivian Fuchs led the British expedition that was the first to cross Antarctica from coast to coast.

Makes plan while stranded

After the war, in 1947, Fuchs was put in charge of the Falkland Islands Dependencies Survey. The Dependencies were a group of islands near Antarctica, and included Britain's claim to part of the mainland of Antarctica. After setting up scientific bases on the Graham Peninsula, Fuchs was marooned in one of them for a year when his supply ship could not land because of weather conditions. During that time he conceived of a plan to fulfill the dream of **Ernest Shackleton** (see entry), the British explorer who had attempted to cross Antarctica from coast to coast.

Takes part in International Geophysical Year

Fuchs's plan was carried out by the British Commonwealth Trans-Antarctic expedition as part of the activities of the International Geophysical Year in 1957-58. The plan involved two parties: led by Fuchs, one party left Shackleton Base on the Filchner Ice Shelf on November 24, 1957; in the meantime, a New Zealand team headed by **Edmund Hillary** (see entry) was establishing food and fuel supply bases starting from McMurdo Sound on the other side of the continent.

Fuchs made slow progress in very bad conditions, with his heavy new Sno-Cat and Weasel vehicles frequently getting stuck in the snow. The British party crossed a very dangerous region of crevasses at the place where the ice-shelf joined the Antarctic continent. Dog teams had to be sent ahead to find a safe route for the tractors, which were always in danger of falling into one of the crevasses. Furthermore, Fuchs's party was engaged in making seismic and gravity soundings all along their route, in order to determine the nature of the land underneath the Antarctic ice cap. This work was extremely slow but it was also extremely valuable: for example, it showed that the ice reached depths of 9,000 feet and that there was a great valley at the South Pole. Establishing this information had been one of the main goals of the International Geophysical Year.

Reaches South Pole

While Fuchs was engaged in this work, Hillary's team

made much faster progress. Originally, the New Zealand team had intended to go only as far as a place called Depot 700, which was 500 miles from the Pole, but Hillary continued on and reached the South Pole on January 3, 1958. He had made such good progress that he saw the possibility of completing the crossing himself. Early in January 1958, he radioed to London headquarters and to Fuchs that Fuchs should turn back in the face of the coming winter. Fuchs refused, however, and continued on to the South Pole, which he reached on January 19, 1958. He was greeted enthusiastically by Hillary and the Americans stationed at the Amundsen-Scott Base.

Honored for achievement

As winter approached, Fuchs and Hillary continued on their very difficult trek from the South Pole. They reached McMurdo Sound on March 2, 1958. It had taken Fuchs 90 days to cover the 2,180 miles from one side of Antarctica to the other. When they reached Scott Base in Victoria Land, Fuchs received word that he had been knighted as a result of his accomplishment. He and Hillary collaborated on writing the story of the expedition in *The Crossing of Antarctica,* which was published in 1958. That same year Fuchs was appointed director of the British Antarctic Survey; in 1959 he received the Hubbard Medal from the National Geographic Society. Fuchs retired from his position with the Antarctic Society in 1977.

Yury Gagarin

*Born March 9, 1934,
Klushino, Russia*

*Died March 27, 1968,
Near Moscow, Russia*

Yury Gagarin was a Soviet cosmonaut who was the first human to travel in space, making one complete orbit of Earth on April 12, 1961.

Yury Alekseyevich Gagarin's successful orbit of Earth was a technical triumph for the Soviet Union that came at the height of the Soviet-American rivalry for dominance in space exploration. His flight is also considered to have inaugurated modern space exploration. Although Gagarin never participated in another space venture, he became a goodwill ambassador and a leader in Russia's cosmonaut training program. His career was cut short when he died in a training mission in 1968.

Gagarin was born on March 9, 1934, in the village of Klushino near the town of Gzhatsk, where his mother and father worked on a collective farm. Gagarin was forced to quit school in 1941 when the Germans invaded the Soviet Union during World War II. For a while the Gagarins lived in a dugout shelter because their home was occupied by Germans. When the Germans retreated, they took two of Gagarin's sisters with them as forced laborers. The sisters were able to return after the war.

Trains as aviator

When he finished school in Gzhatsk, Gagarin moved to a suburb of Moscow where he worked in a steel factory and apprenticed as a foundryman. After a year, however, he was accepted into a technical college in the Russian town of Saratov on the Volga River. During his fourth year in college Gagarin enrolled in aviation courses at a nearby flying school, taking his first ride in an airplane and making a parachute jump. In 1955 he graduated from college with honors and also earned his ground school diploma from the flying school. During the summer of that year, he went to an aviation camp where he learned how to fly.

Gagarin was then accepted for training at the Orenburg Pilot Training School and graduated two years later. He met his future wife, Valentina, in Orenburg. He joined the Soviet Air Force and volunteered for a difficult assignment in the Russian Arctic while Valentina finished her nurse's training in Moscow. They were married in 1957 and had their first child, a daughter, in 1958.

Enters experimental cosmonaut program

After passing a series of tests, Gagarin was secretly accepted into the cosmonaut training school. He had joined the Communist Party in the summer of 1958. Around the time when the Gagarins's second daughter was born, in March 1961, Gagarin revealed to his wife that he had not only been training to go into space, but he had also been selected to become the first man in space.

The Soviets had been preparing for the first manned spaceflight since May 1960, when they launched a series of *Vostok* test rockets. The tests were initially unsuccessful: the first rocket had not been able to return to Earth and the second exploded in midair. The third rocket successfully launched and retrieved two dogs in space; in December 1960, however, two rockets crashed with dogs on board. The program was then shut down for three months while the rockets were redesigned. *Sputnik 9* was launched on March 9, 1961, and *Sputnik 10* on

March 25. Since both launches were successful the decision was made to go ahead with the manned flight.

Prepares for flight

The final assembly of the *Vostok* (East), the rocket to be used in the manned flight, took place at the Soviet space center of Tyuratam in the Republic of Kazakhstan. As part of a plan to keep the preparations secret, the Soviets always referred to it as the Baikonur Space Center; Tyuratam is actually located 200 miles southwest of Baikonur on a spur of the main railroad line between Moscow and Tashkent. Gagarin was scheduled to be the first cosmonaut to enter space on April 8; Gherman Titov was to be his backup. On April 10 at 4 P.M. the Soviet State Commission on Space approved the final plans for launch. At 5 A.M. on April 11 the rocket was towed to the launch pad.

At 1 P.M. on April 11, 1961, Gagarin was driven to the launch pad, accompanied by Sergei Korolov, the chief architect of the Soviet space program. Gagarin was presented to the assembly workers, and he and Korolov spent an hour going through the final checks and procedures. The next morning, Gagarin and Titov were awakened at 5:30 A.M.; sensors were attached to their bodies to monitor pulse, blood pressure, and other functions. Before boarding the *Vostok,* at 7:30 A.M., Gagarin made a brief speech: "Am I happy, setting out on this space flight? Of course I am. In all times and epochs the greatest happiness for man has been to take part in new discoveries."

Takes off into space

After Gagarin had entered the *Vostok,* he had to wait an hour and a half for the final countdown. He would have no control over the spacecraft himself; all procedures would be performed by the ground control crew. If there was a malfunction, a secret code would allow him to operate the controls manually. Gagarin took off at 9:07 A.M. on April 12, 1961. His first recorded word was "Poyekhali!"—"Let's go!" Nine minutes into the flight, the *Vostok* reached maximum pressure at 6 g's, which is six times the weight of gravity. The flight was officially announced on Radio Moscow at 10:00 A.M.

Orbits Earth

During the flight Gagarin went in an orbit that took him across Siberia and over Japan, then southeast to the tip of South America and northeast across West Africa. As the *Vostok* passed over various countries, he radioed greetings from the Soviet people. Gagarin described his flight: "I saw for the first time the spherical shape of the Earth. You can see its curvature when looking into the horizon. It is unique and beautiful." He was the first human to see the roundness of Earth. The age of space exploration had been launched.

Gagarin made one complete orbit of Earth during a flight that lasted 108 minutes and reached an altitude of 327 kilometers. While in orbit, he experienced weightlessness; he also ate and drank in order to test man's ability to perform these acts in space. At 10:25 A.M., the *Vostok* passed over West Africa; retrorockets fired Gagarin back into Earth's atmosphere. He lost radio contact with Earth for a while and his body was subjected to 8 to 10 g's of force. At an altitude of 8,000 meters, the hatch on the *Vostok* blew off and Gagarin fired from his ejector seat. As the parachutes unfolded he drifted down into a potato field near the village of Smelovka not far from the city of Saratov. The first person Gagarin saw as he landed was a woman planting potatoes with her six-year-old daughter. "I must report my return to earth!" he yelled to her.

Honored for achievement

After the safe landing Gagarin was taken to the nearest airstrip where Titov arrived in a plane to greet him. He was then flown to a villa on the Volga to rest and celebrate. On April 14 he was summoned to Moscow where he was greeted by Nikita Khrushchev, leader of the Soviet Union, and an enormous crowd. Gagarin was named a Hero of the Soviet Union and awarded the Order of Lenin; he was also made Pilot Cosmonaut of the Soviet Union. His arrival was broadcast live throughout the world, another engineering first. Gagarin's parents came from their village to greet him, his mother wearing her best shawl and he father a carpenter's cap. Throughout the republic monuments were raised and streets and towns were renamed in his honor.

Heads cosmonaut team

Although Gagarin never had an opportunity to go into space again, he traveled triumphantly all over the world representing the Soviet Union. After his travels he was named commander of the cosmonaut training team in 1963 and elected to the Supreme Soviet. He trained as a backup for *Soyuz I,* which was launched on April 23, 1967. When the cosmonaut who actually flew in *Soyuz I* was killed during reentry, there were rumors that Gagarin had been chosen for the first Soviet landing on the Moon.

Memorialized as space hero

The truth of the rumors was never to be tested. On March 17, 1968, Gagarin and another pilot were killed on a routine jet training flight about 30 miles east of Moscow. Shocked at Gagarin's sudden and unexpected death, the Soviet Union gave him a state funeral. The town of Gzhatsk, where he went to school as a child, was renamed Gagarin. The cosmonaut training center was also renamed in his honor, and his office at the center remains exactly as he left it.

Aelius Gallus

Lived first century B.C.

During the period of classical Greece and the Roman Republic, nothing was known about Arabia other than the trading centers on the northern edges. The Greeks and Romans knew there were caravan routes that went from Aqaba at the head of the Red Sea to southern Arabia and from the Euphrates to the Hadhramaut, in the area that is now Yemen. It was known that there was a central desert, but there was no knowledge of the great inland plateau.

Leads expedition to Arabia

The expedition of Aelius Gallus sent out by Emperor Augustus of Rome was therefore important, not so much for what it accomplished but because it represented a systematic effort to gather information about a part of the world about which there was only scant information. Gallus was the Roman governor of Egypt. He was put in charge of a military expedition of 10,000 troops that was supposed to travel to the

Aelius Gallus was a Roman soldier who led an expedition to southern Arabia.

land of the Himyarites, the pre–Arab inhabitants of southern Arabia. Our knowledge of the expedition comes from the writings of the Roman historian Strabo.

Gallus's army consisted of Egyptian troops, Jews, and Nabataean allies of the Romans who came from the trading city of Petra. The force was assembled around 25 B.C. at Cleopatris in the Gulf of Suez and then sailed down the Gulf of Suez and the northern part of the Red Sea to the port of El Haura in northern Arabia (or Leuke Kome as it was known in classical times). They were forced to stay there through the following summer and winter because many of the troops became ill after eating contaminated food and drinking polluted water. They set out into the desert in the spring of the following year, using camels to carry the water supplies.

Reaches Saudi Arabia

Gallus and his troops traveled for 30 days through the lands of the friendly Areta tribe and then another 50 days more through a desert region that was ruled by the Bedouin king Sabos. At the end of this journey, they reached Najran in what is now the southwestern part of Saudi Arabia. This was a fertile part of the peninsula, and the Roman soldiers stayed there long enough to conquer some of the nearby towns and replenish their supplies.

The army went as far south as the town of Mar'ib in the interior of Yemen; however, their siege of the town was unsuccessful because they ran out of water. Gallus heard that he was only two days' march from what he called the Aromatic region, the source of frankincense and myrrh, which is now the Hadhramaut region of Yemen. He hired a guide named Syllaeus, who then proceeded to spend six months getting the Romans lost in the desert. Gallus blamed all of his problems on the treachery of Syllaeus. By this time many of his troops had died from hunger, thirst, and disease. Gallus was forced to return to Najran.

Unsuccessful, returns to Rome

The return trip to the port of Egra on the Red Sea

required only 60 days. The army crossed over to Egypt and returned home. It is said that only seven men were lost in battle, but it is clear that many more died from hunger or disease, although there is no record of how many. Gallus brought back some information on the Himyarites and the rest of Arabia but otherwise his expedition was a failure. As a result, the Romans gave up any ideas of expanding their empire in that direction. They later created a province in northern Arabia centered on the city of Petra. They pursued peaceful relations with the Arabs through trading caravans out of Palmyra and Petra and by voyages around the coasts of the peninsula.

Vasco da Gama

Born c. 1460,
Sines, Portugal

Died December 24, 1524,
Cochin, India

Vasco da Gama was a Portuguese nobleman who discovered the best way to sail from western Europe around the Cape of Good Hope to India, opening the first trade route to the East.

Little is known about the early life of Vasco da Gama, who was born around 1460 at the seaport of Sines, Portugal, where his father, Estevao da Gama, was civil governor; his mother was of English descent. He probably received the typical upbringing of a young nobleman of his time in military and court life. He studied mathematics and navigation, although there is no record of his commanding a ship before being chosen by King Manuel I for his historic passageway to the East.

When King Manuel I ascended to the Portuguese throne in 1495 at the age of 26, **Bartolomeu Dias** had already rounded the southern tip of Africa and **Christopher Columbus** (see separate entries) had sailed to the Americas three years earlier. Although the pope had granted Portugal first rights to the Orient, the Portuguese feared the Spanish would capture the wealth of the East. The Treaty of Tordesillas, signed between Manuel's father, John II, and King Ferdinand and Queen Isabella of Spain in 1494, divided the world in half, but John died the next year. His son spent his time putting a Spanish marriage in place to realize these plans.

Leads expedition to the East

Manuel chose the courtier Vasco da Gama to lead an expedition to the East and to serve as his ambassador to the rulers of India. Da Gama spent several months planning and equipping the expedition; before sailing, he traveled to Manuel's court at Lisbon to receive best wishes and to swear loyalty. The night before sailing da Gama and his three captains kept a vigil at the chapel Prince **Henry the Navigator** (see entry) had built for sailors on the bank of the Tagus River in Lisbon.

On July 8, 1497, da Gama's party departed on an historic voyage to discover a passageway to the East. The fleet consisted of 170 men and four vessels: two three-masted sailing ships—the flagship *Sao Gabriel* and the *Sao Rafael,* with da Gama's brother Paolo as commander—and two smaller ships, the *Berrio,* commanded by Nicolau Coelho, and a storeship. Bartolomeu Dias accompanied the da Gama expedition on his way to take command of the Portuguese fortress of Elmina on the Gulf of Guinea.

Finds better route to Cape of Good Hope

From the Tagus the fleet sailed to the Cape Verde Islands in the Atlantic Ocean, remaining there for eight days before continuing south to the coast of what is now Sierra Leone, where Dias departed for the Gulf of Guinea. Da Gama steered his ships west-southwest into the open sea. From the time da Gama's party left the Cape Verde Islands on August 3 until November 4, when they reached the southwest coast of Africa, they saw no land. Taking a wide sweep west into the Atlantic enabled da Gama to avoid the contrary winds and currents of the Gulf of Guinea and to take advantage of the favorable winds prevailing at sea.

Da Gama's exact course is unknown, but at its farthest point west the fleet may have been within 600 miles of the coast of South America. Certainly da Gama's strategy was effective, for later captains followed his route into the Atlantic, which became the normal course for ships sailing toward the Cape of Good Hope. Today both the British admiralty and the United States hydrographic office recommend it.

Visits Hottentots

On November 7, the Portuguese reached Saint Helena Bay north of the Cape of Good Hope, remaining there until November 16 and taking on food and water. At Saint Helena da Gama made his first contact with the Hottentot people of South Africa. Adverse winds prevented da Gama from rounding the Cape of Good Hope until November 22; but three days later the expedition was at Mossel Bay and conducted the first trade with the Hottentots—for an ox the explorers found "as toothsome as the beef of Portugal."

While his ships were at Mossel Bay, da Gama erected a *padrao* (stone marker) to mark the expedition's progress; he also ordered the dismantling of the storeship and the redistribution of its cargo among the three remaining ships. Da Gama set sail on December 8, and eight days later passed Dias's last *padrao,* which marked the farthest point reached by a Portuguese ship to that time.

Stops at Mozambique

Soon the explorers arrived at the Quelimane River on the coast of Mozambique, where they erected another *padrao*; they rested for a month, taking on fresh water and repairing the ships. While the fleet lay on the Quelimane, scurvy, which is caused by a lack of vitamin C, broke out among the men and many of them died. Da Gama named the Quelimane the Rio dos Bons Sinais, or River of Good Omens, because he saw the first signs of nearby civilization. Unknown to the Europeans, settlements along the river were on sea lanes traversed by merchant vessels making their way to and from the ports of East Africa. From these commercial centers, grain, ivory, gold, and other African goods were shipped throughout the Indian Ocean; in return came textiles, metals, porcelain, and spices. Since Arabs mainly engaged in this trade, the region was a center of Islamic culture.

Not surprisingly, the Portuguese, who were traditional enemies of the Muslims, did not receive a warm welcome. The sultan of Mozambique provided two pilots to guide da Gama on his way, but one deserted when he found out that his new employers were Christians; da Gama kept the other pilot on board by force. At Mozambique, da Gama had his first sight of the thriving trade of the area—he described four Arab vessels "laden with gold, silver, cloves, pepper, ginger, pearls, and rubies."

Encounters more hostility

At Mombasa, an island off the south coast of Kenya, an attempt was made to seize the Portuguese fleet; they were better received at the next port of call, Malindi, in southeast Kenya. The ruler of Malindi was on poor terms with the neighboring sultan of Mombasa and, thinking da Gama might be an ally, he provided the Portuguese commander with a pilot to guide him across the Indian Ocean. The monsoon winds were favorable for a northeast crossing of the ocean; on May 20, after sailing 23 days out of sight of land, the explorers reached Calicut, a city on the southwestern coast of India.

Da Gama displayed great navigating skills and persevering leadership in successfully completing the voyage, which was over ten months long, three on the open sea. The diplomatic side of his trip was far less successful, however, because the only trading goods available were cheap cloth and trinkets used to barter with natives on the Guinea coast of Africa. These items were highly unsuitable for sale in the sophisticated societies of India and inappropriate as presents for local kings. Although the Zamorin, the ruler of Calicut, and most of his subjects were Hindu, the city's trade was dominated by Muslims hostile to the Portuguese. Da Gama hoped he could negotiate a commercial treaty in India, but no such formal arrangement could be made. He therefore sold his goods at a loss in order to obtain samples of Indian products to take back to Portugal.

Makes difficult trip back to Portugal

A journal of da Gama's voyage, probably written by Alvaro Velho, one of his subordinates, gives an account of the spice trade of Calicut and the superior spices from the Far East as well as information about other Asian countries. According to Velho's account, as the months passed relations between the Portuguese and their hosts steadily deteriorated, so on August 29, da Gama began the journey home. Despite Muslim hostility, da Gama left a *padrao* with the Zamorin to commemorate the visit; in return the Zamorin gave da Gama a letter to carry to Manuel, promising spices and precious stones in exchange for silver, coral, and scarlet cloth.

Da Gama steered his fleet up the Indian coast to Angediva Island, where the Portuguese stopped to repair their ships. They sailed across the Indian Ocean on the first leg of their voyage home; now the winds were against them, and they were three months at sea before sighting Malindi in January 1499. By that time their numbers were so reduced by scurvy that da Gama ordered the burning of the *Sao Rafael* and the redistribution of the crew between the two remaining ships. From Malindi the *Sao Gabriel* and the *Berrio* sailed south, rounding the Cape of Good Hope in March; a month later a storm separated the ships. In July the *Berrio* reached the Tagus River, while da Gama sailed the *Sao Gabriel* to the Azores, where his brother Paolo died. On September 9, 1499, da Gama received a tumultuous welcome as he made his triumphal entry into Lisbon.

Honored for achievement

Manuel rewarded da Gama's achievement with a title and generous annual income. In 1502 da Gama was made Admiral of the Indian Seas. Amid the rejoicing at the discovery of a sea route to India, the cost of the voyage was temporarily forgotten. The expedition had been expensive: two of four ships had been destroyed and only 50 men had returned. The spices da Gama bought in India had cost a fraction of their European price, but the expense of obtaining them far exceeded any savings. In addition, future Portuguese expeditions would be

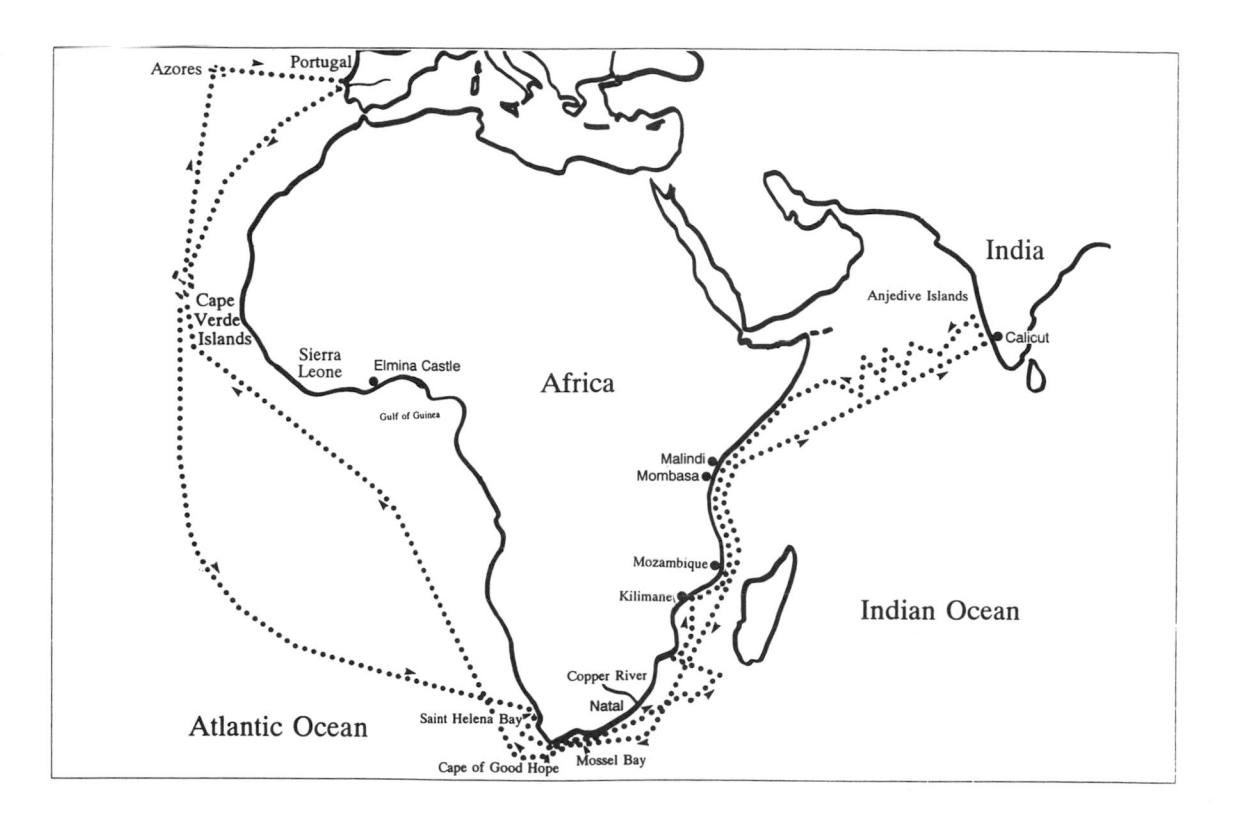

operating in seas controlled by a hostile power, thus increasing the expense to the country. But da Gama had proven that the Cape route to India was navigable and that spices could be obtained cheaply in India; Portugal therefore had a substantial lead over other European countries in the race to establish trade in the East. After da Gama's voyage, Manuel gave himself a title—"Lord of the conquest, navigation, and commerce of Ethiopia, Arabia, Persia, and India."

Although da Gama's second voyage to India was costly, it gave Portugal a lead over other European countries in the race to establish trade with the East.

Makes second voyage to India

In February 1502, da Gama sailed again for India with a squadron of 15 ships that were later joined by another five vessels. The Portuguese had reason to send out a strong fleet: since da Gama's pioneering voyage, a second Portuguese expedition, commanded by Pedro Alvares Cabral, had visited Calicut and established a trading post there; however, a rioting mob had massacred more than 50 people and in retaliation Cabral had bombarded the city. Da Gama's second voyage was intended to impress the world with a new show of Portugal's power.

Da Gama discovered the Amirante Islands in the Indian Ocean and established colonies in Mozambique and Sofala. At Kilwa, a town in Tanzania, he forced the ruler to pay tribute to the king of Portugal. Off the coast of India da Gama took personal revenge on the Muslims with a barbarous act: his fleet overtook a ship laden with pilgrims, including men, women, and children; after seizing its treasure, da Gama set the ship on fire, burning its passengers alive. In Calicut the terrified Zamorins begged for peace, but da Gama rejected his overtures and bombarded the town. At other Indian ports, he loaded his ships with spices, leaving behind a trail of blood and destruction. In February 1503, da Gama set sail for Portugal.

Ends life as viceroy to India

For more than 20 years after his second voyage to India, da Gama lived in retirement. In 1519 he was named count of Vidigueira. In 1524 he was appointed viceroy of Portuguese India and given the task of rooting out administrative corruption; he spent the last months of his life trying to establish an honest government. On December 24, 1524, da Gama died at Cochin in India, the country he had linked with Europe by sea. He was buried in Goa, a port city on the west coast; in 1539 his body was taken back to Portugal to be interred in the Church of Vidigueira. In 1880 the coffin was removed to the Monastery of the Jeronymos at Belém near Lisbon; it was placed in a marble sepulcher on the site of the seaman's chapel at Restello, where da Gama had kept vigil on the night before his first voyage. Several years later it was discovered that the wrong coffin had been put in the sepulcher; so in 1898 da Gama's actual remains were laid to rest at the monastery.

Francis Garnier

*Born July 25, 1839,
St. Etienne, France*

*Died December 21, 1873,
Near Hanoi, Vietnam*

As a supporter of French imperialism, Francis Garnier believed he could advance French power and commercial interests by exploring the Mekong River in what is now Vietnam. Garnier was received as a hero by the French government upon the completion of his first expedition, which covered 7,000 miles and added to European knowledge of Southeast Asia. However, he was blamed for initiating a series of events that led to the French retreat from Hanoi.

Marie-Joseph-François Garnier was born the son of an army officer in St. Etienne, France, on July 25, 1839. The family was strongly traditional and pro-monarchy. After attending the lycée in Montpellier, Garnier went on to the French Naval Academy, where he graduated in 1857. The following year he took part in a French naval cruise to Brazil, Uruguay, Cape Horn, Chile, and Tahiti.

Francis Garnier was a French naval officer who led the first European expedition up the Mekong River in Southeast Asia.

Serves with navy in China

In the mid-nineteenth century war broke out between China and the two main Western imperialist powers, Great Britain and France, over Western efforts to secure favorable trade treaties in Asia. In 1860 Garnier was assigned to the French warship the *Suffren,* which was sent to support the French effort. During the voyage to Asia, Garnier saved a sailor who had fallen overboard; as a result he was promoted and attached to the personal staff of the admiral in charge of the French fleet. Once in China, Garnier was put in charge of building gunboats to ascend the Pei Ho River, which is now the Pai, to attack Beijing. He was present when the Imperial Palace in Beijing was captured by the Western allies in October 1860.

Sent to Cochin China

From China Garnier was sent to Cochin China, a colony France had established in the southernmost part of what is now Vietnam with its capital in Saigon. Cochin China was eager to extend its influence and was constantly engaged in hostilities and negotiations with an area in Vietnam known as Annam. Garnier took part in two minor campaigns in early 1861 before returning to France. After becoming bored with garrison life in France, he requested another assignment in Cochin China. In January 1863 he was sent to Cholon to take over a position of "inspector of native affairs." Cholon is now part of the city of Saigon but was then a separate commercial city with a large Chinese population.

Proposes expedition

Combining his Chinese and Vietnamese experiences, in 1863 Garnier approached the governor of Cochin China with the idea for an expedition up the Mekong River from Saigon into the interior of China. He believed the Mekong might be used to open vast new trade areas for French commercial interests based in Saigon. The promotion brochures he wrote for the project were favorably received in Paris, especially by the

Minister of the Marine, the Marquis de Chasseloup-Laubat. The expedition was approved, but because of Garnier's junior rank the title of commander was given to Ernest Doudart de Lagrée. Garnier was placed second in command, with responsibility for astronomical, meteorological, and geographical observations.

Explores Mekong River

The expedition left Saigon on June 5, 1866, in two gunboats with eight Frenchmen, two interpreters, and 12 Vietnamese soldiers and servants. After stopping in Cambodia to get necessary documents, the party set out again on July 7. They left one of the gunboats behind in Phnom Penh, which is now Pnompenh, and had used the other for only six days until it proved to be too large for the river. At that point the explorers transferred to canoes made of tree trunks with a straw roof to protect them from the sun.

The expedition visited the ruins of Angkor, the former capital of the Khmer kingdom. They continued up the Mekong into Laos where it was halted by the Khon Rapids, the first of a series of rapids that interrupted the flow of the Mekong. Each time the French explorers were obliged to travel around them through the surrounding forest. They did this so often that their boots disintegrated and they had to continue on their way barefoot.

While they were in southern Laos, Garnier made a brief trip back to Saigon to give a progress report and to pick up the mail; he rejoined the party at Vientiane, the former Laotian capital, in April 1867. Later that month they were well received at the royal capital of Luang Prabang.

Gateway to China Remains a Mystery

By this time the Frenchmen had suffered great hardship; in fact, Garnier had nearly died of typhus. They now realized the Mekong could not be navigated by any kind of boat; their hopes of using it as a gateway to China were therefore dashed. Nevertheless, they pushed on, much of the time traveling overland since they could not continue along the river. They entered the northeastern limits of Burma on September 30 and met with Chinese officials in the small town of Cymba, in the province of Yunnan.

Learning that several great river systems come together in Yunnan, Garnier wanted to investigate the upper course of the Red River, which flows into northern Vietnam past the city of Hanoi and empties into the Gulf of Tonkin. He speculated that the Red River might serve as an alternative French route to the interior; however, the French were unable to explore the river because Tonkin, or northern Vietnam, was still controlled by the Emperor of Annam. Garnier sought another approach to the Red by traveling from the south into Kunming, the capital of Yunnan province.

Explores Yunnan province

In December 1867 the French explorers became the first Europeans to enter Kunming from the south. Their passage through Yunnan revealed that it was a vast, well-populated province with an abundance of natural wealth, but its mountains made communications with the rest of China difficult. This isolation gave Garnier even more encouragement to open it up to French exploitation. By this time Doudart de Lagrée was near the point of death, so Garnier took charge of the expedition. He made a side trip to the city of Dali, which was in the control of Chinese Muslims rebelling against rule from Beijing. Dali's inhabitants were hostile, so Garnier quickly returned to Kunming, only to find that Doudart de Lagrée had died in April 1868.

Suggests Red River route

Garnier led the party to the headwaters of the Yangtze River. Traveling by Chinese junk, they sailed to the great city of Hankow, where Garnier met a French arms merchant named Jean Dupuis. He told Dupuis about his idea for a route to the interior via the Red River. What Dupuis did with this information would ultimately cost Garnier his life. From Hankow Garnier and his companions went by steamer to Shanghai, which they reached on June 12, 1868, almost two years to the day after leaving Saigon. They had traveled almost 7,000 miles on boat, canoe, junk, and steamer; they had made 2,500 miles of this trek on foot through jungles and over mountains and plains.

Becomes hero in France

When Garnier returned to France in October 1868, he was greeted as a hero. The British and French geographical societies both gave him gold medals, and the first international geographical congress awarded him one of its two special medals of honor—the other went to the famous African explorer **David Livingstone** (see entry). Welcomed by the French Emperor Napoléon III, Garnier was given a special assignment to write the story of his expedition. The book was published in 1869, the same year the explorer married a young Englishwoman.

When the Franco-Prussian War broke out in 1870, Garnier served with distinction in the defense of Paris. However, because he was outspoken in his criticism of the French for giving in to the Germans, he was passed over for promotion.

Returns to China

Disappointed and resentful, Garnier returned with his new wife to China, hoping to combine exploration with private business interests. He financed his trip from his own resources and those of his French supporters. He also agreed to become a correspondent for a French newspaper. The Garniers arrived in Shanghai in November 1872. From there, Garnier traveled alone to Hankow and Beijing, then through central China as far as Kweichow in the southwest. He returned to Shanghai in July 1873.

In Shanghai Garnier received an urgent telegram from Admiral Dupré, the governor of Cochin China, informing him that Jean Dupuis, the arms dealer Garnier had met in Hankow, was being held hostage by the Vietnamese government. It turned out that Dupuis had decided to pursue Garnier's idea of following the Red River to the sea. He had collected a force of Chinese mercenaries, but was captured in Hanoi. Dupré put Garnier in charge of an official mission to rescue Dupuis. Yet there appears to have been a secret agenda that was contrary to French policy: Dupré may also have instructed Garnier to seize territory in the area of Hanoi, reasoning that if they were successful the French government would approve their actions.

Leads assault on Hanoi

Garnier accepted the assignment. He arrived in Saigon on October 5, 1873, then traveled with an escort of marines to Haiphong, the port of Hanoi, which they reached about three weeks later. In Hanoi he immediately made demands of the Vietnamese commander, but the Vietnamese did not comply. In the early hours of November 20 Garnier stormed the Vietnamese fortress with 110 men while French gunboats bombarded it with shells. After the Vietnamese commander was mortally wounded in the battle his forces capitulated; the French took 2,000 prisoners. During the following two weeks, Garnier sent out his small band of troops to demand the surrender of all neighboring towns and villages.

Dies violently

Garnier's men encountered the largest Vietnamese force at the town of Son-tay, upriver from Hanoi. It was reinforced by Chinese mercenaries and pirates who called themselves the Black Flags. On the morning of December 21, 1873, the Vietnamese and the Black Flags marched to Hanoi, appearing under a huge black flag at the walls of the citadel. The French cannons were easily able to beat them off. Yet Garnier's impetuousness led him into a fatal error: he personally led a party of only 12 men out of the gates of the fortress to pursue the retreating Black Flags. He fell into a ditch and was killed by a volley of spears. Hours later his body was recovered but he had been decapitated and his heart had been removed.

Held in dishonor by French

This disaster eventually led the French to negotiate a withdrawal from Hanoi in 1874; they did not return to take final possession of the city until 1882. Admiral Dupré denied responsibility for Garnier's actions. Blaming Garnier for the misadventure, the French government refused to award a pension to his widow, who had been left behind in Shanghai.

John Glenn

Born July 18, 1921,
New Concord, Ohio

Astronaut John Glenn was the first American to orbit Earth. He was also the first pilot to fly at an average speed greater than Mach 1 (the speed of sound) between the two coasts of the United States.

John Glenn's spaceflight around Earth made him a hero. At the time of Glenn's flight, space was a new battleground in the cold war between the Soviet Union and the United States. The Soviet Union's advantage at the beginning of the space race, as it was called, put pressure on the United States to launch a man into Earth orbit. Mechanical difficulties during Glenn's flight made his accomplishment even more heroic.

War hero

Named after his father, who was a fireman for the B&O Railroad, John H. Glenn, Jr., was born on July 18, 1921, in New Concord, a small town in southeastern Ohio. Glenn's modest background and formative experiences parallel those of another Ohioan, **Neil Armstrong** (see entry), thus giving this midwestern state a unique position in the annals of spaceflight. Like Armstrong, Glenn interrupted his college education to serve his country. In 1939 Glenn enrolled at Muskingum College, located in New Concord. When the United States entered World War II after the bombing of Pearl Harbor, Glenn left college and volunteered for service in the U.S. Marine Corps. He attended flight training at the University of Iowa and at the Naval Air Training Center in Corpus Christi, Texas. Before going overseas, Glenn married his high school sweetheart, Anna (Annie) Castor.

Glenn fought against Japan in the Marshall Islands, and at the end of the war he decided to stay in the marines to receive advanced training. He then flew strafing and bombing missions during the Korean War, protecting marine ground troops. He volunteered for air-to-air combat over the Yalu River, on the border between Korea and China. He shot down three MiG fighter jets during the last few days of the war.

When he returned from Korea, Glenn asked to be assigned to the navy's Patuxent River Test Pilot School in Maryland. He soon gained a reputation as a daring, fearless test pilot by proposing the first flight across North America at supersonic speed. On July 16, 1957, traveling from Los Angeles to New York's Floyd Bennett Field, he became the first pilot to make a coast-to-coast flight at an average speed greater than Mach 1. His F8U aircraft was refueled three times by tankers during the flight, which was 3 hours and 23 minutes long.

Spaceflight pioneer

In 1958 Glenn became involved in experiments testing the reaction of humans to high gravity, which would be necessary if humans were ever to fly in space. He volunteered for runs on the navy's human centrifuge machine in Johnsville, Pennsylvania. In March 1959 Glenn represented the navy's Bureau of Aeronautics in reviewing the progress of the *Mercury* space capsule, designed to take humans into space. These assignments, in addition to Glenn's accomplishments as a pilot, led to his being chosen in April 1959 as one of the "Mercury Seven," the military test pilots who would be the first Americans in space.

The astronauts began training at Langley Air Force Base in Newport News, Virginia, and were then moved to the John F. Kennedy Space Center at Cape Canaveral on the eastern coast of Florida, the launch site for manned space missions. Like each of the six other astronauts, Glenn wanted to be the first American to fly in space, so he was keenly disappointed when he was not chosen for this honor. Instead, Alan Shepard would pilot the first flight, and Glenn would serve with Virgil I. "Gus" Grissom as a back-up pilot.

The U.S. space program suffered a major setback when, on April 12, 1961, cosmonaut **Yury Gagarin** (see entry) of the Soviet Union became the first man to go into space. Gagarin made one complete orbit of Earth in 1 hour and 48 minutes. Shortly thereafter, on May 5, 1961, Alan Shepard became the first American in space when he took off in a *Mercury-Redstone* rocket on a 15-minute flight from Cape Canaveral to a spot 40 miles from Bermuda. He was weightless for only five minutes.

Inspired by this feat, President John F. Kennedy spoke before Congress and asked for a pledge from the United States to put a man on the Moon before the end of the decade. The president's call to action marked the beginning of the *Apollo* program. Once again, Glenn was passed over when Grissom repeated Shepard's flight on July 21, with Glenn serving as backup pilot.

Glenn's orbit of Earth

The Soviets continued to impress the world when cosmonaut Gherman Titov circled Earth 17 times in *Vostok 2*. The United States responded by announcing that Glenn would pilot its first orbital flight. Scheduled for December 20, 1961, at Cape Canaveral, the launch was postponed because of bad weather. It was rescheduled for January 27, 1962, but last-minute difficulties forced an additional two-week postponement. Finally, Glenn's *Mercury-Atlas* rocket, with the space capsule *Friendship* attached, took off from Cape Canaveral at 9:45 A.M. on February 20, 1962.

Millions of Americans watched the launch on national television. As the rocket surged through Earth's atmosphere, Glenn was subjected to six times Earth's normal force of gravity before he achieved weightlessness. The space capsule went into orbit 100 miles above Earth, traveling at a speed of 17,500 miles an hour. "Oh, that view is tremendous!" were Glenn's first words to ground control in Florida. As *Friendship* headed east around the world and as day turned into night, Glenn's one clear picture was of Perth, Australia, where people had stayed up until midnight with their house lights on for his benefit.

Problems in the spacecraft

At the beginning of the second orbit, Glenn experienced difficulty with his spacecraft. The capsule suddenly swung about twenty degrees to the right and stopped before swinging back again; then, as though it had hit a wall, it bounced back and began to sway. The automatic altitude control was obviously not functioning correctly, and Glenn had to prevent the swaying by using manual controls. It was feared that the malfunctioning control would use up too much fuel, endangering the spacecraft's reentry into Earth's atmosphere.

The ground control crew told Glenn he would have to land after only two orbits, but when he flew over the United States he obtained permission to make a third orbit. During preliminary landing procedures ground control radioed Glenn that the spacecraft's landing bag may have been deployed. There was a possibility that the protective heat shield, which was necessary for reentry, could be loose and would be worn off by the atmosphere. If that happened, the capsule would burn up on reentry. Checking his instruments, Glenn concluded everything seemed normal.

Reentry into Earth's atmosphere

As Glenn reached California on his final orbit, the spacecraft's retro-rockets were supposed to fire, thus moving the capsule out of orbit and heading it down toward Earth. This maneuver was the most difficult part of the flight. If the angle was too shallow, the spacecraft would bounce off the atmosphere and head out into space; if it was too steep, the friction of the atmosphere would burn up the capsule. Glenn turned on the automatic controls and found they worked, but he had to continue to correct the craft's sway manually. Ground control informed Glenn that once the retro-rockets fired he should leave the straps of the retropack (auxiliary rockets) attached to the space capsule and then retract the periscope manually. The ground control crew, without telling Glenn, believed this maneuver would help keep the heat shield in place.

Friendship hit Earth's atmosphere when Glenn was flying over Cape Canaveral. During the descent burning chunks of the retropack started to fly by the window. Glenn was dropping at the rate of a thousand feet per second; he could not control the capsule's swaying. The parachute opened automatically just as Glenn hit the manual release. The spacecraft landed near Bermuda about a mile away from the target point and some 300 miles from Cape Canaveral. The time was 2:45 P.M., five hours after Glenn had left.

National hero

The flight had been an obvious success despite the mechanical difficulties. Glenn received a tremendous reception. Vice-President Lyndon Johnson greeted him as he climbed down a ladder from a helicopter at Cape Canaveral, and President Kennedy later flew to Florida to congratulate him personally. Glenn was invited to address a joint session of the U.S. Congress, and during his speech some members of Congress openly wept. In New York City Glenn and his wife, accompanied by the other Mercury Seven astronauts, were treated to a ticker-tape parade.

In 1964 Glenn decided to turn his popularity into a political career by running as a Democrat for the seat of U.S. senator from Ohio. Before the campaign began, however, he sustained middle ear damage when he fell in the bathtub at his home. Glenn retired from the Marine Corps in 1965, and the next year Royal Crown Corporation hired him as a vice-president and then as president of Royal Crown International.

Glenn ran for Senate again in 1970 but lost the Democratic primary election to Howard Metzenbaum, a wealthy Ohio industrialist. Glenn and Metzenbaum faced each other again in the 1974 primary, and this time Glenn won the contest; he was also the victor in the general election, which marked the beginning of his long career as a U.S. senator. In 1984 he unsuccessfully sought the Democratic nomination for president. Because of his military and space background, Glenn was appointed to positions on influential congressional committees.

Glomar Challenger

Commissioned 1968
Decommissioned 1980

The Glomar Challenger *was an American oceanographic research ship that pioneered the study of the earth's geology by taking sample cores of the ocean floor.*

An outgrowth of preliminary drilling made during Project Mohole, the Deep Sea Drilling Project began on August 11, 1968, with the commissioning of the research ship *Glomar Challenger.* Project Mohole had been proposed by the U.S. National Academy of Sciences in 1957 to drill all the way through the outer crust of the earth. During the project a hole was drilled thousands of feet below the surface of the water, but the technology was not sufficiently advanced to achieve the project's goals. Its failure led to the building of the *Glomar Challenger,* a ship constructed especially for underwater drilling.

Designed for deep drilling

Glomar Challenger was designed by a California offshore oil-drilling company, Global Marine, Inc. The first part of the ship's name is an acronym for that company; the second part was taken from **H.M.S.** *Challenger* (see entry), the world's pioneer oceanographic vessel. When completed, the *Glomar Challenger* looked like an oil-drilling derrick perched on top of a ship.

From the derrick it was possible to lower up to 20,000 feet of pipe into the open ocean, bore into the seafloor, and then bring up samples (or "cores") of the earth beneath the ocean. One technical problem encountered immediately was that as the pipe was raised out of the ocean, the core fell out and as much as two-thirds of the material collected was lost. One of the geologists arrived at an ingenious solution: he designed little plastic fingers that bent outward when the drilling was being done and then folded inward when the core was being pulled out of the ocean. Eventually, upwards of 90 percent of the material was retained by this method. Each plastic finger cost one cent to manufacture.

Launched on drilling voyages

On its first drilling voyage, the ship traveled from Galveston, Texas, to New York. At the second drilling site scientists found a salt dome in water 11,750 feet deep. Oil often accumulates inside of salt domes, as in this case, but no one thought that salt domes existed at such great depths. Thus, almost immediately, the *Glomar Challenger* proved it could be commercially as well as scientifically valuable.

Proves Earth once single landmass

On its third drilling venture the ship proved something that has become the basis of theories of the geological structure of the world: the land area of the earth once formed one great mass. Over hundreds of millions of years the continents were formed as this landmass broke up and the pieces moved apart; in fact, the continents are still moving. On Christmas Day 1968 in the mid-Atlantic Ocean, *Glomar Challenger* took samples that showed the ocean floor was youngest at the mid-ocean divide and became progressively older the farther one went from the divide.

Shows dating ocean floor possible

Glomar Challenger advanced scientists' ability to test these theories by making it possible to take core samples of bottom sediments at depths no ship could reach before. By dating the fossils of the tiny organisms that constantly rain down on the ocean floor, it is possible to date the formation of the seafloor itself. The *Glomar Challenger* proved that the oldest seafloors, which are about 160 million years old, are much younger than the oldest land rocks, which are estimated to be as much as four billion years old.

Discovers shifting of Mediterranean floor

On Leg 13, which started in August 1970, the *Glomar Challenger* proved that Africa is slowly moving north, closing in the Mediterranean Sea. Core samples taken on the ship documented this movement, which is folding and displacing the floor of the Mediterranean Sea. For instance, calculations showed that Africa is moving away from South America at the rate of about one inch a year. The same movement is pushing the Alps higher. *Glomar* scientists speculated, however, that the force of erosion would keep the Strait of Gibraltar from closing, thereby creating an inland sea. This expedition also showed that the Mediterranean, which contains meager fossil remains, is an oceanic "desert" compared to the rest of the world's seas.

Revealed geological plate movement

During the course of other expeditions, the drilling showed that the main geological plate beneath the Pacific Ocean is moving north, thus causing the underwater volcanoes that erupted to form the islands of Hawaii and that are still erupting and gradually increasing the size of the islands. The *Glomar Challenger* continued its work until it was decommissioned in 1980.

Isabel Godin des Odonais

Born 1728,
Riobamba, Ecuador
Died September 28, 1792,
Saint-Amand, France

Isabel Godin des Odonais triumphed over the death of most of her loved ones and survived starvation, betrayal, and, finally, the jungle. She was eventually reunited with her husband after a harrowing journey and a long separation; the couple settled in France and enjoyed their final years together.

Marries Jean Godin

Jean Godin des Odonais was employed as a chain-bearer, or carrier of a chain used for calculating scientific measurements, in an expedition to Ecuador led by the French explorer Charles Marie de La Condamine. While La Condamine's party was staying in the Andes, Godin met Isabela de Grandmaison y Bruna, the daughter of a local dignitary who was of French origin. When they married in 1735, Jean was 30 years old and Isabel (the French form of her name) was 13.

When La Condamine left Ecuador in 1743, he decided to travel eastward over the Andes and then down the Amazon

Isabel Godin des Odonais, a native of Ecuador, made an epic voyage through the Andes Mountains and down the Amazon River system to rejoin her French husband.

| Isabel Godin des Odonais

and its tributaries to the port of Belém and then across the Atlantic to France. The Godins were supposed to leave with him, but Isabel was pregnant and could not travel. Along the way La Condamine left word that the couple would be following shortly.

Left alone in Ecuador

Since Isabel was either pregnant or was nursing young children for the next few years, the Godins were unable to follow La Condamine. Growing impatient, Jean set out alone in March 1749 to travel across the continent to French Guiana. He promised to return for Isabel as soon as possible. Godin followed La Condamine's route down the Amazon until he reached Cayenne in French Guiana in April 1750; he had traveled over 2,000 miles.

Once he was in Cayenne, Godin seems to have run into difficulties with the Portuguese when he attempted to travel through their territory to the Spanish city of Quito, Ecuador, and back. Godin wrote to La Condamine and the French government asking for their help, but in spite of their efforts, nothing happened; he remained in Cayenne for 13 years, until 1763.

Godin then conceived of a plan for expanding French territory in Guiana by seizing the entire Amazon basin from the relatively weak Portuguese. He felt his idea might be of interest to the French foreign minister because France had recently lost its North American empire at the conclusion of the Seven Years' War. Godin wrote to the minister, who received the letter but never bothered to reply. Godin therefore suspected that the Portuguese had intercepted his plan.

Jean attempts reunion with Isabel

After a number of years the Portuguese government finally paid attention to the French government's request for assistance in the Godin case. In 1765 a small boat arrived in Cayenne to take Godin up the Amazon to Quito and bring him and his wife back. Because Godin was still convinced that the

Portuguese had intercepted his letter to the French foreign minister, he thought the offer was a trap. Consequently, the boat stayed in Cayenne harbor for a year until the governor, furious at Godin's rejection of help, ordered it to leave.

Realizing this was probably his last chance to be reunited with his wife, Godin hired another man to pilot a boat upriver to the port of Lagunas on the Marañón River. He gave the man money and letters that instructed Isabel to make the journey to Lagunas and meet him in Cayenne. Although the messenger stole the money and the letters never reached Isabel, the boat did travel to Lagunas.

Isabel plans to find Godin

Back in Ecuador, Isabel heard rumors about the boat and sent a trusted servant, Joachim, to Lagunas. It took Joachim two years to travel to Lagunas and return to Ecuador. So it was not until 1769, 20 years after her husband had left, that Isabel prepared to go meet him: she was now 40 years old. In the meantime, all of her four children had died and she lived with her father, Pedro Grandmaison, in the town of Riobamba.

Grandmaison decided to travel to Lagunas first and pave the way for her. He sent back letters describing the route and making arrangements along the way for her to be boarded and cared for. When Isabel finally left Riobamba at the end of 1769, she traveled with a party of 31 Native Americans, Joachim and three other servants, two of her brothers, and a 12-year-old nephew. They were joined at the last minute by three Frenchmen who were traveling back to France.

Encounters hardship and betrayal

The trip was difficult from the beginning. The party traveled through continuous rain during the first leg of the journey from Riobamba to Canelos, a mission station at the head of the Bobonaza River. They slipped and fell along the path as they tried to reach the safe haven of Canelos. When they arrived at the village they found it had been destroyed by smallpox. Someone in Grandmaison's party had carried the virus into Canelos, and all of the inhabitants had either died or fled. Since Native Americans were especially prone to the disease, all 31 of the Native Americans who had been traveling with Isabel left as well.

Isabel found that the canoes Pedro de Grandmaison had chartered for her were also gone. After finally locating a canoe and a raft, the party started down the Bobonaza River. Almost immediately they began having difficulties. When the Frenchman who was steering the raft fell overboard, both he and the raft were lost. Then the canoe struck a log and capsized. No one drowned and the canoe was recovered, but some of the supplies were lost. To make matters worse, one of the Frenchmen offered to take the canoe and go with Joachim to seek help at Andoas, the next stop along the way. The Frenchman had no intention of returning.

Stranded alone in the jungle

The party waited four weeks for help that never came. They ran out of food, and Isabel's young nephew became ill. They constructed a raft and set off again, but the raft hit a tree almost immediately and fell apart and the remaining supplies were lost. Exhausted, hungry and sick, the members of the party began to die—first the nephew, then two of the servant women, the third Frenchman, and finally Isabel's two brothers. The remaining servant wandered into the forest. Isabel fell into unconsciousness for two days. When she awoke, she was surrounded by rotting corpses.

Dazed but determined to survive, Isabel managed to make a pair of sandals from the shoes of her dead brothers before stumbling off into the forest. She wandered aimlessly for nine days; later, she could not remember if she had eaten. In the meantime, Joachim had returned to look for her. He had traveled to Andoas with the Frenchman, who then stole the canoe. Joachim borrowed another canoe from the missionaries at Andoas and set out to search for Isabel's party. When he discovered the dead bodies at the site from which Isabel had only recently wandered away, he fled in horror back to Lagunas to tell Grandmaison that his whole family was dead. He then sent the news downriver to Jean Godin in Cayenne, and Godin wrote to La Condamine in Paris.

Shows amazing survival skills

But Isabel was still alive. During her dazed and aimless trek through the jungle she encountered two Native Americans who fed her and took her to the mission at Andoas during the first week of January 1770. She rewarded them with two gold chains she was wearing around her neck. When the priests at the mission took the gold away from them, Isabel was so incensed that she told her rescuers she wanted to leave immediately. She was wearing the clothes the Native Americans had given her and "the soles of the shoes of her dead brothers."

Isabel went downstream to another mission station where the priest offered to equip her for a return trip to Riobamba, but she refused, vowing to continue the search for her husband. Word was sent to her father, who was still at Lagunas. He used the boat the Portuguese had provided five years before and met her at the juncture of the Marañón and Pastaza rivers. They made the long journey together down the Amazon system to the Atlantic Ocean and on to Cayenne.

Godins reunite and return to France

In the harbor of Cayenne, the Godins met for the first time in 20 years. As Jean put it, "On board this vessel, after twenty years' absence and a long endurance on either side of alarms and misfortunes, I again met with a cherished wife whom I had almost given up every hope of seeing again." The Godins, Grandmaison, and Joachim stayed in Guiana for three years.

In 1773 they returned to France, which Jean had left 38 years before. By this time, the story of Isabel's amazing adventure was well known, and the Godins became celebrities. But the hardships had taken their toll on Isabel; her face was scarred from insect bites and she had developed a nervous tic that became worse when she talked about those terrible days on the river. The only souvenir Isabel had from her trip was a pair of soles from her brother's shoes, which she kept in an ebony box. The Godins lived at Jean's family home in central France in the town of Saint-Amand. Some years later the son of one of Isabel's dead brothers came to live with them; he married and stayed in the town, where his descendants still live. Jean died on March 1, 1792, and Isabel died on September 28 of the same year.

Abu al-Kasim Ibn Ali al-Nasibi Ibn Hawkal

Born c. 920,
Nisibis, Upper Mesopotamia

Died c. 990

Abu al-Kasim Ibn Ali al-Nasibi Ibn Hawkal was born in Nisibis in Upper Mesopotamia, which is present-day Iraq. According to his own account, he left Baghdad on Thursday, 7 Ramadan 331 (May 15, 943) with the intention of learning about other lands and peoples and of engaging in trade. He then spent the next 30 years traveling; he later wrote about his experiences in a book called *On the Shape of the World*.

Goes to Spain

In 947 Ibn Hawkal reached Mahdia on the east coast of Tunisia, then traveled across North Africa to Morocco. The following year he sailed across the Strait of Gibraltar to Spain, which was ruled by the Muslim Umayyad dynasty and had been united by the Caliph Abd al-Rahman III from his capital at Cordoba. In his book Ibn Hawkal gave a lengthy description of Cordoba, a great cultural and intellectual center and probably the largest city in Europe at the time. He also said

In the year 943 Ibn Hawkal of Baghdad set out on a long journey that lasted 30 years and took him to all parts of the Muslim world.

that Spain was economically strong but militarily weak. These reports led to speculation that he was sent as a spy for the Fatimids, a North African Shi'ite dynasty that was then in the process of military expansion.

Travels in Africa

From Spain Ibn Hawkal turned back to North Africa, reaching Sijilmasa at the southern edge of Morocco in 951. From Sijilmasa he headed south to the ancient African kingdom of Ghana in what is now Mali, where he stayed in the commercial center of Awdaghost, which he said was fabulously rich. He reported seeing a check there made out in the sum of 42,000 dinars to a merchant in Sijilmasa. Ibn Hawkal gave the first account of Accra, the capital of Ghana, on the edge of the Sahara; he also saw the Niger River. Since the river was flowing to the east, he concluded it was the upper course of the Nile.

Journeys throughout Middle East

On his way north to Egypt, Ibn Hawkal noted that the most direct route from Ghana to Egypt had been interrupted by Berber raiders. His presence in Egypt at a time when it was being invaded by the Fatimids further supports the idea that he was a Fatimid spy. In 969 Egypt was finally captured by the Fatimids, who founded the city of Cairo and made it their capital.

From Egypt Ibn Hawkal continued eastward, journeying to the northernmost region of Islam, Armenia and Azerbaijan, which he reached in 955. He observed that Islamic fervor was lacking on this religious frontier. Ibn Hawkal then traveled to Al-Jazira in western Syria. By 961 he was in Basra in southern Iraq and from there he headed east to Khuzestan and Fars in southern Iran. In 969 he visited Gorgan in northern Iran, from there crossing the Amu Darya River, which is now the Oxus, into central Asia. He went as far as the city of Samarkand, where he saw topiary gardens in which bushes and trees were trimmed to look like animals. He noted that irrigation water at

Samarkand was strictly regulated, and he listed the salary scale for public officials.

Went to Sicily on final trip

From Samarkand Ibn Hawkal returned in 969 to Basra and Khuzestan. The last of Ibn Hawkal's recorded trips was to Sicily—he writes that he was in Palermo on April 16, 973, having been there since the previous year. Sicily had been conquered by the Arabs starting in the year 825 and remained Muslim until it was taken by the Christian Normans in 1061.

Left valuable geographic and cultural records

Ibn Hawkal copied some of his geographic descriptions from the work of another famous Arab geographer, al-Istakhri, but he seems to have corrected al-Istakhri's work with his own observations of the various places that he visited. In his book Ibn Hawkal recounted how he met al-Istakhri, who asked him to correct the errors in his book. Ibn Hawkal then went beyond that and replaced some of the original maps and some of al-Istakhri's descriptions with his own. In fact, his goal seems to have been to update the body of knowledge that then made up Arab geography. The point was not to compose an individual work but to pass on a corrected version of accumulated information.

Ibn Hawkal took care to state the situation in a country or region at the time that he himself visited. Therefore, it has great value to historians. He was also the first Arab geographer to discuss the basic facts of the production and economy of the places he visited. In the course of his work he discussed such diverse subjects as the market for vegetable oils in the Mediterranean region, the difficulties of handicraft producers in Egypt, the price of pens in Spain, the decline of Armenian bakeries, trade in coral and dates, and the monopoly on the tar trade in Cyrenaica.

Sven Hedin

Born February 19, 1865,
Stockholm, Sweden

Died November 26, 1952

Sven Hedin, a Swedish explorer and prolific writer, made five important expeditions into central Asia, contributing significantly to Western knowledge of Asian geography. He was also an influential figure in European politics during the two world wars.

Sven Anders Hedin was born into a prominent family in Stockholm, Sweden. While in high school he became interested in geography and mapmaking. After showing an exceptional talent for mapmaking, he was asked to produce a map for the Swedish Geographical Society to illustrate a lecture on the expeditions of Russian explorer **Nikolay Przhevalsky** (see entry). Another famous explorer, the Arctic adventurer Nils Adolf Erik Nordenskiöld, complimented Hedin on his mapmaking skills.

Early voyages

At the age of 20 Hedin moved to Baku—the capital city of present-day Azerbaijan, located on the Caspian Sea—where he served for eight months as a tutor to the son of a Swedish engineer working in the region's oil fields. During that time he studied Farsi (the language of Iran, which was then known as Persia) and Turkish. Using money he had saved, he left Baku and traveled alone 2,000 miles through Iran and Iraq. On his return to Sweden he wrote an account of his recent journey, the first of many books he would write throughout his life.

Hedin later enrolled in Swedish and German universities to study geography. At the University of Berlin he had the opportunity to study under Ferdinand von Richthofen, a prominent Asian explorer, who recognized Hedin's talents as a mapmaker and linguist. He soon left the university, however, to serve as interpreter on a diplomatic mission to Tehran (in Iran). When it was time to leave Tehran, Hedin did not return to Stockholm; instead, he telegraphed the king of Sweden to request permission to explore Russian central Asia and Chinese Turkistan.

Leaving Tehran in September 1890, Hedin traveled via the cities of Mashhad, Iran, and Tashkent, Uzbekistan, across the Pamir Mountains to Kashgar, the westernmost town in the Chinese Empire. On his return trip he trekked over the Tien Shan range in western China to Lake Issyk-Kul. While exploring the area around Lake Issyk-Kul, he visited the grave site of Przhevalsky, who had died in the nearby town of Karakol on his final expedition to Lhasa, the capital of Tibet. Hedin returned to Stockholm in the spring of 1891, spending some time there to write books about the mission to Persia and his own journey through central Asia. He was invited by Richthofen to address the Berlin Geographical Society. The following year he received his doctorate in geography from the University of Halle in Germany.

Leader of scientific expedition

Shortly after earning his degree, Hedin began making plans for his first scientific expedition, which was financed in part by King Oscar II of Sweden. The trip was delayed, however, by the recurrence of a vision problem that had been plaguing him; he eventually lost sight in one eye. Not to be discouraged, Hedin started on his trip as soon as he was able to travel. His first stop was Tashkent, and in January 1894 he crossed into China. He spent over a year exploring the region around Kashgar and the Pamir Mountains, a vast range that extends into several countries in central Asia.

In February 1895 Hedin headed east with his local guide into the great Takla Makan Desert of western China. Starting near the town of Khotan, he crossed the desert from south to north. Along the way his party ran out of water, and one of the guides died. Hedin and his companions were near collapse when they found a well at the edge of the desert. In later years, after Hedin had become a well-paid lecturer, his story about crossing the Takla Makan Desert was always popular with his audiences.

Important discoveries

Hedin and his party were finally able to reach Kashgar, where they recuperated. They set out again in January 1896, heading east through part of the Takla Makan to the Tarim Basin, another great desert. Near the town of Khotan, Hedin found traces of ancient cities; these sites contained artifacts that were influenced by Persian and Indian cultures. His reports, which stirred archaeologists into investigating the sites, helped reconstruct the early history of this area. Hedin continued to the western shore of Lop Nor, a desert lake on the eastern end of the Tarim Basin, where he tried to solve the mystery of why the lake was constantly changing in size and location.

In November Hedin reached the town of Tankar, where he met the Canadian missionary **Susie Carson Rijnhart** (see entry) and her husband, who were also on an exploring expedition to Lake Nor. They were the first Westerners he had seen in ten months. Leaving Tankar, Hedin journeyed on to Peking (now known as Beijing), the capital of China; he then turned north and crossed the eastern end of the Gobi Desert to Mongolia, arriving at the Russian border town of Kyakhta. Traveling via the Trans-Siberian Railroad, he reached St. Petersburg, Russia, where he had an audience with the Russian czar, Nicholas II, before returning to Sweden.

Attempt to reach Lhasa

Two years later, in 1898, Hedin set out on his next journey, this time accompanied by four Cossacks, noted Russian horsemen, whom Nicholas II had sent to escort him. Hedin traveled via Kashgar and Yarkand to the Tarim River, which he sailed down for a return visit to Lop Nor. Turning south from Lop Nor, he crossed the A-erh-chin Shan-mo range and reached the Plateau of Tibet. In March 1901 he discovered the remains of the ruined city of Lou Lan.

At this point in his journey, Hedin disguised himself as a Mongol, hoping he would be able to enter Lhasa, which was forbidden to Westerners. But when he was still more than 150 miles from Lhasa, Tibetan officials forced him to turn back. He headed west to Leh, the capital of Ladakh, the region on the border of Tibet and Indian Kashmir. After a subsequent visit to Calcutta, India, he retraced his steps to Kashmir and returned to Sweden by way of Russian central Asia and St. Petersburg. Upon his return he was awarded a title of nobility, the last ever granted in Sweden.

Hedin stayed in Sweden to oversee publication of the six books he had written about his 1899-1902 travels. For the first time since gaining prominence as an explorer and scientist, he became involved in political affairs. He warned his countrymen about Russian expansionism and tried unsuccessfully to prevent the breakup, in 1905, of the union between Sweden and Norway.

Second journey to Tibet

The explorer set out for Asia again in October 1905. This time he chose to travel east through Iran and India. His aim was to go back to Tibet, which he hoped to reach via its southern border with India. He traveled back to Leh and then managed to slip across the border into western Tibet.

Exploring expanses of unmapped territory, Hedin reached Shigatse, the second-largest city in Tibet. During his exploration he mapped a previously uncharted mountain range—the Kailas—and reached the source of the Brahmaputra River. He also confirmed the sources of the Indus and Sutlej rivers, which had never been visited by Westerners. Hedin returned to India and then traveled to Japan, where he was received by the Japanese emperor.

With his expedition a success, Hedin returned to Sweden. When his boat docked in Stockholm in January 1909, the royal family, the prime minister, and all the members of the Swedish cabinet were there to greet him. In the following years Hedin became more deeply involved in Swedish politics. Profoundly conservative, he supported Swedish ties to Germany, and he advocated Swedish rearmament to counter what he saw as the Russian threat. He wrote a speech for King Gustav V that called for military preparedness and that caused the downfall of the liberal Swedish government in 1914.

Sino-Swedish Scientific Expedition

When World War I broke out, Hedin accepted German invitations to visit both the western and eastern fronts. The books he wrote about his trips were translated into German and used as war propaganda. He was in Berlin when the war ended and wrote an article praising the German emperor, who had fled the country. After World War I Hedin spent most of his time writing and lecturing. He later made a trip around the world that included a visit to the newly formed Soviet Union.

In 1925 Hedin went to Germany at the invitation of Hugo Junkers, an airplane manufacturer, to discuss the possibility of setting up regular air service between Europe and Asia. Junkers hired Hedin to survey sites in Asia for weather stations and to help plan routes. The Chinese government, which was skeptical of the project and insisted that Hedin's mission be called the Sino-Swedish Scientific Expedition, placed several restrictions on its activities. This project was quite different from Hedin's previous expeditions. He headed a large group of scientists and specialists who traveled widely over central Asia. Hedin did not always personally accompany the scientists, and he was often in Europe or North America, rather than in Asia, handling fund-raising and administration for the project.

The Sino-Swedish Scientific Expedition has been counted as Hedin's greatest success. When it ended in 1933, the participants had accomplished an enormous amount of work, having gathered information in a wide variety of fields. After returning to Stockholm, Hedin began editing the scientific reports of the expedition. In order to finance the publication of these reports, he made a lecture tour of Europe. At the invitation of Nazi leader Adolf Hitler, he made one of the opening speeches at the 1936 Olympic Games in Berlin; he was the only non-German to be accorded this distinction.

Final years

During World War II Hedin maintained close ties with the Nazis and had several meetings with Hitler; he also wrote two books supporting the views of the German leadership. His friendship with Nazi officials enabled him to save the lives of 13 Norwegian resistance fighters and a Jewish colleague at a German university.

After the war Hedin wrote five more books, including one about his wartime missions to Germany and a memoir about famous people he had met during his career. Toward the end of his life an operation restored the vision he had lost in his eye 60 years earlier. Hedin died on November 26, 1952, when he was nearly 88 years old.

Henry the Navigator

Born March 4, 1394,
Pôrto, Portugal

Died November 13, 1460,
Cape St. Vincent, near Sagres, Portugal

Prince Henry the Navigator was a member of the Portuguese royal family who used his private fortune to sponsor expeditions of discovery in the Atlantic Ocean and down the coast of Africa.

Although he was called Henry the Navigator by the English, Prince Henry never actually sailed on any of the many voyages of discovery he sponsored to the Madeira Islands and the west coast of Africa. He used his wealth to establish a maritime school for the study of the arts of navigation, mapmaking, shipbuilding, and maritime commerce. His goals were to test and gain scientific knowledge, find a route to the rich spice trade of the Indies, and spread the Christian faith. Henry was the third son of King John I of Portugal and Philippa of Lancaster, the daughter of John of Gaunt of England. Under the supervision of their parents, Henry and his brothers were taught soldiering, statecraft, and literature.

Recognized for valor

During the Crusades, much of Portugal and Spain had been conquered by the Moors. By Henry's time, Portugal was devoutly Catholic but the Portuguese still feared Muslim domination. In 1415 Henry took part, along with his father and brothers, in an assault on the port of Ceuta in northern Morocco. In recognition of his distinguished service, Henry was named Duke of Viseu by King John.

While fighting in Morocco, Henry had become interested in Africa; in 1416 he established a base for exploring the continent at Sagres in southwest Portugal, which was conveniently located near the port of Lagos. By 1418 he had begun sponsoring voyages, and over the next two years he had excellent results: one of his navigators rediscovered the Madeira Islands, which had been discovered and abandoned by the Romans. Henry's expeditions were also exploring the west coast of Africa.

Establishes navigation school

After Henry was appointed governor of the Algrave, Portugal's most southern province, he constructed a school for navigation at Sagres. Under his direction a new and lighter ship known as the Portuguese caravel was developed. He surrounded himself with scientists and experts on navigation and began to formulate a plan for the systematic exploration of the west coast of Africa. He was intrigued with stories he had heard of gold in Africa and hoped to locate the legendary kingdom of Prester John, a Christian priest and king who reputedly ruled over an empire in either Asia or Africa.

In 1420 Henry was made grand master of the Order of Christ, which was sponsored by the pope and dedicated to converting pagans to Christianity. This group financed many of Henry's voyages; his ships were easily identified by distinctive white sails emblazoned with large red crosses.

Backs important voyages to Africa

Henry had difficulty persuading his captains to go beyond Cape Bojador on the coast of what is now the western Sahara. According to legend, only dangerously churning water would be found beyond this point. It took 14 voyages over a period of 12 years to overcome this psychological barrier. In

1434 Gil Eannes, one of his navigators, finally had the courage to sail round the cape.

Following Eannes's achievement Henry's ships advanced over 250 miles farther down the coast in the next two years. Henry was disappointed when the pope granted the Canary Islands to Spain in 1436. The following year, Henry took part in an abortive attack on Tangier in Morocco with his younger brother, Ferando. Taken hostage, Ferando died in captivity in 1443.

Continuing to make progress in exploring Africa, Henry's ships reached Cape Blanco, midway down the west coast, in 1441. During an expedition in 1443 the Portuguese discovered the Bay of Arguin; they built a fort and warehouse on nearby Arguin Island, thus founding the first European trading post in Africa. It was soon being used for the slave trade, which Antao Gonçalves initiated when he brought captives back to Portugal from the Rio De Oro area. (In 1455 Henry would forbid the kidnapping of Africans for the slave trade.)

Continues exploration of Africa

During the two-year period from 1444 to 1446, Henry intensified exploration of Africa, sending between 30 and 40 of his ships on missions. Dinis Dias, brother of **Bartolomeu Dias** (see entry), sailed as far as the Senegal River near the present-day city of Dakar. In 1444 Henry sent out a large fleet to attack and destroy the Moroccan fort at Tider. After the victory, a ship under the command of Alvaro Fernandes continued on to reach the Cape of Masts near the Gambia River. Rounding the cape, Alvise da Cadamosto discovered the Cape Verde Islands soon thereafter. The last voyage sponsored by Henry was captained in 1460 by Pedro de Sinta, who sailed as far south as Sierra Leone, 1,500 miles down the African coast.

During this period of pioneering exploration Henry lived and studied at his home in Sagres. He never married and he is usually described as a highly disciplined person who was entirely devoted to his religion and his mission of discovery. His voyages in the mid-fifteenth century are generally regarded as having launched Portugal's golden era of colonial and maritime expansion.

Upon Henry's death in 1460, one of his captains, Diogo Gomes, wrote:

In the year 1460 the lord infant Henry fell ill in his town at Cape St. Vincent and died of the illness on the 13th November ... and on the night of his death, he was taken to the Church of St. Mary at Lagos and there honorably buried. And the King Afonso ... was very saddened, both he and his people, by the death of so great a lord, because he spent all his revenues and all he got from Guinea in war and continual fleets at sea against the Saracens [Muslims] for the faith of Christ.

Matthew A. Henson

Born August 8, 1866,
Charles County, Maryland

Died 1955,
New York

Matthew A. Henson was an American who accompanied Robert Peary on his Arctic explorations; he was a member of the first expedition to reach the North Pole.

Matthew A. Henson was invited to go along with **Robert Edwin Peary** (see entry) when Peary became interested in Arctic exploration. Henson subsequently became the first person to officially raise the American flag over the North Pole. He was well liked by the native Inuit, easily learning their language and adapting to their customs. As racial attitudes in the United States slowly changed, he gradually received the recognition he deserved. Henson was the first black member to be elected to the Explorers Club in 1937; he received the Navy Medal in 1945. He was also honored by Presidents Harry Truman and Dwight Eisenhower.

Henson was born in Charles County, Maryland, on August 8, 1866, a time when most African Americans were enslaved; however, his parents had been born free. The family soon moved to Washington, D.C., but both of Henson's parents had died by the time he was seven. He was raised by an uncle and attended a segregated school for six years. At the age of 13, he went to Baltimore and found a job as a cabin boy on a ship bound for China. Befriended by the ship's captain, he soon became an able-bodied seaman. During that time he sailed to China, Japan, the Philippines, North Africa, Spain, France, and Russia. When the captain died, Henson, who was 17, decided to seek work ashore.

Joins Peary

In 1888, while working in a clothing store, Henson met a young U.S. Navy lieutenant, Robert Edward Peary, who had come in to buy a tropical helmet. Peary offered to hire him as a valet. Henson did not like the idea of becoming a personal servant, but he thought it would be worthwhile to accompany Peary to Nicaragua where he was going to survey for a possible canal across Central America. They spent a year in Nicaragua. When Peary was assigned to the League Island Navy Yard, Henson worked there as a messenger. Peary became interested in Arctic exploration and had previously traveled to Greenland in the hope of being the first person to cross the Greenland ice cap. He was beaten by the Norwegian explorer **Roald Amundsen** (see entry).

Frustrated by this turn of events, Peary vowed he would be the first person to reach the North Pole. Henson accompanied Peary to Greenland in June 1891, along with Peary's wife, Josephine, and a party that included the Arctic explorer Frederick Albert Cook. During this trip Henson began to study the Inuit who lived at the northern end of Greenland. He learned to speak their language and he studied their customs and methods of Arctic survival. Henson soon became popular with the Inuit, who nicknamed him Maripaluk, which means "kind Matthew."

Makes yearly trips to Greenland

When Henson returned to Greenland with Peary in 1893 he adopted a young Inuit orphan and taught him to speak English. During this expedition Peary and Henson crossed the northern end of Greenland from their base at Etah to the northeastern corner of the island at Independence Bay in "Peary

Land." Henson later wrote, "The memory of the winter and summer of 1894 and 1895 will never leave me ... the recollections of the long race with death across the 450 miles of the ice-cap of North Greenland in 1895 ... are still the most vivid." The party left in September, and Henson vowed that he would never return.

But he did return. In fact, except for one summer, Peary and Henson returned to Greenland every year from 1896 onward. In July 1905 they made plans to travel over the polar ice cap to the North Pole. Starting in early 1906, they crossed the frozen sea by dogsled. Since the winter turned out to be unusually warm and spring came early, they encountered too many stretches of open water to continue their trip. Yet they did come within 160 miles of the Pole, the point farthest north anyone had reached at that time.

Makes another attempt to reach North Pole

On July 6, 1908, Peary and Henson tried again with an expedition that included 21 explorers and 50 Inuit who were to help set up supply bases on the route to the Pole. Sailing on the *Roosevelt,* they left Cape Columbia at the northern end of Ellesmere Island on the morning of March 1, 1909. The expedition was organized into support teams that either accompanied the main party or went ahead to scout a trail. A scouting team led by Professor Ross Marvin of Cornell University set up its last supply depot 230 miles from the Pole, then headed back to Cape Columbia. Marvin did not return with his team. An Inuit named Kudlukto said Marvin had fallen into a stretch of open water and drowned. Years later Kudlukto confessed he had shot Marvin and dumped his body in the water after he refused to let one of Kudlukto's young cousins ride on a dogsled.

Chosen to go with Peary to the Pole

On March 31, Peary and other members of the expedition were at 87°47', about 150 miles from the Pole. At that point Peary ordered Captain Bob Bartlett, commander of the *Roosevelt,* to return to Cape Columbia, saying Henson would accompany him from that point onward. Bitterly disappointed, Bartlett headed south. It made sense for Peary to take Henson: he had much more Arctic experience and was an acknowledged master with the dog teams. But there have always been suggestions that Peary sent Bartlett back because he did not want to share the honor of reaching the Pole with another white person. Given the racial prejudice at the time, Henson and the four Inuit did not "count."

Two days later, as Henson was crossing a lane of moving ice, a block of ice he was using for support slipped and he fell into the water. Fortunately one of the Inuits pulled him out immediately or he would have drowned. The normal daily procedure was for Peary to leave the night camp early in the morning and push ahead for two hours, breaking the trail ahead. The others would break camp and catch up with Peary; then Peary (who at age 52 was already suffering from the leukemia that would later kill him) would ride in one of the dogsleds while Henson went ahead and broke a trail. They would not see each other until the end of the day. The details of this routine would become important when the time came to give credit to the person who saw the North Pole for the first time.

On April 6, 1909, Henson arrived at a spot that, just by calculating the distance the party had traveled, he thought must be the North Pole. When Peary arrived 45 minutes later, Henson greeted him by saying, "I think I'm the first man to sit on the top of the world." Peary was furious. Peary then attached an American flag to a staff and the members of the party went to sleep. At 12:50 P.M., when there was a break in the clouds, Peary was able to take a reading of their location. It showed they were three miles short of the Pole. After a nap Peary—without telling Henson—took another reading, then set out with Henson and two Inuits, Eginwah and Seegloo, to the site where he thought the Pole must be. After they spent 30 hours in the vicinity of the Pole, Henson officially raised the flag over the spot that Peary's calculations indicated was the North Pole. Whether it really was the Pole or not has been a source of controversy ever since.

Peary and Henson and the four Inuit met the *Roosevelt* at Cape Columbia on April 23. They had to wait until July 17 for the ice to melt enough for the ship to steam into open water. They telegraphed news of their triumph from Labrador on September 6, 1909. By that time the world thought Frederick Cook had been the first one to reach the Pole. Peary spent the next few years defending his claims and eventually won the fight.

Faces racial discrimination

By the time Henson returned to the United States he had lost 43 pounds; he spent several months recuperating. For a while Henson traveled with Peary on lecture tours wearing Inuit clothing. In 1912 he wrote a book about his experiences, *A Negro at the North Pole,* but it never sold well and he was forced to take a job as a porter working for $16 a week. Through the efforts of politically influential friends, he was later given a job in the United States Customs House in New York at a salary of $20 a week; eventually it raised to $40 a week.

When Henson retired in 1936, there was an unsuccessful effort to award him the Congressional Medal of Honor. Recognition and honors finally came, but not without personal humiliation. In 1945, when all the survivors of the North Pole expedition received the Navy Medal, Henson's medal was awarded privately. When he attended a banquet in his honor in Chicago in 1948, none of the downtown hotels would allow him to register because of his race. His election to the Explorers Club was a triumph, and a first, and his reception at the White House by two presidents in the years before his death was a great honor. Henson died in New York in 1955 at the age of 88. In 1988, when his achievements received more publicity, he was reburied at Arlington Cemetery with full military honors in a plot next to Peary's.

An interesting footnote to this story is that, although it was not widely known at the time because both Peary and Henson were married, they had liaisons with Inuit women. Dating from the 1905 expedition, Peary fathered two sons and Henson a boy named Anaukaq. This information was discovered in 1986 when it was revealed that the small Greenland village of Moriussaw was largely made up of Henson's descendants, who had prospered as traders and hunters.

Herodotus

Born c. 484 B.C.,
Halicarnassus, Greece

Died c. 425 B.C.,
Thurii, Greece

H erodotus is known as the father of history. His *History,* an account of the Persian-Greek wars, is considered to be the first attempt at historical writing. Herodotus was born at Halicarnassus, a Greek colony on the coast of Asia Minor (now Turkey), where his parents, Lyxes and Dryo, seem to have been prominent citizens. Herodotus exhibited intense curiosity about the Greek world, and he began to travel extensively as a young man.

Travels through the ancient world

Although the exact period of his travels has not been determined, Herodotus apparently left Halicarnassus around 454 B.C. and journeyed to the Aegean island of Samos. He may have returned briefly to Halicarnassus before going to Athens. He then traveled to Asia Minor, the Aegean Islands, Greece, Macedonia, Thrace, the coast of the Black Sea as far as the Crimean Peninsula, Persia (modern-day Iran), Tyre (in Lebanon), Egypt,

The most famous classical Greek historian, Herodotus accurately described important places in the ancient world, many of which he apparently visited.

Scylax of Caryanda

Scylax was an ethnic Greek from the town of Caryanda in Asia Minor. He was a naval commander in the fleet of the great emperor Darius I of Persia. After ascending to the Persian throne in 521 B.C., Darius set out to expand his empire in several directions. He wanted to invade India, so he sent Scylax out to visit the mouth of the Indus River and to find the best sea route from the Persian Gulf to India.

To accomplish his goal, Scylax started out from the reverse direction—at the source of the Indus River in the Hindu Kush Mountains of Afghanistan. Some historians have said he started from as far upstream as Kabul, the capital of modern Afghanistan. But the river is not navigable at that point, and he probably started out near the meeting of the Kabul and Indus rivers not far from the modern town of Attock, Pakistan.

Scylax sailed down the Indus River to its mouth near present-day Karachi and then followed the coastline of Pakistan to the Gulf of Oman, crossing it to reach Arabia. Darius made use of the information that Scylax brought back to him. He conquered Sind, the region through which the Indus flows.

and Cyrene (in Libya). During this time he collected historical, geographical, ethnological, mythological, and archaeological material, which he used for writing his *History*.

In 447 B.C. Herodotus returned to Athens, the intellectual center of the Greek world, where he gave public readings from his book. He later joined the colony of Thurii, which was founded by Athenians on the Gulf of Taranto in southern Italy in 443 B.C. From Thurii he visited Sicily and southern Italy. It is possible that he traveled back to Athens after civil strife broke out in Thurii. Since the *History* mentions the Peloponnesian War, which started in 431 B.C., it is thought that Herodotus finished writing the work in the final years of his life.

Importance of the *History*

The *History* is the most comprehensive early history of the ancient world. It tells about the wars between the Greeks and their neighbors, beginning with the conquest of the Greek colonies in Asia Minor by Croesus, the king of Lydia (in modern-day Turkey). It continues with a history of Lydia, Persia, Babylon, Iraq, and Egypt, concluding with an account of the two wars between the Persians and the Greeks. Included in the book is the story of Queen Artemisia, an ally of the Persians, who ruled Halicarnassus at the time of Herodotus's birth. Following the defeat of the Persians in Ionia in 478 B.C., the throne passed to her son Lygdamis, who became involved in a civil war that resulted in the death of Herodotus's uncle.

The *History* is distinctive for many reasons. For instance, it shows that Herodotus was an astute geographer. During his time people thought the world was divided into three equal parts—Asia, Europe, and Africa (which he called Libya)—but he did not accept this view. He thought Europe was as wide as the other two continents, although he knew nothing about northwestern Europe (Britain and Scandinavia). While his concept of Asia went only as far east as the Indus River, he was the first geographer to realize the Caspian was a great inland sea and not the gulf of an ocean that encircled the world.

Herodotus described a supposed voyage by the Egyptian king Necho that circumnavigated Africa around the year 600 B.C., thus suggesting that he thought the continent was surrounded by water. Yet he made two major mistakes. First, he thought that the Nile River rose in the Atlas Mountains and then flowed eastward through what would be the Sahara Desert before turning north into Egypt (it flows northward from Lake Victoria). His other error is more surprising. He was aware of the voyage of Scylax of Caryanda, a Persian naval commander who had sailed southwest down the Indus River into the Arabian Sea and then around Arabia to Egypt. But Herodotus still described the Indus as flowing southeastward.

Despite these two misconceptions, Herodotus's observations, interspersed throughout the *History,* give the most thorough and accurate account of classical geography. Significantly, his book also shows that he had visited many of the places he described.

Chronology of Exploration

As an aid to the reader who wishes to trace the history of exploration or the explorers active in a particular location, the major expeditions within a geographical area are listed below in chronological order.

Africa: across the continent

1802-14	Pedro João Baptista and Amaro José
1854-56	David Livingstone
1858-64	David Livingstone
1872-73	David Livingstone
1873-77	Henry Morton Stanley
1877-80	Hermenegildo de Brito Capelo and Roberto Ivens
1884-85	Hermenegildo de Brito Capelo and Roberto Ivens
1888-90	Henry Morton Stanley
1896-98	Jean-Baptiste Marchand
1924-25	Delia Akeley

Africa: coast

1416-60	Henry the Navigator
1487-88	Bartolomeu Dias

Africa: east

1490-1526	Pero da Covilhã
1848	Johannes Rebmann
1848-49	Johann Ludwig Krapf
1848-49	Johannes Rebmann
1849	Johannes Rebmann
1851	Johann Ludwig Krapf
1857-59	Richard Burton and John Hanning Speke (with Sidi Mubarak Bombay)
1860-63	John Hanning Speke and James Augustus Grant (with Sidi Mubarak Bombay)
1862-64	Samuel White Baker and Florence Baker
1865-71	David Livingstone
1870-73	Samuel White Baker and Florence Baker

1871-73	Henry Morton Stanley (with Sidi Mubarak Bombay)
1883-84	Joseph Thomson
1905-06	Delia Akeley
1909-11	Delia Akeley

Africa: south

1849	David Livingstone
1850	David Livingstone
1851-52	David Livingstone

Africa: west

1352-53	Abu Abdallah Ibn Battutah
1795-99	Mungo Park
1805	Mungo Park
1827-28	René Caillié
1850-55	Heinrich Barth
1856-60	Paul Du Chaillu
1861-76	Friedrich Gerhard Rohlfs
1863	Paul Du Chaillu
1867	Paul Du Chaillu
1875-78	Pierre Savorgnan de Brazza
1879	Henry Morton Stanley
1879-81	Pierre Savorgnan de Brazza
1883-85	Pierre Savorgnan de Brazza
1891-92	Pierre Savorgnan de Brazza
1893	Mary Kingsley
1894	Mary Kingsley

Antarctica

1819-21	Fabian Gottlieb von Bellingshausen
1837-40	Jules-Sébastien-César Dumont d'Urville
1839-40	Charles Wilkes
1907-09	Ernest Shackleton

1910-12	Roald Amundsen
1914-16	Ernest Shackleton
1921-22	Ernest Shackleton
1928	Hubert Wilkins
1928-29	Richard Evelyn Byrd
1929	Hubert Wilkins
1933-34	Lincoln Ellsworth
1933-35	Richard Evelyn Byrd
1935-36	Lincoln Ellsworth
1937	Lincoln Ellsworth
1939-40	Richard Evelyn Byrd
1946-47	Richard Evelyn Byrd
1956	Richard Evelyn Byrd
1956-58	Vivian Fuchs
1989-90	Will Steger

Arabia

25 B.C	Aelius Gallus
1812-13	Hester Stanhhope
1854-55	Richard Burton
1877-78	Anne Blunt and Wilfrid Scawen Blunt
1879-80	Anne Blunt and Wilfrid Scawen Blunt
1913	Gertrude Bell

Arctic (see also North America: Northwest Passage)

1827	Edward Parry
1893-96	Fridtjof Nansen
1902	Robert Edwin Peary
1905-06	Robert Edwin Peary (with Matthew A. Henson)
1908-09	Robert Edwin Peary (with Matthew A. Henson)
1925	Roald Amundsen
1925	Richard Evelyn Byrd

1926	Roald Amundsen and Umberto Nobile
1926	Louise Arner Boyd
1926	Richard Evelyn Byrd
1926-27	Hubert Wilkins
1928	Louise Arner Boyd
1928	Hubert Wilkins
1931	Hubert Wilkins
1940	Louise Arner Boyd
1955	Louise Arner Boyd
1958	U.S.S. *Nautilus*
1986	Will Steger

Asia: interior

1866-68	Francis Garnier
1870-72	Nikolay Przhevalsky
1876	Nikolay Przhevalsky
1883-85	Nikolay Przhevalsky
1893-95	Sven Hedin
1895-97	Isabella Bird
1899	Fanny Bullock Workman
1899-1901	Sven Hedin
1900	Aurel Stein
1903-05	Sven Hedin
1906	Fanny Bullock Workman
1906-08	Aurel Stein
1913-15	Aurel Stein
1927-33	Sven Hedin
1934-36	Sven Hedin
1953	Edmund Hillary
1977	Edmund Hillary

Asia/Europe: link (see Europe/Asia: link)

Asia, south/China: link

629-45 B.C.	Hsüan-tsang
138-26 B.C.	Chang Ch'ien

1405-07	Cheng Ho
1407-09	Cheng Ho
1409-11	Cheng Ho
1413-15	Cheng Ho
1417-19	Cheng Ho
1421-22	Cheng Ho
1433-35	Cheng Ho

Australia

1605-06	Willem Janszoon
1642	Abel Tasman
1644	Abel Tasman
1770	James Cook
1798-99	Matthew Flinders
1801-02	Matthew Flinders
1801-02	Joseph Banks
1802-03	Matthew Flinders
1839	Edward John Eyre
1840-41	Edward John Eyre
1860-61	Robert O'Hara Burke and William John Wills

Aviation

1927	Charles Lindbergh
1928	Amelia Earhart
1930	Beryl Markham
1930	Amy Johnson
1931	Amy Johnson
1931	Wiley Post
1932	Amelia Earhart
1932	Amy Johnson
1933	Wiley Post
1935	Amelia Earhart
1936	Amelia Earhart
1936	Beryl Markham
1947	Chuck Yeager
1986	Dick Rutan and Jeana Yeager

Europe/Asia: link

454-43 B.C. Herodotus
401-399 B.C. Xenophon
334-23 B.C. Alexander the Great
310-06 B.C. Pytheas
1159-73 Benjamin of Tudela
1245-47 Giovanni da Pian del Carpini
1271-95 Marco Polo
1280-90 Rabban Bar Sauma
1487-90 Pero da Covilhã
1492-93 Christopher Columbus
1497-99 Vasco da Gama
1502-03 Vasco da Gama
1537-58 Fernão Mendes Pinto
1549-51 Saint Francis Xavier
1595-97 Cornelis de Houtman
1598-99 Cornelis de Houtman
1697-99 Vladimir Atlasov
1787 Jean François de Galaup, Comte de La Pérouse

Greenland

982 Erik the Red
1886 Robert Edwin Peary
1888 Fridtjof Nansen
1891-92 Robert Edwin Peary (with Matthew A. Henson)
1893-95 Robert Edwin Peary (with Matthew A. Henson)
1931 Louise Arner Boyd
1933 Louise Arner Boyd
1937 Louise Arner Boyd
1938 Louise Arner Boyd

Muslim World

915-17 Abu al-Hasan 'Ali al-Mas'udi
918-28 Abu al-Hasan 'Ali al-Mas'udi
943-73 Abu al-Kasim Ibn Ali al-Nasibi Ibn Hawkal
1325-49 Abu Abdallah Ibn Battutah

North America: coast

1001-02 Leif Eriksson
1493-96 Christopher Columbus
1497 John Cabot
1498 John Cabot
1502-04 Christopher Columbus
1508 Sebastian Cabot
1513 Juan Ponce de León
1513-14 Vasco Núñez de Balboa
1518-22 Hernán Cortés
1524 Giovanni da Verrazano
1534 Jacques Cartier
1534-36 Hernán Cortés
1535-36 Jacques Cartier
1539 Hernán Cortés
1541-42 Jacques Cartier
1542-43 João Rodrigues Cabrilho
1584 Walter Raleigh
1585-86 Walter Raleigh
1587-89 Walter Raleigh
1603 Samuel de Champlain
1604-07 Samuel de Champlain
1606-09 John Smith
1608-10 Samuel de Champlain
1609 Henry Hudson
1610 Samuel de Champlain
1614 John Smith
1792-94 George Vancouver

North America: Northwest Passage

1610-13 Henry Hudson
1776-79 James Cook
1819-20 Edward Parry

1821-23	Edward Parry	1621-23	Étienne Brulé
1824-25	Edward Parry	1657	Pierre Esprit Radisson
1845-47	John Franklin	1659-60	Médard Chouart des Groselliers
1850-54	Robert McClure		
1903-06	Roald Amundsen	1659-60	Pierre Esprit Radisson
		1669-70	René-Robert Cavelier de La Salle

North America: sub-Arctic

1654-56	Médard Chouart des Groselliers
1668	Médard Chouart des Groselliers
1668	Pierre Esprit Radisson
1670	Pierre Esprit Radisson
1679	Louis Jolliet
1682-83	Médard Chouart des Groselliers
1684	Pierre Esprit Radisson
1685-87	Pierre Esprit Radisson
1689	Louis Jolliet
1694	Louis Jolliet
1789	Alexander Mackenzie
1795	Aleksandr Baranov
1799	Aleksandr Baranov
1819-22	John Franklin
1825-27	John Franklin

North America: west

1527-36	Álvar Núñez Cabeza de Vaca (with Estevanico)
1538-43	Hernando de Soto
1539	Estevanico
1540-42	Francisco Vásquez de Coronado
1611-12	Samuel de Champlain
1613-15	Samuel de Champlain
1615-16	Samuel de Champlain
1615-16	Étienne Brulé

1672-74	Louis Jolliet
1678-83	René-Robert Cavelier de La Salle
1684-87	René-Robert Cavelier de La Salle
1769-71	Daniel Boone
1775	Daniel Boone
1792-94	Alexander Mackenzie
1792-97	David Thompson
1797-99	David Thompson
1800-02	David Thompson
1804-06	Meriwether Lewis and William Clark
1805-06	Zebulon Pike
1806-07	Zebulon Pike
1807-11	David Thompson
1811-13	Wilson Price Hunt and Robert Stuart
1823-25	Jedediah Smith
1824-25	Peter Skene Ogden
1825-26	Peter Skene Ogden
1826-27	Peter Skene Ogden
1826-28	Jedediah Smith
1828-29	Peter Skene Ogden
1829-30	Peter Skene Ogden
1842	John Charles Frémont
1843-44	John Charles Frémont
1845-48	John Charles Frémont
1848-49	John Charles Frémont
1850-51	Jim Beckwourth
1853-55	John Charles Frémont

Northeast Passage

1607	Henry Hudson
1918-20	Roald Amundsen
1931	Lincoln Ellsworth

North Pole (see Arctic)

Northwest Passage (see North America; Northwest Passage)

Oceans

1872-76	H.M.S. *Challenger*
1942-42	Jacques Cousteau
1948	August Piccard
1954	August Piccard
1960	Jacques Piccard
1968-80	*Glomar Challenger*
1969	Jacques Piccard

Pacific; south

1519-22	Ferdinand Magellan
1577-80	Francis Drake
1642-43	Abel Tasman
1721-22	Jacob Roggeveen
1766-68	Samuel Wallis
1766-69	Philip Carteret
1767-69	Louis-Antoine de Bougainville
1768-71	James Cook (with Joseph Banks)
1772-75	James Cook
1776-79	James Cook
1785-88	Jean François de Galaup, Comte de La Pérouse
1791	George Vancouver

1826-29	Jules-Sébastien-César Dumont d'Urville
1834-36	Charles Darwin
1838-39	Jules-Sébastien-César Dumont d'Urville
1838-42	Charles Wilkes
1930	Michael J. Leahy
1931	Michael J. Leahy
1932-33	Michael J. Leahy

South America; coast

1498-1500	Christopher Columbus
1499-1500	Alonso de Ojeda
1499-1500	Amerigo Vespucci
1501-1502	Amerigo Vespucci
1502	Alonso de Ojeda
1505	Alonso de Ojeda
1509-10	Alonso de Ojeda
1519-20	Ferdinand Magellan
1526-30	Sebastian Cabot
1527	Giovanni da Verrazano
1528	Giovanni da Verrazano
1594	Walter Raleigh
1595	Walter Raleigh
1617-18	Walter Raleigh
1831-34	Charles Darwin

South America; interior

1524-25	Francisco Pizarro
1526-27	Francisco Pizarro
1531-41	Francisco Pizarro
1540-44	Álvar Núñez Cabeza de Vaca
1541-42	Francisco de Orellana
1769-70	Isabel Godin des Odonais
1799-1803	Alexander von Humboldt
1903	Annie Smith Peck
1904	Annie Smith Peck
1908	Annie Smith Peck

1911	Hiram Bingham
1912	Hiram Bingham
1915	Hiram Bingham

Space

1957	*Sputnik*
1958-70	*Explorer 1*
1959-72	*Luna*
1961	Yury Gagarin
1962	John Glenn
1962-75	*Mariner*
1963	Valentina Tereshkova
1967-72	*Apollo*
1969	Neil Armstrong
1975-83	*Viking*
1977-90	*Voyager 1* and *2*
1983	Sally Ride
1990-	Hubble Space Telescope

Tibet

1624-30	Antonio de Andrade
1811-12	Thomas Manning
1865-66	Nain Singh
1867-68	Nain Singh
1879-80	Nikolay Przhevalsky
1892-93	Annie Royle Taylor
1898	Susie Carson Rijnhart
1901	Sven Hedin
1915-16	Alexandra David-Neel
1923-24	Alexandra David-Neel

Explorers by Country of Birth

If an expedition were sponsored by a country other than the explorer's place of birth, the sponsoring country is listed in parentheses after the explorer's name.

Angola

Pedro João Baptista (Portugal)
Amaro José

Australia

Michael J. Leahy
Hubert Wilkins

Canada

Louis Jolliet
Peter Skene Ogden
Susie Carson Rijnhart

China

Rabban Bar Sauma
Chang Ch'ien
Cheng Ho
Hsüan-tsang

Ecuador

Isabel Godin des Odonais

England

Samuel White Baker
Joseph Banks
Gertrude Bell
Isabella Bird
Anne Blunt
Wilfrid Scawen Blunt
Richard Burton
Philip Carteret
H.M.S. *Challenger*

James Cook
Charles Darwin
Francis Drake
Edward John Eyre
Matthew Flinders
John Franklin
Vivian Fuchs
Henry Hudson (Netherlands)
Amy Johnson
Mary Kingsley
Thomas Manning
Beryl Markham (Kenya)
Edward Parry
Walter Raleigh
John Smith
John Hanning Speke
Hester Stanhope
Annie Royle Taylor
David Thompson
George Vancouver
Samuel Wallis
William John Wills (Australia)

Estonia

Fabian Gottlieb von Bellingshausen (Russia)

France

Louis-Antoine de Bougainville
Étienne Brulé
René Caillié
Jacques Cartier
Samuel de Champlain
Médard Chouart des Groselliers
Paul Du Chaillu (United States)
Jacques Cousteau
Alexandra David-Neel
Jules-Sébastien-César Dumont d'Urville
Francis Garnier

Jean François de Galaup, Comte de La Pérouse
René-Robert Cavelier de La Salle
Jean-Baptiste Marchand
Pierre Esprit Radisson

Germany

Heinrich Barth (Great Britain)
Alexander von Humboldt
Johann Ludwig Krapf
Johannes Rebmann
Friedrich Gerhard Rohlfs

Greece

Herodotus
Pytheas
Xenophon

Hungary

Aurel Stein (Great Britain)

Iceland

Leif Eriksson

India

Nain Singh

Iraq

Abu al-Kasim Ibn Ali al-Nasibi Ibn Hawkal
Abu al-Hasan `Ali al-Mas`udi

Ireland

Robert O'Hara Burke (Australia)
Robert McClure
Ernest Shackleton

Italy

Pierre Savorgnan de Brazza (France)
John Cabot (Great Britain)
Sebastian Cabot (England, Spain)
Giovanni da Pian del Carpini
Christopher Columbus (Spain)
Marco Polo
Giovanni da Verrazano (France)
Amerigo Vespucci (Spain, Portugal)

Macedonia

Alexander the Great

Morocco

Abu Abdallah Ibn Battutah
Estevanico

Netherlands

Cornelis de Houtman
Willem Janszoon
Jacob Roggeveen
Abel Tasman

New Zealand

Edmund Hillary

Norway

Roald Amundsen
Erik the Red (Iceland)
Fridtjof Nansen

Nyasaland

Sidi Mubarak Bombay (Great Britain)
James Chuma (Great Britain)

Portugal

Antonio de Andrade
Hermenegildo de Brito Capelo
João Rodrigues Cabrilho (Spain)
Pero da Covilhã
Bartolomeu Dias
Vasco da Gama
Henry the Navigator
Roberto Ivens
Ferdinand Magellan (Spain)
Fernão Mendes Pinto

Romania

Florence Baker

Rome

Aelius Gallus

Russia
(*see also* Union of Soviet Socialist Republics)

Vladimir Atlasov
Aleksandr Baranov
Nikolay Przhevalsky

Scotland

David Livingstone
Alexander Mackenzie
Mungo Park
Robert Stuart (United States)
Joseph Thomson

Spain

Benjamin of Tudela
Álvar Núñez Cabeza de Vaca

Francisco Vásquez de Coronado
Hernán Cortés
Vasco Núñez de Balboa
Alonso de Ojeda
Francisco de Orellana
Francisco Pizarro
Juan Ponce de León
Hernando de Soto
Saint Francis Xavier

Sweden

Sven Hedin

Switzerland

Auguste Piccard
Jacques Piccard

Union of Soviet Socialist Republics

Yury Gagarin
Luna
Sputnik
Valentina Tereshkova

United States of America

Delia Akeley
Apollo
Neil Armstrong
Jim Beckwourth
Hiram Bingham
Daniel Boone
Louise Arner Boyd
Richard Evelyn Byrd
William Clark
Amelia Earhart

Lincoln Ellsworth
Explorer 1
John Charles Frémont
John Glenn
Glomar Challenger
Matthew A. Henson
Hubble Space Telescope
Wilson Price Hunt
Meriwether Lewis
Charles Lindbergh
Mariner
U.S.S. *Nautilus*
Robert Edwin Peary
Annie Smith Peck
Zebulon Pike
Wiley Post
Sally Ride
Dick Rutan
Jedediah Smith
Will Steger
Viking
Voyager 1 and 2
Charles Wilkes
Fanny Bullock Workman
Chuck Yeager
Jeana Yeager

Wales

Henry Morton Stanley (United States)

Index

Bold denotes figures profiled

Ahvaz, Iran 595, 597
Ainu 40, 42, 105
Air Mountains 71
Akeley, Carl 1-2
Akeley, Delia 1-4
Alabama River 770
Alarcón, Hernando de 270
Ala Tau Mountains 706
Albany, Australia 356-357
Albany, New York 226
Albi 508
Albigensian heresy 95
Albuquerque, Afonso de 291
Aldrin, Edwin "Buzz," Jr. 29, 37-38
Aleppo, Syria 108, 596
Aleutian Islands 266, 600, 612
Alexander 639
Alexander Aegus 13
Alexander Archipelago 63
Alexander I 63, 91
Alexander I Land 92
Alexander the Great 5-13, 218, 808
Alexandretta, Syria 108
Alexandria, Egypt 7, 76, 97, 152, 289, 785, 789
Alfonso (of Portugal) 287
Algerian Memories 862
Algiers, North Africa 281, 737
Algonquin (tribe) 216-217, 765
Alima River 134
Al-Jazira, Syria 416
Al-Kufrah 738
Allahabad 462
Allumette Island 216
Almagro, Diego de 628, 670
Almagro, Francisco 673
Almanzor 571
Alps 87, 408, 450, 475, 654
Altai Mountains 185, 219, 707
Alvarado, Hector de 271-272
Alvarado, Pedro de 176, 275-276, 279, 672
Amazon Basin 337
Amazon River 304, 409-410, 413, 474, 477, 481, 627-629, 631
Ameralik Fjord 606
American Fur Company 82

American Geographical Society 132
American Highlands 339
American Museum of Natural History 2, 3
American Philosophical Society 529
American Revolution 120, 127, 192, 508, 529
American River 760
American Samoa 510
Amirante Islands 392
Amon-Ra 7
Amritsar, India 105
Amsterdam, Netherlands 455, 458, 486
Amu Darya River 8, 808
Amundsen Gulf 17
Amundsen, Roald 14-22, 56, 130, 158, 160, 337, 429, 641, 747, 859
Amundsen-Scott Base 377, 804
Amur 705
"Amy, Wonderful Amy" 492
Anabasis 868, 870
Anadyr River 41
Añasco Bay 248
Andalusia, Spain 287
Andaman Islands 693
Anders, William 28
Anderson, William R. 611, 613
Andes Mountains 99, 101, 157, 174, 299-301, 409, 479, 654, 768
Andrade, Antonio de 23-25
Andronicus II 67
Andronicus III 77
Andros Island 697
Angareb River 45
Angediva Island 390
Angkor, Cambodia 395
Angmagssalik, Greenland 342
Angola 57, 137-138, 313, 500
Angostura 479
Annam, Vietnam 394
Annapolis Royal, Nova Scotia 214
Antarctica 90-93, 158, 160-163, 325-329, 336, 375, 452-453, 744-747, 801, 804, 853, 856

Aztec 276-279
Azua, Dominican Republic 275

B

Baalbek, Lebanon 97, 787
Baalbek, Syria 597
Babylon 8, 868
Back, George 366, 367
Back River 368
Bactria 8-9, 219, 461
Badakhshan, Afghanistan 690
Badrinath, India 24
Baffin Bay 368, 603, 645
Baffin Island 525, 640-642
Bafuka, Zaire 4
Bagamoyo 773, 792, 794
Baghdad, Iraq 67, 76, 88-89, 97,
    108, 110, 184, 490
Bahía Bariay, Cuba 245
Bahia Blanca, Argentina 297-298
Bahia, Brazil 303
Bahia dos Vaqueiros 312
Bahía San Miguel 616
Bahr-al-Ghazal River 582
Bahr-el-Salam River 45
Baikonur Space Center 380, 778,
    818
Baja, California 28, 177, 281,
    834
Baker, Florence 43-51, 114,
    156, 776
Baker, Samuel White 43-51,
    114, 156, 580, 776
Bakongo (tribe) 581
Baku, Azerbaijan 418
Balboa, Vasco Núñez de (see
    Núñez de Balboa, Vasco)
Balchen, Bernt 338
Bali 304, 457
Baliem River 522
Balkan Peninsula 5-6, 44
Balkan Wars 856
Balkh 462
Baluchistan 808
Bamako, Mali 634, 636
Bamian 462
Bancroft, Ann 802
Banda Sea 487

Bangala (tribe) 796
Bangkok, Thailand 491, 666
Bangladesh 575
Bangui 581
Banks Island 601-602
Banks, Joseph 52-56, 91, 257,
    262, 360, 575, 601, 632-633,
    635, 638
Bantam 456-457, 486-487
Baptista, Pedro Joâo 57-60,
    139
Baranof Island 63
Baranov, Aleksandr 61-64
Baranov, Peter 62
Barbosa, Duarte 571
Barcelona, Spain 95, 247
Bari 50
Barka Khan 688
Barker, Frederick 794
Barotse 548
Barrow, John 638-639
Barrow Strait 639
Barrow Submarine Canyon 612
Bar Sauma, Rabban 65-68
Barth, Heinrich 69-74, 737
Bartlett, Bob 430-431, 648, 652
Basel, Switzerland 503-504
Basra, Iraq 77, 89, 416-417
Bass, George 360
Bass Strait 360
Basundi (tribe) 581
Batavia, Dutch East Indies
    (Djakarta, Indonesia) 64, 261,
    733, 810
Bates, Henry Walter 304
Bathori, Sigismund 763
Bathurst, Australia 302
"Battle" of Cahuenga 83
Battle of Coruña 784
Battle of Las Salinas 673
Battle of New Orleans 365
Battle of Okeechobee 83
Battle of Omdurman 583
Battle of Trafalgar 365
Battle of Wounded Knee 532
**Battutah, Abu Abdallah Ibn 75-
    80,** 181
Batu 184-186
Baudin, Nicolas 362
Bauer, Ferdinand 361

D